This book is dedicated to our students, past, present, and future.

Preface

Philosophy Applied to Education: Nurturing a Democratic Community in the Classroom is designed for students taking foundations courses in teacher education programs. It does not assume students have a philosophical background, but it encourages them to realize they have the ability to understand and apply philosophical theories because of their ability to reason and discuss ideas with others.

Historically, much has been written concerning the individual self and how it relates to communities. Whole fields of study are devoted to looking at how the self develops (e.g., psychology) and how social life affects individual selves (e.g., sociology). From a philosophical perspective, answering the question "What is the relation between individual selves and communities?" involves people in social/political, ethical, and epistemological questions. We seek to address these kinds of questions by using the overall framework of individual selves in relation to others. We examine classical as well as current perspectives on this issue, and address the concerns current teachers face as well as those prospective teachers will likely encounter in the course of their careers. **Using the metaphor of a caring, democratic community to describe a school setting, *Philosophy Applied to Education* translates philosophical perspectives to actual classroom contexts so that the theoretical can be more easily understood and teachers can see how theory is translated into practice.**

Philosophy Applied to Education offers an example of a teacher's philosophy of education and how it applies to the classroom. Our goal is to help students understand philosophical issues through the example of one particular perspective. Rather than presenting a comprehensive philosophical text that summarizes major philosophical schools of thought, we are sharing our perspective and the reasons to support it, as well as the problems and issues such a perspective must address. We hope this book will model for students the kinds of questions all educators must face when trying to explain their philosophy of education.

Approach

The authors hope that *Philosophy Applied to Education* offers students and instructors a valuable and meaningful model of an educator's philosophy of education that demonstrates how theory relates to practice. The model of a caring, democratic community is offered as one that has distinct advantages because it is flexible, adaptable, and inclusive of individual needs and the needs of others. The model offered strives to remain humble and aware of human fallibility, so that it does not marginalize others or become open to ideological abuse. Such a model has the possibility of being inclusive and affirming, of being balanced and holistic as well as allowing for dissonance and discord, striving to meet the needs of individuals and groups and offering hope for finding ways to achieve harmony and peace in our efforts to live together, and meet the needs of individuals from differing social classes, races, religious backgrounds, sexual orientations, genders, ages, and abilities.

This book presents an alternative theory of knowledge termed a "relational epistemology." **A relational epistemology views knowledge as something that is socially constructed by embedded, embodied people who are in relation with each other.** These assumptions are what make this a **social** theory.

The metaphor of a democratic classroom community reflects our view that knowledge is relational. Unlike traditional individualistic theories, a democratic social theory suggests that being is directly connected to knowing, a **pragmatic** view. Because this democratic approach to teaching highlights the interactive connection between social beings and ideas, it becomes necessary to look at the kinds of relationships people experience in the classroom community. Ethical and political issues also need to be addressed in a philosophy of education that looks at knowledge as being created by **people**. A community theory must also consider the quality of the social relationships people have and make the **feminist** case that these social relationships need to be caring, reasonable, equitable, democratic ones. The quality of the social relationships in a community affects both the ideas being constructed and whether the ideas have the opportunity to be expressed. The perspective offered here is a **pragmatic social feminist** view, calling for active engagement, aiming at democratic inclusion, joining theory with praxis, striving for awareness of context and values, tolerating vagueness and ambiguities.

Organization of the Text

Philosophy Applied to Education is the authors' attempt to apply this relational theory to schools and classroom settings in a way that makes philosophy of education a field of study that is approachable and understandable to teachers and future

Philosophy Applied to Education
Nurturing a Democratic Community in the Classroom

Barbara J. Thayer-Bacon
Bowling Green State University

with Charles S. Bacon

Merrill,
an imprint of Prentice Hall
Upper Saddle River, New Jersey　　　*Columbus, Ohio*

Library of Congress Cataloging-in-Publication Data

Thayer-Bacon, Barbara J.
    Philosophy applied to education : nurturing a democratic community in the classroom/Barbara J. Thayer-Bacon; with Charles S. Bacon.
        p.   cm.
    Includes bibliographical references and index.
    ISBN 0-13-242413-4 (p)
    1. Education—Philosophy. 2. Knowledge, Theory of. 3. Teaching.   I. Bacon, Charles S. II. Title.
    LB14.7.T53   1998   97-8914
370'.1—dc21   CIP

Cover photo: Bob Grant, Comstock
Editor: Debra A. Stollenwerk
Production Editor: Patricia S. Kelly
Design Coordinator: Karrie M. Converse
Text Designer: Pagination
Cover Designer: Proof Positive/Farrowlyne Assoc., Inc.
Production Manager: Laura Messerly
Electronic Text Management: Marilyn Wilson Phelps, Matthew Williams, Karen L. Bretz, Tracey B. Ward
Director of Marketing: Kevin Flanagan
Marketing Manager: Suzanne Stanton
Advertising/Marketing Coordinator: Julie Shough

This book was set in ITC Leawood and News Gothic by Prentice Hall and was printed and bound by R. R. Donnelley & Sons Company. The cover was printed by Phoenix Color Corp.

© 1998 by Prentice-Hall, Inc.
Simon & Schuster/A Viacom Company
Upper Saddle River, New Jersey 07458

Printed in the United States of America

10 9 8 7 6 5 4 3

ISBN: 0-13-242413-4

Prentice-Hall International (UK) Limited, *London*
Prentice-Hall of Australia Pty. Limited, *Sydney*
Prentice-Hall of Canada, Inc., *Toronto*
Prentice-Hall Hispanoamericana, S. A., *Mexico*
Prentice-Hall of India Private Limited, *New Delhi*
Prentice-Hall of Japan, Inc., *Tokyo*
Simon & Schuster Asia Pte. Ltd., *Singapore*
Editora Prentice-Hall do Brasil, Ltda., *Rio de Janeiro*

teachers. Theories related to individuals and others are addressed from a sociopolitical perspective in Chapter 1. Chapter 2 describes other epistemological perspectives in comparison with the relational perspective presented there. Chapter 3 considers the advantages and disadvantages of different ethical perspectives in terms of justice and care. The tools and skills that are needed to construct knowledge are addressed in Chapter 4. How a democratic classroom community can address individuals, others, and the diversity that exists in communities is the focus of Chapter 5. For Chapters 2 and 4, the theoretical discussions are framed around metaphors other than a classroom to increase readers' understanding. Therefore, we have included an "Implications for Education" section at the end of those chapters to bring classrooms and schools specifically back into the discussion.

Features of the Text

Philosophy Applied to Education supplies key **examples of classical philosophical theories** from the past and shows how these theories relate to current situations in schools. For example, in the Chapter 1 discussion of how individuals are related to others, classical individualistic perspectives such as Rousseau's are discussed and shown to support the types of classroom models teachers and students are most familiar with, ones that focus on an individual student's needs rather than on group needs.

Second, the text presents **examples of current philosophical perspectives** on significant issues and problems teachers must deal with and shows how they relate to classical philosophical perspectives. For example, in the Chapter 3 discussion of different ethical perspectives, the book considers Mortimer Adler's proposal that schools offer only a liberal arts curriculum, relating his perspective to Aristotle's and Plato's. In Chapter 1, Johnson and Johnson's cooperative learning theory is compared with classical perspectives that emphasize group needs over individual ones.

Third, an **extensive bibliography** appears at the end of the book, in addition to **endnotes** for each chapter that include **suggestions for other readings**. Instructors can use the suggested readings as a guide for generating more in-depth discussions, and students can use them as resources for individual research papers or small-group presentations. An **index** is also included for finding desired information in the text.

Fourth, *Philosophy Applied to Education* offers at the end of each chapter a section entitled "In the Classroom," **suggestions for activities** that will enhance students' understanding of the concepts discussed. For example, activities dramatizing typical problems facing teachers in their classrooms (such as a student not having completed an assignment on time or a parent calling to complain that having to work with so-and-so is causing her child to get behind in his own studies) and how teachers deal with these problems, depending on their own philosophical perspectives concerning the relationship of self to others, appear at the end of Chapter 1.

Fifth, each chapter closes with a summary to help readers step back from the detailed discussions within the chapter and gain a holistic, large-picture perspective of the chapter's philosophical focus. Readers will also find that each chapter begins with a summary of what has been discussed so far in the book. This **summary technique** should function like a road map to help readers find their way through the text without getting lost or losing track of where they have been.

Ways to Use This Text

Philosophy Applied to Education offers instructors the opportunity to use this book in a variety of ways. It can be used as required reading to address philosophical issues within a class that addresses foundations from more than just a philosophical perspective (one that must also attempt to include historical, sociological, and comparative theories, for example) or from more than one philosophical perspective (as in a graduate philosophy of education course). This book can also be included as a supplemental text since it is reader-friendly and offers students applied examples of philosophy in education. Because of its scope and presentation of theories and issues, this text might also be used as the main text in a shorter course, such as a summer session foundations course.

Acknowledgments

The following works have been reprinted by permission of the organizations that originally published the material.

- Thayer-Bacon, B. J. (1989). How the child reasons. *Philosophical Studies in Education,* 107–116. Reprinted by permission.
- Thayer-Bacon, B. J. (1991, May). Egocentrism in critical thinking theory. *Inquiry: Critical Thinking across the Disciplines,* 7(4), 30–33. Reprinted by permission.
- Thayer-Bacon, B. J. (1992, Spring and Summer). A feminine reconceptualization of critical thinking theory. *Journal of Thought,* 27(3 & 4), 4–17. Reprinted by permission.
- Thayer-Bacon, B. J. (1993, Summer). Caring and its relationship to critical thinking. *Educational Theory,* 43(3), 323–340. Reprinted by permission.
- Thayer-Bacon, B. J. (1995). Caring democratic communities. *Philosophical Studies in Education,* pp. 139–151. Reprinted by permission.
- Thayer-Bacon, B. J. (1995, Spring). Constructive thinking: Personal voice. *Journal of Thought,* 30(1), 55–70. Reprinted by permission.
- Thayer-Bacon, B. J. (1995, Winter). Doubting and believing: Both are important for critical thinking. *Inquiry: Critical Thinking across the Disciplines,* 15(2), 59–66. Reprinted by permission.

■ Thayer-Bacon, B. J. (1996). Democratic classroom communities. *Studies in Philosophy and Education,* 15, 333–351. Reprinted by permission of Kluwer Academic Publishers. Printed in the Netherlands.

■ Thayer-Bacon, B. J., & Bacon, C. S. (1996, Spring). Caring in the college/university classroom. *Educational Foundations,* 10(2), 53–72. Reprinted by permission.

■ Thayer-Bacon, B. J., & Bacon, C. S. (1996, October). Caring professors: A model. *Journal of General Education,* 45(4), 255–269. Copyright 1996 by The Pennsylvania State University. Reproduced by permission of The Pennsylvania State University Press.

■ Thayer-Bacon, B. J. (1997). The nurturing of a relational epistemology. *Educational Theory,* 47(2) (in press). Reprinted by permission.

We wish to thank Scott Bieniek, Thayer-Bacon's research graduate assistant in 1994–1996, for his careful reading and editing of Chapters 1 through 3. We also thank Cathy Long, the Department of Educational Foundations and Inquiry secretary, for her secretarial assistance throughout this process. Many others have given us feedback and suggestions along the way, who are acknowledged for their contributions in the original articles that were previously published and thanked again here as well.

We also thank the reviewers of this text: Richard J. Altenbaugh, Slippery Rock University; Richard A. Brosio, Ball State University; Clinton Collins, University of Kentucky; Bernice Goldmark, Sonoma State University (Emerita) and Fromm Institute-University of San Francisco; Gunilla Holm, Western Michigan University; Scott Hopkins, University of South Alabama; David N. Mielke, Appalachian State University; and Ann H. Stoddard, University of North Florida.

Finally, thank yous need to go to people at Merrill/Prentice Hall: Penny Burleson, editorial assistant, for offering her assistance and advice; Laura Larson, our freelance copyeditor, for her careful and professional work; and Debbie Stollenwerk, our editor, for believing in our project and being as excited about it as we are.

Brief Contents

Contents

Chapter 3
Justice and Care   79

Chapter 4
Constructive Thinking   125

Chapter 5
Cultural Diversity in a Democratic Classroom   **169**

About the Authors

Barbara J. Thayer-Bacon is an associate professor of philosophy of education at Bowling Green State University, in the department of Educational Foundations and Inquiry. Her major interests are critical thinking, epistemology, feminist theory, ethics, and social/political philosophy, all as they relate to education and school reform. She received her Ph.D. in philosophy of education from Indiana University and an M.A. in education from San Diego State University. She holds a B.A. in philosophy from Pennsylvania State University and Rutgers University. Dr. Thayer-Bacon also holds elementary teaching credentials from three states and the American Montessori Society. She has taught for fourteen years, seven in elementary schools and seven at the university level. She is an active member in and regular presenter for the American Educational Research Association, the American Educational Studies Association, and the Philosophy of Education Society. She also has published numerous articles in *The Journal of Thought, Journal for a Just and Caring Education, Educational Theory, Studies in Philosophy and Education, Inquiry, Educational Foundations,* and *Educational Studies.* With her husband, Dr. Charles Bacon, Dr. Thayer-Bacon conducts a teachers' workshop at Bowling Green entitled "Building Community in the Classroom," on which this book is based. She is the mother of four children ages 6–22.

Charles S. Bacon worked as an assistant professor of educational psychology at Indiana University/Purdue University in Fort Wayne for seven years. He has taught educational psychology and measurement/evaluation for Bowling Green State University and psychology for the University of Toledo. His primary academic research interests are affective issues in education and motivation. He has recently finished writing his first novel and is now looking for a publisher while he begins work on his second novel.

Individual Selves and Communities

This book is intended to give teachers, would-be teachers, and other educators such as counselors an example of how philosophical theory applies to education. Most students are required to take a social foundations course of some kind to qualify for a teaching credential, as well as an undergraduate or graduate degree in education. Many students understand the value in learning about the history of American education or how it is students learn (educational psychology), but it is our experience that there seems to be general confusion and even distaste or fear for a course that addresses philosophical issues. Yet understanding why we do what we do, and being able to give reasons to support our practice and explain to others the value of what we do, are what help educators be able to define themselves as professionals. Professionals, in any field, understand the theory behind their practice, so that they can explain to others why they make the decisions they do. Philosophical theory offers educators the opportunity to understand the **why** to their practice. It also helps educators attempt to envision how things should be ideally, what **should** be the case for a teacher or counselor to reach their intended aims of education. Philosophy also provides educators ways to **critique** what is and address the problems that exist in the settings they attempt to teach, such as in our schools. We hope to show readers not only that philosophy is not necessarily scary or too abstract and oblique to be understood but that it is an exciting, important field of study for anyone, especially professional educators.

Our goal is to introduce central areas of study in philosophy by offering a concrete example of a philosophy of education and how this might translate into a classroom setting. As readers begin to understand the model being offered here, they will learn that the distinctions made in the preface describing each chapter's content are not so easily separated and categorized. In fact, one of the basic tenets of this philosophy of education is that sociopolitical perspectives and cultural concerns are very much connected to and overlapping with epistemological and ethical issues; they are all interrelated and affect each other. We are pulling apart strands of a rope that only functions as a rope because these strands are connected and work together. We urge readers to keep this in mind.

With these goals in mind, let us begin to describe our philosophy of education. We start with sociopolitical concerns of how people associate with and influence each other, what forms of association are ideal, and what problems can and do occur with these various types of association. Sociopolitical concerns address individuals in relation to others and issues such as power, oppression, freedom, and justice.

Sociopolitical Philosophical Issues

Is it possible for a form (or forms) of community to emerge that does justice to particularity and universality? Because we live in a time when our situation, a postmodern situation as Habermas (1982) describes it, is one in which "both revolutionary self-confidence and theoretical self-certainty are gone," is there hope for achieving communities based on undistorted communication, dialogue, communal judgment, rational persuasion, nonviolence, and an ethic of care (p. 22)?

In this chapter, we explore democratic communities as potential forms of community that do justice to individuals and others. With democratic communities, we will argue, there lies the possibility of achieving communities that are reasonable, inclusive, affirming, just, and caring. It is vital, however, that we analyze carefully the necessary ingredients for that hope to be realized. We use the metaphor of a school classroom to help further our understandings. We look at the necessary ingredients and attempt to describe a classroom that can function as a model of a democratic community. Such a classroom is what we recommend that educators should be striving to create.

Communities Reexamined

Problems with Community

Richard Bernstein (1983) describes the paradox of the modern age as follows: "the coming into being of community already presupposes an experienced sense of community" (p. 226). The modern age is defined as one in which people believe any science can legitimate itself by making an appeal to a grand narrative, a theory, such as Reason, or the Scientific Method, or Dialogue. Bernstein demonstrates how major modern philosophers fell prey to this problem and points to this paradox in their philosophical work. We, as human beings, desire types of dialogical communities in which practical rationality can flourish, and this desire is deeply rooted in human aspiration. It can be found expressed as far back as the times of Aristotle and Plato. This longing for community is vital "in understanding our own humanity and our solidarity with our fellow human beings" (Bernstein, 1983, p. 230).

If the modern age is defined in terms of how it legitimates itself, by use of theories to explain its theories (meta-theories), the postmodern age has been defined as being "incredulous towards metanarratives" (Lyotard, 1984, p. xxiii). As one postmodern philosopher, Jean-François Lyotard (1984, pp. xxiv–xxv), describes this, the question postmodernists struggle with is "Where, after the metanarratives, can legitimacy reside?" If we cannot defend our theories by appeal to some greater force, such as what's Right, Real, or True, how can we defend them? Does this make all theories of equal worth? Does this make philosophers no different than prophets and poets? Let us look at what two postmodern feminist philosophers have to say about the modern concept of "community."

In Lynda Stone's (1992, pp. 93–101) "Disavowing Community," she expresses dissatisfaction with the meaning of community and argues that 'community' is a modernist term relying on a contradiction. The grand theory for 'community' relies on a positive valuing of sameness. The contradiction is that community, as defined in the Western modern world, is a collective unit, which relies on the components of individualism, rationality, and choice, which are separate units (Stone, 1992, p. 95). In "The Ideal of Community and the Politics of Difference," Iris M. Young (1990) suggests that the ideal of community "privileges unity over difference, immediacy over mediation, sympathy over recognition of the limits of one's understanding of others from their point of view" (p. 300). Both authors express an understanding of the longing for community, even acknowledging that they also feel this longing, but both find **community** problematic. Young argues that the dream for community is problematic because "those motivated by it tend to suppress differences among themselves or implicitly to exclude from their political groups persons with whom they do not identify" (p. 300). Stone agrees with Young, elaborating on this problem: "Community bounds in a way that simultaneously includes and excludes, including on the basis of sameness and excluding on the basis of difference" (p. 96).

Where Stone and Young differ, at first glance, is when they propose a solution to the problem of community. Young suggests "that instead of the ideal of community, we begin from our positive experience of city life to form a vision of the good society. Our political ideal is the unoppressive city" (p. 317), which she further defines as "openness to unassimilated otherness" (p. 319). Stone suggests we disavow 'community' "because the concept itself carries the historical and ideological baggage of the failures of western liberal association." Instead, she suggests we use the term 'heteromity' (p. 98), which she defines as "a human association on the basis of difference" (p. 99). Stone claims that her concept of 'heteromity' does not retain the community concept and the foundation of sameness but that Young's concept of "the unoppressive city" does retain the concept of community. Yet, Young's "unoppressive city" relies on the same conceptualization as Stone's, one that sees associations as embodying difference. As Young describes city life, it is "the 'being-together' of strangers" (p. 318). Association is temporary and shifting, boundaries between groups are fluid, and the freedom of anonymity is available.

At a second glance, Young and Stone seem to propose similar solutions to the problem of individuals and others. That they have successfully eluded 'community' is questionable. What they have appeared to do is rename 'community'. Maureen Stout (1992) points out in her review of Stone's paper that "othering" occurs whenever social practices exist that "create and sustain privileged forms of social discourse at the expense of others. . . . "'[O]thering' as a concept is not a function of 'community' based on a notion of sameness, . . . but exists between individuals at all levels and in all forms of social life—we are all someone else's 'other'. Simply emphasizing difference will not, I fear, eradicate the ongoing practices of 'othering' in which we are all, without exception, implicated" (pp. 103–104).

Assumptions about Community

Although problems and contradictions are embedded in the concept of 'community', it appears that replacing the concept 'community' with other concepts such as 'unoppressive city' or 'heteromity' does not solve these problems and contradictions. Perhaps the effort to solve them is itself misguided. Postmodern philosophers argue that problems and contradictions are inevitable and a necessary condition of life. Maybe the best we can hope for is to continually reexamine the concept 'community' and strive to envision this association with others in new forms. We propose to do this with this book, beginning in this chapter with an effort to define 'community' and questioning the assumptions we attach to this concept.

First, both Young and Stone seem not to address the fact that everyone is born into a community. We cannot avoid this. We all start our lives in relation with someone else, at least one other person: our mothers. Even if our mothers give us up for adoption, someone else then steps in to care for us, or we do not survive. A community is often assumed to be a group of people, with shared interests, who interact with each other. A newborn child could be a member of a community consisting of only one other person, his or her mother, or some other person functioning as a mother. (Imagine for the first example a mother and child shipwrecked on a deserted island. For the second example, imagine a child raised by animals, such as Victor, the Wild Boy raised by Itard in France[1] or Mowgli of the Rudyard Kipling [1992] stories.) The number in a community can be as small as two. It is also possible to imagine that the only shared interest between beings in a community is survival, as it is initially with any newborn child.

Other than needing to have more than one being for a community to exist, the only other necessary ingredient appears to be some kind of shared interest. One can imagine two people who share a common locality but not a common culture and who are unable to communicate through a common language. In our current pluralistic world, this kind of situation is not unusual. These two people can be neighbors, and yet without any shared interest, one would not call them a community. If they begin to try to communicate with each other and can establish a shared interest (e.g., maybe danger lurks and they try to help each other for survival's sake, or their children start playing together), then a community begins to develop. Stone (1992) uses Elizabeth Fox-Genovese's definition of community as "a state of being shared or held in common. . . . a group based on merging . . . on shared attributes" (p. 93).[2] This definition fits the examples and characteristics given here.

Qualities attached to 'community' such as individual membership, rationality, equality are all ones people have added to the basic concept. Our dictionary defines *community* as "a group of people living in the same locality and under the same government" (Morris, 1970, p. 270). We can see from this definition that it assumes a community is a group of people living in the same locality, yet is it not possible to be a member of a community that does not live together at all? In our current world of technology and transportation, scholars come from around the world to be together at annual conferences and consider themselves a community; people communicate with each other through the Internet and form communities, even though they never physically come in contact with each other. The same government or a shared locality are not necessary for a community to exist.

What about joining a community? Is it necessary to join a community willingly to be a member, or may a person be a member of a community even if he or she does not desire such membership? We can think of examples of communities that are very exclusive and difficult to join, such as professional organizations and clubs or fraternities/sororities. However, it is possible to be a member of a community against one's will, as with German citizens associated with the Nazis or children born into a family that belongs to the Ku Klux Klan or the Mafia. Membership to a community can be for many reasons, not all of which are voluntary. Membership can be very fleeting and temporary, or it can last a lifetime.

Community's root word is *common*. Whereas a community may entail a social group having common interests, similar living conditions, and a shared language and culture, it does not necessarily entail anything more than sheer membership due to a common interest/experience/trait, which could be as basic as survival. Although Stone and Young are critical of 'community' as a concept that emphasizes sameness over difference, if only difference is emphasized, there is no community, even in the form of an unoppressed city or as heteromity. Community must have some form of commonness to exist. How commonalty is developed among people who are uniquely different is something we will need to discuss.

We began this section with a quotation that highlights the fact that human beings assume a sense of community, in their discussions on community. Both Stone and Young express a longing for community, even as they draw our attention to the dark underside of romantic notions of community, in their efforts to redescribe or disavow 'community'. The need to feel connected to others is strong with human beings most likely because we could not survive without the help of others. Stone's and Young's concern that we search for a type of community that does justice to individuals and others, to sameness and difference, is based on the very real understanding that not all forms of community are good.

John Dewey (1916/1966, p. 82) points out in his discussion on communities in *Democracy and Education* that people tend to assume 'community' is something good, but many different types of community are possible, some of which are harmful and unjust. Perhaps in Dewey's time more people tended to assume community was an intrinsically good concept because they were experiencing communities in positive forms, but this is doubtful. Oppressive, unjust, cruel communities are not new to these modern or postmodern times. Many children grow up without a sense of community, in Dewey's praiseworthy sense of a "community of purpose and welfare, loyalty to public ends, mutuality of sympathy" (p. 82). Many people are well aware that communities come in a variety of shapes and forms, not all of which are intrinsically good. Communities can and do exclude other people from membership. Communities can be authoritarian and destructive to individuals who are members, in the name of the common good.

Dewey examined different types of communities in trying to define an ideal community as a democratic one. We will use the classroom metaphor to help reexamine a democratic community. We will consider two different types of communities that can be found within an elementary classroom to uncover key assumptions about individuals in relation to communities. We also want to uncover key values and aims for education that are held, depending on the type of community. We would then like to examine a third type of community, a democratic classroom community, to determine what it might look like. We will use Dewey's definition of democracy as a starting place to reconsider the basic qualities of a democratic community, extending it in a way that we believe our times requires, which Dewey's times may have assumed. We are hoping that such reconsideration and extension of democracy as a concept will increase the opportunities for a caring democratic community to be realized and experienced by more children in American schools, as well as elsewhere. First we must present the case in support of using the classroom as a metaphor for community.

Schools and Classrooms as Communities

Why look at classrooms in schools as a way of reexamining democratic communities? Whereas families (in all varieties of forms) are the first communities children experience, school classrooms are often children's second community experience. Many children today actually spend more time consistently in a school classroom than they do with their main caregivers.[3] A school classroom certainly fits the definition of community as described earlier. Multiple persons are in association with each other, sharing at least the common attribute of being enrolled in Ms. Smith's class. One cannot necessarily assume that these students have more than enrollment in common, which is yet another reason that classrooms make a good example of community.

The people in a school classroom comprise a community because they are together, sharing time and experiences whether they like it or not. Individual members of a class will decide what roles they will assume and how they will interpret their shared experiences. This does not alter the fact that people are often members of communities not of their own choosing. All of us were born into certain families, which automatically made us members of that family. We did not choose our families or where they lived, our neighborhood or city, which made us members of other communities, against our consent. Whether a person continues association as a member of his or her family or town of birth does become a matter of choice at some point, as existential philosophers like Jean-Paul Sartre have reminded us so well. It is the same with a classroom in a school building. Students and teachers are often told they will be together, then they must choose whether to honor that assignment. Some teachers and students remove themselves from the classroom and school altogether; some request a transfer to another classroom.

We choose to look at an elementary classroom, as that is the first school community most children will consistently experience. The elementary classroom is the place where the same children are likely to spend the most time together, with the same teacher. Whether or not a teacher looks at her or his classroom as a community of people, which can take on many forms, it is a reality that she or he will be sharing the same space with many people (say, 30) for 5 to 6 hours, 5 days per week, for an average of 180 days per year (with proposals being offered to extend the school day and the school year, e.g., Sizer's (1984, 1992) Coalition of Schools). An elementary teacher spends approximately 1,260 to 1,400 hours with the 30 children who walk in her or his classroom the first day of school (some come and go, but many remain with the group the entire school year).

The people who walk into a teacher's classroom do not come in without a past. All students bring the context of their lives with them and their effects. They each have unique family backgrounds, their own genetic makeup and health conditions, their own cultural backgrounds, such as their language and customs, and their own unique experiences and interpretations of them by the significant others in their lives. Not only do all 30 students have unique, complex contexts, but so does the teacher in this classroom. All of this adds to the complexity of looking at a classroom as an example of a community.

Even if we examine a small private-school classroom with people of the same economic level and same religious faith, for example, we will find the members of the classroom are different, though likely many similarities will exist. The larger the geographic area is from which the school receives students, the more diversity there will be within the school itself. One can see this modeled on a large scale with boarding schools and colleges/universities, many of which potentially derive their student bodies from the world at large, and great diversity can be found on the campus. A classroom of students and a teacher (or teachers, if one is coteaching or has an aide) is a good example of a community because of all the context and complexity they bring to their shared space.

As we have mentioned, people do not have to share the same space to form a community (consider the Internet example), but doing so certainly offers opportunities for association. The teacher(s) and students in a classroom all share the same space for extended periods. For a community to exist, it must have the **opportunity** to do so. Spending time with each other offers opportunities for shared interests to develop. One could say elementary children spend 1,260 to 1,400 hours **living** in their particular classroom, within their school building. While they are there, those children share not only the same locality but also the same form of government, typically meaning the rules that the administrators and teachers in the building have designed for the school and classrooms. This adds another dimension of commonalty to the classroom members.

If we take the model of an elementary classroom and attempt to apply it with older students in secondary settings or at the college level, we will find the classroom still fits the definition of community being used here: there is more than one person in association with an other(s), having shared interests in common. But as the number of people involved increases and the opportunity to develop shared interests decreases, a classroom will more likely function as a community only in a weaker sense. Teachers and students have less of an opportunity to be a richly developed community, although the school certainly does have this chance.

A secondary teacher spends about 180 to 200 hours with each classroom of 30 students, in a school year. Secondary teachers have an average of 150 to 180 students they teach daily. College professors spend an average time of 45 hours per semester in class with their students. They can have as few as 30 students per semester or quarter, if they teach only graduate classes, or they may have an average of 250 students per semester or quarter, if they teach undergraduate classes.

Although the chances for establishing more shared interests as a community lessen as the opportunity to know each other and be able to participate in community activities decreases, the opportunity for commonalty at the secondary or college level can become realized at a larger scale. Many secondary schools are trying to devise "teams" or "homes" within their larger school as a way of creating more of a sense of belonging, so that students feel they are known by other people in the building (Sizer, 1984, 1992). Many colleges use their students' living spaces as the place to create a sense of community, and they assign resident assistants to live with the students in the same dormitory, for example. These resident assistants will sponsor get-togethers and opportunities for students to meet and interact with each other.

Examples of Classroom Communities

Assumptions about how selves are formed in relation to others affect how one relates to individuals within a classroom community. What teachers value and are striving for, what they see as the purpose or aim of education, also affects the decisions teachers make, the actions they take, and the way they choose to relate to others. These beliefs are examined in this section via three common classroom models.

Individualistic Communities

Let us begin by describing the type of classroom community people are most familiar with, as it is very common in our schools. We will look at the assumptions and values that underlie this type of classroom community and their effects on the members of this community. We label this first type of classroom an **individualistic** classroom.[4] Individualistic models are what have been valued traditionally in the United States because of their focus on individualism and freedom. In individualistic classrooms teachers focus on students as individuals and do not concern themselves so much with the class of people, as a whole, the community these individuals make up.

Individualistic classrooms are designed in many ways, but their general aim is to help each individual child learn and develop the necessary skills to be an autonomous person, able to take care of him- or herself. The goal of these models is to help all individuals achieve their full potential and become their own authentic persons (Maslow, 1962). Individualistic models are also concerned that the children receive the knowledge the state deems necessary for them to become good citizens to the country, but this is a secondary consideration, after the concern of becoming self-actualized adults. Any citizenship concern is tempered by the individualistic belief that individuals voluntarily enter into agreement with others to form communities because it benefits them, individually, to do so. (This is what philosophers have labeled **social contract theory**. Classic examples can be found in the work of John Locke [1823/1960] and Jean Jacques Rousseau [1762/1968].) It is to the individual's advantage to give up some freedoms to have the security and aid to his or her own life that living with others produces. But those benefits come at a loss of individual rights, and individualists are always on their guard to make sure they do not give up too many freedoms.

Loss of freedom is a most significant evil for individualists. Therefore, individualists are always weighing the pros and cons concerning whether they want to join up with others, for communities tie them down and limit their choices. Individualists view the needs of their community and their membership role as secondary to their own individual needs. For individualists, going to school is something their children do because it will benefit them in the long run to do so. However, for the children, going to school is a painful experience that creates a loss of individual freedom to play and do as they choose each day.

In individualist classroom communities, teachers must be primarily concerned that each child be able to reach his or her full potential, and the teachers strive to maximize each student's own opportunities. Individualistic parents worry about what happens in the classroom in terms of how it affects their individual child. For example, they ask, "Is my child in the highest reading or math group? Will my child get behind in her studies if special education children are brought into her classroom?" Concern for the group is usually due to how the group affects the individual, in the negative sense of limiting the individual child's freedom.

A good teacher in an individualistic model is someone who is able to control the class, keep the students quiet and in line, and get as many students as possible to pass the tests and move on to the next grade. Students most often work by themselves at their own desks and are not allowed to talk to each other or help each other (that would be cheating). The aim is to help each student obtain the most knowledge possible. The teacher is viewed as the model of authority and wisdom and as an instrument to help the individual child obtain success. The teacher does not seem to have a life outside the classroom, or at least it is not acknowledged. This is the case for the children as well. We are not saying that teachers' and students' lives outside the classroom are not shared and discussed in the classroom but rather that life outside the classroom is not intentionally included in the teaching/learning that goes on in the classroom. Teachers' and students' outside lives are not usually the school's concern.

This is certainly **not** a model that encourages the development of a community within the classroom. It does not seem to encourage contributions by each other for the benefit of the group or the expression of concern for one another's well being. In fact, as Jean Jacques Rousseau (cited in Cahn, 1970), a classic example of an individualist, recommended in *Émile:*

> True happiness comes from equality of power and will. The only man who gets his own way is the one who does not need another's help to get it: from which it follows that the supreme good is not authority, but freedom. The true freeman wants only what he can get, and does only what pleases him. This is my fundamental maxim. Apply it to childhood and all the rules of education follow. (pp. 159–160)

Individualistic models view the self as an individual who can develop on his or her own, naturally, without much help from others. Continuing with the example Rousseau offers in *Émile,* an individualist will likely argue that people left to their own devices will develop quite nicely; problems arise when others get involved and try to shape things. Not only is community development not encouraged, but communities are viewed as a hindrance to individual development. "Everything is good as it comes from the hands of the Maker of the world but degenerates once it gets into the hands of man" (p. 155).

Rousseau recommended that Émile be educated by allowing him to grow up exploring nature and developing on his own. Émile is a solitary student educated by a tutor; there are no others. The teacher is described as an observer who sets up situations for Émile to learn from. The lessons are to come from Émile's own experiences, with the understanding that "[t]he more children can do for themselves the less help they need from other people" (p. 158).

Rousseau argues that a child's first impulses are always right. If a child were allowed to develop his own voice and follow his natural impulses, he would only choose what is right.

> There is no original perversity in the human heart. Of every vice we can say how it entered and whence it came. The only passion natural to man is self-love, or self-esteem in a broad sense. This self-esteem has no necessary reference to other people. In so far as it relates to ourselves it is good and useful. It only becomes good or bad in the social application we make of it. (p. 162)

One can see that an individualistic position, such as Rousseau's, assumes that people are by nature selfish and self-centered, but this is not bad. People naturally make decisions that are for their own best interest, hoping to "maximize their pleasure and minimize their pain."[5] Only when others, such as social communities, become involved can self-interest be made to look as something evil.

From individualistic perspectives, it is right that teachers should place their focus on individual students and each individual's self-development. Placing the focus on others is harmful to individual students; it slows down their progress, forces them to wait, and so forth, because of others' needs. Each child should have the opportunity to develop to his or her full potential, and the teacher needs to be a resource for making that happen and protect each student from harm by others (society) as much as possible. Left to their own resources, with opportunities for experiences, all children will develop into independent, authentic adults.

Problems with Individualistic Views

Many problems with individualistic theories can be seen by looking at them as a model of a community in a classroom. One is that children do not attend classrooms where they are the solitary person, so they are going to have to deal with being around others, whether they like it or not. Countries and people do not have the resources to hire individual tutors for each individual child, as Rousseau recommended for Émile. The children who come closest to individualized school experiences are children with special needs, such as gifted and talented children and special education children. Many of these children receive individualized educational plans (IEPs) and often are pulled out of regular classrooms and given individualized instruction. However, the majority of children in schools experience curricula designed to reach as many people as possible, at the same pace, with the same objectives. The curriculum most likely reflects the majority viewpoint, with selected minority views represented. It does not necessarily represent the experience of each individual student, and it is assumed that such a goal would be impossible, just as it is assumed that writing an IEP for each individual student would also be impossible.

Not only do educators and parents assume that individualized education is impossible, unless they are wealthy enough to afford their own tutors, but many parents also question whether such a goal is necessarily one they wish to achieve. We can see the questioning of the valuing of individualized instruction in the movement in the United States toward "inclusion." After the Civil Rights movement in the 1960s, which focused on racial issues, other groups have fought for equal treatment before the law and within America's institutions. In the 1970s, parents of children with special needs made great headway toward insisting their children have the opportunity to a free, public education, just as children without special needs (e.g., the passing of PL 94-142 in 1975 and PL 99-457 in 1986). One of the goals for these parents was to allow their children to spend as much time as possible in a regular classroom, affording their children the opportunity to be members of the regular classroom community. (In PL 94-142, this was described as placing children in the "least restrictive environment," which quickly became known as "mainstreaming"; Hallahan & Kauffman, 1988.)

In the 1990s, the push has been to have all children, except those with the most severe cases in which health will not permit it, included in the regular classroom communities for the entire day ("inclusion or "full inclusion"). Why have people pushed for this opportunity? Some say, rather cynically, that it is to save money, as meeting the requirements of each student with special needs in an individualized way is an impossibility. But those who are drafting the inclusion proposals are aiming to have a special education teacher and a regular teacher in each classroom, with all the resource people still available to meet individual needs (see National Education Association [NEA], 1992). Such proposals would not save money but increase costs.

In an NEA report, people argue for inclusion because they say it is important for children to be members of classroom communities, not separated or isolated from others. They present the case that only by having children grow up around each other can they learn about each other, understand each other, not be afraid of each other, and learn how to help their fellow classmates. These people recognize the value of others, as well as particular needs, and present the case that by being with others the opportunities for individual learning and growth can actually be increased. They say that children learn more from being in a community than they learn by being isolated by themselves, as Rousseau recommended. We will come back to more discussion on what kinds of skills people learn in communities in the democracy section.

Another problem for individualistic models is that a child does not walk into a classroom out of a state of nature but rather walks in having already experienced social influence and limitations on his or her development. Individualists tend to view the development of self as something that happens independently for each of us and does not need external assistance. It is as though we are each born with a self intact, just needing the opportunity to emerge, rather than viewing the self as something that develops through interactions with others. George Herbert Mead (1934; often described as the "father of sociology" in the United States) turned the whole notion of how the self develops upside down by arguing that it is impossible for individuals to develop and become as we know them by themselves. Mead argues that we are social beings, first, and members of a community, and then, out of that community, we develop a sense of who we are as separate and autonomous individuals. "According to Mead, the self is not present in the individual at birth but emerges and develops in and through the life of the physical organism. And the mechanism for this emergence and development can be found in the process of social activity" (Hanson, 1986, p. 14).

Let us take a closer look at a child's development. We need only think of a newborn child's situation to realize a child's development, while in utero, is totally dependent on the mother's well-being. If the mother is sick or does not get enough to eat, the baby inside of her suffers too. Children are born everyday who remind us of this fact, children who are born addicted to cocaine or heroin or born sick and undersized because of the tobacco or alcohol their mothers ingested. Once a child is born, she or he is still totally dependent on someone else's care for survival. Someone must nurse the baby or give the baby a bottle. Someone must keep the baby warm and dry, protected from the elements. Someone must hold and cuddle the baby, for touch and loving embrace are as important as food and rest. A newborn baby will not survive without another's care. The need to be cared for, and then to care for others, is embedded in this relational reality.[6] We will return to a further discussion on caring in the section on democracy.

Translating the issue of self-development to the classroom community, children arrive in a classroom having received different levels of care and having experienced different kinds of opportunities, or lack of opportunities, to develop a sense of self. Who the caretakers are, for these children in the classroom, has a significant impact on what kind of person each child is. Much research has found that a child does not begin with a sense of self. At first the child is not able to distinguish between him- or herself and the environment. This is the concept of egocentrism as Piaget described it, uniquely that of young children before they have learned that they are separate beings not connected to their caretaker or their blanket or bed (Thayer-Bacon, 1989). Through day-to-day interactions with others, babies begin to learn about the culture they have been born into and about themselves by how others relate to them. How a child comes to know, for instance, language and the ability to express thoughts is through these relationships the child is experiencing. That each child is born with some genetic predispositions is probably true, but it is certainly also true that a child is greatly affected by her or his environment. What each child knows, when that child walks into a classroom, is contextual and pertains to content; it is historical, psychological, political, and social (Kuhn, 1970; Rorty, 1979).

Social Constructivist Communities

For the classroom community that places its emphasis on the group instead of the particular individual, we label this a **social constructivist** model, in honor of the contributions made by sociologists such as Mead (1934) and Berger and Luckmann (1966). Social constructivist classroom communities aim to shape people into good citizens, aware of how they influence each other and how social institutions influence them. A modern example can be found in cooperative learning classrooms; a more classic example, in Plato's *Republic*.

In cooperative learning classrooms (Johnson, Johnson, & Holubec, 1992), teachers are concerned about how they structure their classroom environment, for they are aware that such structure affects how their students interact with each other. Research on cooperative classrooms has focused on academic achievement, intergroup relations, willingness to work with mainstreamed students, self-esteem, or other concerns such as how students feel about school, signifying that teachers may be using cooperative learning to achieve a variety of ends (Slavin, 1991). Doing things such as seating students at tables instead of desks, placing desks so they face each other and form small tables, or arranging desks in a horseshoe shape so that all students can see each others' faces allows students the opportunity to work with each other more and increases the chances that all students will interact and actively contribute to classroom discussions.

Teachers using cooperative models structure their academic lessons so that students work in pairs or small groups rather than individually, when the student's tasks and goals for learning are independent of others'. Students are often assigned different roles/tasks within the groups, and rather than receiving an individual grade, students often receive a grade with their group. In this model, the teacher is not viewed as the only human resource available in the classroom for gaining knowledge but as one of many resources available, the other human resources being the other students in the classroom. The teacher structures the lessons

> so that students work together to accomplish shared learning goals. In this cooperative learning situation, the goals of the students are positively correlated, so students perceive that they can reach their learning goals if and only if the other students in the learning group can also reach their learning goals. Students seek outcomes that are beneficial to all those with whom they are cooperatively linked. (Johnson et al., 1992, p. 37)

The kinds of values a social constructivist model hopes to teach are such things as recognizing the importance of equality and fairness, getting along with and helping others, and viewing oneself as an important, responsible, contributing member to a larger group, community, or society. Through such lessons it is hoped the individual also benefits, for the individual who learns how to work with others learns relational and communication skills and finds her or his self-esteem raised through feeling like an important member of the classroom community. Rather than ignoring the social influence on individuals, social constructivist communities emphasize that such an influence exists. They aim to take that social influence and use it in positive ways, rather than allow it to be used in oppressive, destructive ways.

We find parents of students in cooperative classrooms concerned about how their children are getting along with others. They will want to make sure no child is being excluded from the group and that all the groups are fairly distributed. They are excited to find their children gaining in self-confidence and self-esteem and note how their children seem actually to achieve greater academic success when they feel more valued as members of the classroom.

If we turn to Plato's *Republic* (cited in Cahn, 1970) for a classic example of the social constructivist community model, one will find that Plato also places his emphasis on how society shapes the individual and what the individual's role is in support of society. He views the individual as first of all a citizen of the state. The *Republic* centers around the issue of how a state should educate its citizens so they will become virtuous people able to contribute to the state. Plato's educational plan is designed to afford every citizen the opportunity of a free, public education, primarily so the state can shape the kind of citizens it needs for its survival and, second, as a way of sifting and sorting through the people to find the ones most qualified to become philosopher-kings/queens (guardians), able to lead the state wisely.

> Will he [the guardian] not also require natural aptitude for his calling?
>
> Certainly.
>
> Then it will be our duty to select, if we can, natures which are fitted for the task of guarding the city?
>
> It will. (cited in Cahn, 1970, p. 51)

Plato is not so concerned about helping each individual person reach her or his full potential. He does argue, though, that setting up an educational system like the one he proposes, one in which all people find out what they are suited to do, will offer everyone the opportunity to develop their own natural talents. "[W]e must infer that all things are produced more plentifully and easily and of better quality when one (person) does one thing which is natural to him and does it at the right time, leaving other crafts alone" (p. 46).

Individualistic theories focus on the individual and consider the community's role to be to protect the individual from infringements of his or her own rights (e.g., making sure no child hits another child) and taking care of things for the individual so that the individual is freed up to develop more on his or her own (e.g., making sure the classroom is quiet and orderly so the individual child can concentrate and learn). Social constructivist theories focus on how the state should support an individual's development (e.g., allowing all students the opportunity to attend the same classes and participate in lessons in capacities they are able to) so that individuals can contribute to the state in a way that best suits them (e.g., offering students the opportunity to participate in group lessons by assigning students different roles and responsibilities).

Problems with the Social Constructivist View

Social constructivist theories also present many problems. Again, we can begin to see them by looking at these theories as a model of a community in a classroom. Students who work in group settings in classrooms often complain that they spend a lot of time helping others, and this process slows down their own learning. Working with others is not necessarily a very efficient way to get anything done. Anyone who has served on committees may know this is true! Committees will take forever (so it seems) to accomplish what one person could do alone in half the time. Often the chair of the committee ends up doing most of the work anyway, because that person is considered responsible for the end product, and it is easier to do it alone than to gather everyone together to accomplish the task. The sheer organizing of a group can take tremendous amounts of time and effort.

This leads to another complaint from students in these kinds of settings. They complain that getting only a group grade does not necessarily reflect the contribution each of them made to the group project. Students will find that although they may have done the bulk of the work, they get the same grade everyone else in the group gets. One student in particular may contribute very little to the project and yet will receive the same high grade, without having earned it. Or, worse, that same one person may not do what he agreed to do, and the whole group project will suffer as a result, causing every student to receive the same bad grade.

Cooperative learning advocates claim that these problems are examples of teachers not successfully using the cooperative learning method. They cite research that says cooperatively instructed students show "greater student achievement, higher quality work, more independence in pursuing individual learning and helping others in the group learn, and greater cooperation and awareness of skills needed to be successful in cooperative activities" (Johnson et al., 1992, p. 44).

Social constructivists point out that it is difficult to learn how to structure classrooms cooperatively because what the vast majority of teachers experienced as students themselves was an individualistic model. In other words, teachers and parents have been socialized to be focused on individual needs over community needs and therefore find it very difficult to change. They must relearn ways of relating with others, so they can teach their children and those children can then arrive at schools ready and able to participate in classroom activities in positive and constructive ways.

A third concern, which parents often raise, is that in the name of equality and sameness, instead of improving individual student learning, we end up lowering the quality of learning for everyone. One often hears parents make this claim about public education, in general: that it becomes a minimalist level of education, instead of a maximalist, and instead of discriminating against some children, it hurts all of them. We all end up getting the same lousy education. Others have pointed out that making all children take the same curriculum, as Plato recommended and other modern-day philosophers such as Adler (1982), Bloom (1987), and Hirsch (1987) have recommended, ignores the fact that all children have different talents. Maybe we need to learn to value each child's unique talents.

We could say Plato was proposing exactly that kind of differentiation in the *Republic*. He was suggesting simply a means of sifting and sorting people into their best possible occupations, ones in which they would be happiest and best able to contribute to the community at large. We could argue that Plato was not saying that one type of person should be valued over another in the *Republic*. The problem is, if one were to ask people what they would prefer to be in Plato's *Republic,* most people probably would rather be classified a gold person (a philosopher-king/queen, a guardian) than a silver (soldier) or bronze one (craftsperson). Just having the opportunity to procreate would be enough to create the desire to be gold for most people![7]

Underlying these sample problems for social constructivist views is a problem with the assumption that the self is shaped by the community. Individualistic views describe the self as developing on its own and then deciding whether to join up with others and become a member of a community. The focus is on the particular, the individual, at the expense of the general, the community. Social constructivist views tend to focus on the community and argue that if the community's needs are met, so are the individual's needs met. This theory does justice to the group, potentially at the individual's expense.

Some philosophers have focused on the community and how it shapes individuals, but not in a positive way as Plato or cooperative learning scholars have argued. Rather, the approach has been to show how communities, and institutions formed by social groups, are oppressive to individuals. Karl Marx offered powerful criticisms for individualistic views that people are by nature self-centered (Marx & Engels, 1848/1964). He called his socialist theory "communism" to distinguish it from other utopian socialist theories, such as that of the British socialist philosopher Robert Owen (1813/1948). Socialists question the notion of "human nature," saying instead that people are shaped to become who they are by their social settings. Of the social institutions that affect our lives, Marx focused on the church and economic institutions. He viewed all history as a history of class struggle, a series of contradictions and their resolutions through class struggle, with each new society establishing new classes and new forms of oppression and exploitation. Marx predicted that a social revolution was going to occur and that this was historically determined—nothing could be done to stop it. All we could do was either speed up or slow down the process.

Marx's theory has been criticized for concentrating social conflict on *a priori* privileged agents (the working class, or proletariat). Marx classified people in terms of their worker status, denying that within the worker status people were also distinguishable (and exploited) because of gender (men, women), sexual orientation (heterosexual, homosexual, bisexual), culture (Asian, African, South American), and so forth, as well as because of distinctions within these (e.g., Mainland Chinese and Taiwan Chinese, North and South Korean, Japanese and Okinawan), for example. Marx has also been criticized for assigning a character of inevitability to resistance against oppression. Marxism is too mechanistic, it does not take into account the unique differences of individuals, and it is too simplistic, for there is "nothing inevitable or natural in the different struggles against power, and it is necessary to explain in each case the reasons for their emergence and the different modulations they may adopt" (Laclau & Mouffe, 1985, p. 152).

Since Marx, other "Marxists" (often also called critical theorists or radical democratic philosophers) have discussed the role of other institutions in our lives. China's Chairman Mao was critical of economic, state, family, and educational institutions. Some Marxists such as Ivan Illich (1973) and Paulo Freire (1970, 1985) have focused on schools as social institutions that shape our individual lives.[8] A closer look at Freire's work will help us understand one critical theorist perspective concerning schooling.

One of Freire's most significant philosophical works to date is *The Pedagogy of the Oppressed,* which he wrote in Chile while he was living in exile from Brazil. Freire has devoted his adult life to adult education, in particular teaching adults how to read. He began this career by going to small, poor, isolated villages and offering his services as a teacher. He asked his adult students, "What do you want to learn how to read?" Their answer was, "The newspaper." When the adults learned to read the newspaper, they began to look critically at their world and how their views were shaped by the institutions in their lives. They started to see how this shaping had limited and oppressed their lives. They also began to consider ways to take action against the exploited elements of their lives. Freire labeled this "learning to perceive social, political, and economic contradictions, and to take action against the oppressive elements of reality" by the Portuguese term *conscientização* (Freire, 1970, p. 19). The development of *conscientização* in his adult students caused the Brazilian government to perceive Freire as a threat when a military coup occurred in 1964. Freire was serving as head of the National Literacy Program of the Brazilian Ministry of Education and Culture at the time.

Freire labeled the common "banking" method of teaching as one that teaches students to be passive receivers of knowledge (others have labeled this "direct teaching," or what college students know so well as "lecturing"). "Education thus becomes an act of depositing, in which the students are the depositories and the teacher is the depositor" (Freire, 1970, p. 58). The banking method allows educational institutions (teachers, administrators, and schools and the governments that make the rules they must follow) to shape students' lives, and this shaping is oppressive because it hinders students' pursuits of self-affirmation as responsible people (p. 40). "Implicit in the banking concept is the assumption of a dichotomy between man and the world: man is merely *in* the world, not *with* the world or with others; man is a spectator, not re-creator" (p. 62).

Instead of using the banking method of teaching, Freire (1970) proposed using "problem-posing" as an instrument of liberation. When teachers use a problem-posing method, they treat their students with respect, as colearners who are capable of "authentic thinking, thinking that is concerned with *reality*" (p. 64). They enter into dialogue with their students. Problem-posing education takes questions and concerns that are real for students and focuses on trying to solve these issues. The teacher's role is to help empower students to think and act for themselves (Freire's **praxis**). Problem-posing helps students develop "a deepened consciousness of their situation" and leads them "to apprehend that situation as an historical reality susceptible of transformation" (p. 73).

As Freire (1970) describes his liberating view of education: "Education as the practice of freedom—as opposed to education as the practice of domination—denies that man is abstract, isolated, independent, and unattached to the world; it also denies that the world exists as a reality apart from men" (p. 69). People are not individuals, separate from their social communities, as individualistic theories argue. People are also not just shaped by a world that is separate from them, as social constructivist theories argue. By describing education this way, Freire clearly has moved away from a social constructivist theory, to what Laclau and Mouffe (1985) call a "post-Marxian terrain." According to Laclau and Mouffe, "It is no longer possible to maintain the conception of subjectivity and classes elaborated by Marxism, nor its vision of the historical course of capitalist development, nor, or course, the conception of communism as a transparent society from which antagonisms have disappeared" (pp. 2–3). The world we live in is pluralistic, diverse, and multifarious. It is also a transactive world where individuals affect their social groups **and** social groups affect individuals.

If we take another look at the newborn child described previously and at the child's relationship with the family, his or her first community, we find that the child affects the family as powerfully as the family affects the child.[9] The picture painted earlier pointed out how dependent the child is on others for care because children are physically helpless. But they are socially strong (Dewey, 1916/1966). A baby developing in utero can cause a mother to change her eating and exercising habits so that her baby will be born healthy and strong. The baby will enter into her plans and relationships with others as she tries to prepare for its arrival. She may commit to a relationship or decide to end one, so that a good support system will be there to help her when the baby arrives. She will definitely have to make changes in her work schedule, even if only temporarily, because a time will come when she will not be able to work at all. If she is not planning to be the child's main caretaker, she will have to make plans for who will be. Her life will also be financially affected by the child, before the child is even born.

After a birth, even more changes happen to the family because of a child's presence. Basic human patterns of living, such as when to eat or sleep or bathe and dress, change because of one small, physically helpless human being! Much stress, learning and growth, and tremendous feelings of love can develop because of this small living being who really is not an individual with a sense of self yet. But even that does not take too long. At 2 years, a child can very adequately express his or her needs and desires verbally, and a basic personality has already begun to emerge. Even at 1 year, one child reacts to a situation by crying, and another reacts to the same situation by laughing. One is shy and timid around strangers; another reaches out for them and gives them a hug or at least a smile; a third screams if they come near. Parents with several children tell about how differently their children reacted to the same environment in their house and the same guidelines and rules for coexistence.

Our point, Freire's, and Laclau and Mouffe's, is that social constructivist theories of the individual and community make the opposite mistake of individualistic theories. Where individualistic theories give the individual the all-powerful role of affecting the community, social constructivist theories tend to give the community the all-powerful role of affecting the individual. The reality is that it is an interactive, interrelational process (Dewey, 1916/1944). Dynamic changes take place with the self and the community, because of their interaction with each other, and all are affected. One can see this very clearly in a classroom community.

Many children arrive at school hungry, tired, sick, or worried about problems at home. They need tending to before they can learn. Arriving under such conditions, students can be distracted, disruptive, argumentative, or even just listless and unable to attend to what is going on, let alone to contribute in class. If some children in a classroom are suffering, usually everyone suffers as a result. Little learning can take place if children are hurting each other or disrupting the environment. The classroom is dependent on the individual's well-being to function best, and the individuals are dependent on the group's well-being to function best. The children arriving to school each day need their classroom to be a place that notices how they are doing and a haven they can turn to for support and help if they need it. These children, our children, may walk past winos and druggies on the way to school. They may hear gunfire and see violence and crime all around them. Children, and their families, need to know that people in their school community look out for them, notice whether they are missing, care about them, and will help them. In such a school environment, children will have an opportunity to heal, if they need to, and thrive and contribute in positive ways to the learning of others, as well as learn themselves.

Communities—for example, one's family and later on one's school community—teach children skills such as their language and social customs and help children develop a sense of self, a voice. Then children turn around and contribute those voices to the conversations. They add their insights and unique perspectives as well as their actions and energies to communities. And communities are changed because of the children. Realizing this is the first step toward working to help build healthy democratic communities in our classrooms, communities full of loving, caring, reasonable people who help each other and teach and learn from each other. There is hope for achieving communities based on undistorted communication, dialogue, communal judgment, rational persuasion, and an ethic of care, if we can begin to see how dependent communities are on the welfare of their individuals, and how dependent individuals are on the community, for their welfare.

Democratic Schools and Classrooms

We learned from Young and Stone that problems and contradictions are embedded in the concept of community. We also learned that problems of "othering" exist between individuals at all levels and in all forms of social life. Emphasizing difference does not appear to eradicate the ongoing practices of "othering." In fact, proposing forms of association based on difference as a way of solving problems of **exclusion** highlights how important **inclusion** is for all of us. We seem to need to be members of some form of community, at least in our early years. We suggested earlier that rather than trying to disavow or rename 'community', we should continually reexamine the concept 'community' and strive to envision this association with others in new forms.

Dewey offered a description of a democratic community that uses 'democratic' to describe a type of social grouping, as we use the term. By 'democratic' we do not mean a certain political party or style of political governing. Rather, we use 'democracy' to describe a form of community, like Dewey's description, that recognizes the interactive, interrelational, interdependent qualities of individuals and others.[10] Amy Gutmann (1987) reexamines Dewey's description in *Democratic Education*. Let us start with Dewey's description, then turn to hers, and see whether we can envision a democratic community in new forms, through our use of the classroom metaphor.

Dewey's description of a democratic community highlights the type of community that encourages the contributions of unique voices to the conversation. It also recognizes the interaction and relationship between the individual and the group. The two criteria Dewey (1916/1966) gives in *Democracy and Education* to measure the worth of a form of social life are "the extent in which the interests of a group are shared by all its members, and the fullness and freedom with which it interacts with other groups" (p. 99). The first criterion points out the importance of connection and relationships within the group, and the second points out the importance of interaction within the group and with others outside the group. Such interaction helps the democratic community be able to adapt and change continually to meet the needs of its individual members. A democratic society is "a society which makes provisions for participation in its good of all its members on equal terms and which secures flexible readjustment of its institutions through interaction of the different forms of associated life" (p. 115). A democratic community is dependent on the contributions of its individuals as well as on the recognition of each one's value and worth. Because each voice is needed, the opportunity for dialogue, for conversation that is undistorted and relies on rational persuasion, is vital.

When Dewey (1900/1956) turns to applying his democratic theory to education, he advises, "[W]hat the best and wisest parent wants for his own child, that must the community want for all of its children" (p. 7).

Gutmann (1987) uses Dewey as inspiration for her democratic theory but says she differs in at least one way: she points out the inconsistency with a theory of democratic education that insists (note Dewey's term *must*) it be done a certain way. Gutmann's point is that "the enforcement of any moral ideal of education, whether it be liberal or conservative, without the consent of citizens subverts democracy" (p. 14). She argues it is necessary to add principles to support a broader democratic standpoint, one that is not just individualistic, for even democratic communities can be repressive and discriminatory. The two principles she recommends are principles of nonrepression and nondiscrimination. The principle of nonrepression assures "the freedom to deliberate rationally among different ways of life" (p. 44), and the principle of nondiscrimination assures that "all educable children must be educated" (p. 45).

> A democratic society must not be constrained to legislate what the wisest parents want for their children, yet it must be constrained *not* to legislate policies that render democracy repressive or discriminatory. . . . A society that empowers citizens to make educational policy, moderated by these two principled constraints, realizes the democratic ideal of education. (p. 14)

When we turn to the classroom community for assistance in envisioning a democratic community, we have trouble finding examples. Dewey started a Laboratory School at the University of Chicago, which he ran from 1896 to 1903 (it still exists today).[11] Teachers at the Lab School were treated as colleagues and met weekly with Dewey to discuss school issues such as curriculum. Teachers also had free time built into their daily schedule so they could meet with other teachers to discuss their work. However, students did not have the freedom or authority to influence educational decisions concerning the curriculum the way the adults did. They were encouraged to participate in decisions that took place (teachers had "council meetings" with students at the beginning of the day), but they were not treated "as the political or intellectual equals of [the Lab School's] teachers" (Gutmann, 1987, p. 93).

A. S. Neill's Summerhill, founded in 1921 and still in existence, is a famous example of a school designed to be democratic in form, but the classrooms at Summerhill have never been highlighted as examples of democratic classrooms. It is the boarding school, itself, that is uniquely democratic. Summerhill shows its democratic qualities through the weekly town meetings the school has to discuss issues and decide policy. The children share in the governing of their school. As Neill (1960) describes:

> Summerhill is a self-governing school, democratic in form. Everything connected with social, or group, life, including punishment for social offenses, is settled by vote at the Saturday night General School Meeting.
>
> Each member of the teaching staff and each child, regardless of his age, has one vote. My vote carries the same weight as that of a seven-year-old. (p. 45)

In Summerhill's town meetings, one can see the focus is on interaction and the free exchange of ideas, democratic qualities described by Dewey. Children at Summerhill are encouraged to develop their communication skills as well as their relational skills. The school recognizes that each voice in the town meeting is important and must have the opportunity to be heard. Summerhill's town meetings encourage students to learn the art of rational persuasion, so that they can persuade other students to vote on issues the way they are hoping, to win the results they desire. The school also encourages students to think for themselves and learn to be critical thinkers, able to judge whether reasons offered are sound and whether arguments are valid.

> The educational benefit of practical civics cannot be overemphasized. At Summerhill, the pupils would fight to the death for their right to govern themselves. In my opinion, one weekly General School Meeting is of more value than a week's curriculum of school subjects. It is an excellent theatre for practicing public speaking, and most children speak well and without self-consciousness. I have often heard sensible speeches from children who could neither read nor write. (Neill, 1960, p. 55)

Summerhill also shows the democratic characteristics of being flexible, able to adjust to the needs of its population. The children are free to come and go as they choose and get involved or not in activities that are going on around the campus. If the children want to play all day and not attend any classes, they are free to do so. Neill's basic philosophy was that children should not be coerced to learn. He believed very strongly that children have a natural curiosity and desire to learn and that it is schools, as we have structured them, that kill in children the desire to learn. He also believed children have a lot they can teach adults and deserve to be treated with respect and dignity.

> My view is that a child is innately wise and realistic. If left to himself without adult suggestion of any kind, he will develop as far as he is capable of developing. (Neill, 1960, p. 4)

> The function of the child is to live his own life—not the life that his anxious parents think he should live, nor a life according to the purpose of the educator who thinks he knows what is best. All this interference and guidance on the part of adults produces a generation of robots. (p. 12)

The democratic characteristic of acknowledging the worth and value of individuals and allowing for their contributions (Gutmann's principles of nonrepression and nondiscrimination) are common traits that can also be found in another type of school, a Montessori school.[12] Montessori classrooms and schools do have many democratic community traits. In a Montessori classroom, the teacher functions as a facilitator and resource person. Maria Montessori called her teachers "directresses." The teacher observes students as they work and notes what their interests are. He or she gives the children the opportunity to be drawn to the curriculum materials that are in the room according to the students' own interests. This involves a level of trust of the teacher's part, that the teacher is able to step back, not try to control the curriculum but allow the students to choose their own work. If nothing seems to attract a child's interest, the teacher often tries to show the child some different materials or spend more time observing and talking to the child, to try to get ideas for new materials he or she may design and bring into the classroom. In the Montessori classroom, the adults function as models for learning themselves and as resource people and guides to help students in their explorations.

Like those at Summerhill, the children in Montessori classrooms choose what they want to learn and when. Montessori classrooms offer children the opportunity to move freely throughout the room, working by themselves or with others who share similar interests. There is as much opportunity for full, free interaction with others as the students desire. Opportunity for dialogue in group situations is also offered. Although both Summerhill and Montessori schools start with children and staff who may have nothing more in common than membership (and for the children that membership is not necessarily voluntary), they both provide many opportunities for the members to get to know each other more and develop shared interests. They also both offer opportunities for the members to decide they do not want to participate. The associations in these schools can be temporary and shifting, the boundaries within the schools are fluid, and there is freedom of anonymity (all characteristics Stone and Young desire in a community). Summerhill and Montessori schools seem to address Stone's and Young's concerns of sameness and difference and still offer a model of community.

Teachers mention how much they enjoy the working conditions in Montessori classrooms and at Summerhill, for these schools are ones in which children learn how to treat each other and the environment with respect, and the children learn self-discipline and independence. Teachers do not have to worry that they must always supply external control on the classroom community; the structure of the setting itself does so, and the children encourage each other to follow the general rules, so that the classroom community functions effectively. If someone does not take care of the materials, others will not be able to choose that work. If someone is too noisy or disruptive, others will not be able to concentrate on their own projects. In our experience, the only children who seem to struggle in a Montessori classroom are those who have trouble developing self-discipline and need the teacher to supply them with more external structure then the Montessori classroom itself offers. Neill (1960) also mentions these same type of children struggling at Summerhill; they were what he calls "the bullies."

We can see from the examples of Summerhill and Montessori schools that a democratic perspective values a view of people who are not ruled by self-interest alone. Neill stressed the difference between freedom and license at Summerhill. Children are allowed to vote on what time they go to bed, but they may not ride another child's bicycle without permission or walk on Neill's piano. In a democratic community, people have to be reasonable. They must be able to see how their decisions and actions affect others. They have to be able to be critical of themselves, as well as of others, for self-criticism is the essence of self-growth. In choosing to value a democratic perspective, one has to believe that everyone can be reasonable and that all human beings have dignity. It may be that we are not born rational, but the belief is that we can **learn** to be through education.

Education has a very important role in a democratic community. The aim of education is to teach people to be rational, reflective thinkers. According to Dewey (1916/1966), "Such a society [a democratic society] must have a type of education which gives individuals personal interest in social relationships and control, and the habits of mind which secure social changes without introducing disorder" (p. 99). Gutmann (1987) adds, "All societies of self-reflective beings must admit the moral value of enabling their members to discern the difference between good and bad ways of life" (p. 43).

Problems with Democratic Schools/Classrooms

We now outline some problems with Summerhill and Montessori classrooms that will help us see what is a potential weakness in the classical view of democracy as Dewey described it. This weakness is something Gutmann points to with her two principles. Neill (1960) described "one perennial problem that can never be solved" as the problem of "the individual vs. the community" (p. 53). He saw this problem in the form of one child becoming a gang leader and leading children by encouraging them to be nuisances and harm others. At Summerhill these individuals were attacked at the General Meetings.

> Strong words are used to condemn her [Jean's, a student] misuse of freedom as license. . . . As to the condemnation by the school meeting, one simply cannot sacrifice other children to one problem child. . . . On a very few occasions I [Neill] have had to send a child away because the others were finding the school a hell because of him. I say this with regret, with a vague feeling of failure, but I could see no other way. (pp. 53–54)

Summerhill and Montessori schools struggle with how to balance the needs of individuals and the group. Both types of schools work at great length to try to address individual needs, but they must also be concerned with the larger group, as they are responsible for all the children in their schools and depend on the enrollment of many children to survive (as private schools).

In Summerhill and Montessori classrooms, the focus can tend to be more on the individual than on the group. It certainly is the case that interrelationships and interconnections between the self and others are acknowledged (e.g., in how the children are taught to care for the materials and the classroom or school environment), but the value of learning skills such as self-discipline are often seen as being valuable mainly to the individual child's development. Also, the value of having an environment in which children are free to choose their own work is often seen as important mainly to the individual. Although learning how to work with others is valued and encouraged, learning how to be an independent, self-reliant, autonomous decision maker who is a reflective thinker is often more highly prized.

One can find Montessori classrooms in which teachers value the community as much as the individual, but there is much room for variation within the Montessori method, and what one finds in terms of a democratic classroom community depends greatly on the individual teacher's influence. What weakens the chances of a Montessori classroom being a democratic community is a greater focus on individual freedom than on the development of shared, common interests. Because the children at Summerhill live together, they have even more opportunities to develop shared interests, but that does not mean those shared interests will not be harmful to individuals (e.g., bossing others around).

Is there a way to redescribe this problem of valuing the individual's needs as well as the community's needs, other than through principles of nonrepression and nondiscrimination (Gutmann's suggestion)? We would like to suggest that one way out of this problem might be to recognize the importance of teaching and encouraging people in communities to **care** for each other as well as to be reasonable, self-disciplined individuals.

We use the word *care* after a great deal of consideration of whether it adds clarity or confusion to the model of a democratic community. We realize *care* is used in many ways, and many different meanings are associated with it. *Care* is used to mean "love" when people say, "I care for you very much." We also use *care* to mean "I have affection for you," but not as strongly as the term *love* signifies. We say, "I care for you" meaning, "I like you." *Care* is also used to mean the "meeting of someone's basic needs," as when people say, "I am caring for my mother because she is ill."

Feminist scholars have made the case that historically, we have associated the care of others as being mainly a female responsibility. *Care* is also associated with people of lower social class and minority status, as when wealthy families will hire other people to care for their property and children (nannies, gardeners, and housekeepers). *Care* does not always have a positive, supportive, relational association, either. Many times parents will say things to their children such as, "It is because I care so much for you that I am punishing you for what you did." From a child's perspective, the parents' caring may feel like manipulation or control, like someone else is telling them what they can or can not do. They may wish their parent did not care so much!

We acknowledge the many ways we use the term *care* and the many associations attached to the word, some of which seem harmful rather than helpful to further development of a theory concerning democratic communities. Yet, if we examine the different meanings associated with *care,* we notice they do all point to an aspect of relationships that reason does not seem to highlight. *Care* points to the affective side of relationships; it emphasizes the need to consider emotional feelings of worth and value. Caring is a valuing of the other as someone who is worth attending to (Thayer-Bacon, 1993a). Caring for another does not have to entail loving the other or even liking the other. Caring does not have to entail certain gendered or social classed people. What caring does insist on, in all its forms, is that to care for another, one must be willing to try to understand the other. Trying to understand another requires learning a shared language so that communication can take place. Trying to understand another requires attempting to see the world through the other's eyes, suspending one's own beliefs and trying to believe what the other is attempting to communicate, before critiquing or dismissing the other (Thayer-Bacon, 1995c). Nel Noddings (1984, 1992) describes caring as being "receptive" to the other and as a form of "engrossment."

Remember, **a democratic community is one that has shared interests, with full, free interaction among its members**. Individual selves are dependent on others to help them develop and grow, but so are others, that is, communities, dependent on the contributions of individuals to be able to thrive and flourish. Democratic communities especially rely on having their members contribute of their own free will. What causes an individual to want to contribute to a community? To want to contribute to a community, a member needs to feel like she or he is a valued member. A valued member is someone who feels cared for.

In his discussion of different types of communities (e.g., a gang of thieves), Dewey (1916/1966) noted that from the two traits of **shared interests** and **interaction**, standards could be derived. "How numerous and varied are the interests which are consciously shared? How full and free is the interplay with other forms of association?" (p. 83).

Through an examination of the standards Dewey offered, especially the standard of full interaction with others, one can uncover the necessary ingredient for a democratic community of **caring**. Even if people have opportunities to form associations with others (Gutmann's principle of nondiscrimination), people have to want to do so. Even if people have the opportunity to interact freely with others within their community as well as with other communities (Gutmann's principle of nonrepression), they have to make an effort to attend to each other and feel there is value in opening up to others. People have to **care**, to desire hearing what another has to say, for full interaction to take place. When a person is excluded from a community or is a member of a community that is oppressive, she or he likely experiences the community as being cruel and unreasonable. To achieve democratic communities in which people enjoy having shared interests and appreciate their opportunities for full, free interaction, both rationality and caring must be stressed, and the community must find a way to balance these. Let us explain further.

A child can be a member of a Montessori classroom community or attend Summerhill school, share the same locality as other students, live with the same rules as every other student, and that child may choose not to interact with others or develop any further shared interests than the membership of that school community. The child may just focus on his or her own individual needs, and the teachers and staff would have to honor that choice. This is because the Montessori method and Summerhill school (to a lesser degree because it is a boarding school) stress independence and self-initiation over mutual aid and cooperation with others.

A democratic community perspective that includes caring as a value (as well as reasonableness) strives to be balanced and harmonious as well as allow for dissonance and discord. It wishes to honor an individual's right to be different, which might mean honoring an individual's decision not to participate. Yet it also is aware of issues concerning exclusion and 'othering' that occur within communities, so it seeks to make the community a welcoming place where individuals feel invited to join, if they so choose. It focuses on the importance of relationships and the need to affirm others, so that they will feel encouraged to contribute to the conversation rather than be excluded or silenced. Also, because of the relational quality of the people in a democratic community, it is vital that the community embrace an ethic that relies on caring about each other, showing concern for each other's well-being, and getting to know each other.

A Democratic Classroom Community Redefined

Montessori classrooms may be excellent examples of democratic classroom communities, which value individuality and others equally. In many Montessori classrooms, a democratic community feeling develops, but not necessarily directly because of the methods being used by the teachers or the values being stressed. Support for the development of a caring democratic community is built into the very structure of the Montessori classroom. Two factors that indirectly help a sense of democratic community thrive in Montessori classrooms are the facts that students are typically in mixed-age classrooms and are members of that classroom community for 3 years. (One can see, in many special education classrooms, English as a Second Language classrooms, art, music, and physical education classrooms, as well as one-room schools, the same two factors. Because of limited resources, many schools have the same few teachers responsible for these same subject areas for the entire range of students, for several years.) Montessori classrooms, at preschool or elementary levels,[13] usually have an age span of 3 years (3- to 6-year-olds, 6- to 9-year-olds, 9- to 12-year-olds) with an average of 30 children in a classroom, around 10 children of each age. There are usually two adults per classroom.

In a democratic classroom community redescribed, the teacher strives to teach students the importance of equality and fairness, and she or he strives to teach students how to get along with and help others and to view oneself as an important, responsible, contributing member of a larger group, community, or society. Because Montessori schools are designed to place children of mixed ages and abilities in the same classroom for 3 years with the same teachers, the structure fosters caring for others. Because Summerhill is a boarding school with children of mixed ages living together for potentially 12 years, this structure also encourages caring for others. The Montessori classroom and Summerhill foster a tendency toward mutual aid and cooperation with others, even if the teachers' focus is more on independence, self-initiation, and rationality.

When a Montessori teacher teaches children for 3 years, she or he has a lot of opportunity to get to know the students and their families (keep in mind, one does not have the same group of 30 for 3 years; each year some of the children graduate and move on to another class, and younger students become new members of the class). Sometimes it takes a year for a teacher to build a relationship of trust and mutual respect with a student and her or his family. With the Montessori method, that same student walks back into the classroom the next school year, and all the groundwork that was laid the past year in terms of relationships is in place. The structure of having children in the same class for several years affords one **time to develop relationships**, which appears to be a vital ingredient for a caring, democratic community. As stated in the prior discussion of classrooms as models of communities, the opportunity to develop shared interests is important, and having more time further enhances that opportunity.

Knowing that the Montessori teacher will have the same child return to the classroom the next year brings out another important quality. When the teacher and students know they only have a short amount of time together, they do not necessarily have to make much of an effort to get along and learn how to solve their relational problems. It is not too difficult to stall and survive the experience without it affecting members too much. When people know they will not be together for very long, they may avoid forming a caring, democratic community within the classroom, if the students and teachers so desire. But when teachers and students know they will be together for several years, if they do not learn how to get along with each other, they will find the experience miserable and will likely leave the classroom community. Because of its unique structure, the Montessori classroom (and Summerhill) becomes like an extended family, and the teachers and students often find that they make friends in their classroom community who become lifelong friends. Having enough **time** together not only offers people the opportunity to develop relationships with each other, but it also makes it very uncomfortable for them to be together so much, if the relationships people develop are not caring, reasonable ones.

A Montessori (or Summerhill) teacher is forced to face another important factor to a caring, democratic community, owing to the structure of the school. Because the teacher has each student in his or her classroom for several years, the teacher has a greater responsibility to the child and the parents than other teachers experience. If she or he does not do a good job, it will be noticeable. One may not be a very good teacher and people may not realize that when one teaches for short amounts of time. But the longer students occupy the same space with the same teacher, the harder it is for the teacher to go undetected if she or he is not fulfilling responsibilities. The good news is that spending a greater amount of time together also gives a teacher increased opportunities to understand students, diagnose their needs, and find ways to meet those needs. In a Montessori classroom the teacher has **greater responsibility** for ensuring the success of the classroom community, but she or he also has **more opportunities** to find ways to develop the community successfully.

Students in Summerhill and the Montessori classroom find they also have greater responsibilities. If they are having problems getting along with others, those problems do not go away and are not easily ignored. Because of the amount of time the students and teachers spend together, problems in relationships can also have a greater impact on all the people in the classroom (or school). The classroom is designed to be interactive and foster opportunities for relationships to develop. If students are having trouble developing positive relationships with others, it will be apparent to all: teachers, fellow students, parents, and themselves.

The good news for students is that, although their responsibilities increase in a caring, democratic community, so do their opportunities to learn the skills they need to nurture positive relationships. The relational skills people need to develop caring relationships include communication skills (e.g., the ability to listen attentively to others and attempt to understand their point of view, the ability to express one's own point of view so that others can understand), mutual respect, and helping others feel validated and valued (Burbules & Rice, 1991; Rice & Burbules, 1993). When students spend 3 years (or more in Summerhill) in a caring, democratic classroom with other people, they have many opportunities to get to know others better and develop a better sense about themselves. They have many opportunities to develop a sense of mutual trust and respect with others, where they can feel safe to be the people they are becoming. They have lots of chances to practice their communication skills and learn how to express their voices, knowing others will listen to what they have to say.

Having children of mixed ages assigned to one classroom community for several years affords other advantages. Because the Montessori classroom and Summerhill are structured this way, they open the door to a greater variety of people and an increased range of skill levels within the community. With the increase of age range comes more room for children to grow and develop in their own unique ways and still feel like they are functioning within a range of normalcy. When only 7-year-olds are in a classroom together, if one is not reading yet and all the others are, that child is likely to feel "behind" in comparison and have his or her self-esteem affected. But, when there are ten 6-year-olds, ten 7-year-olds, and ten 8-year-olds, whether a student is reading "at grade level" will not be as noticeable, as there will probably be others who are not reading as well. What age the child is does not matter so much. With the increase in variety and range it becomes more likely that all children will be able to find some skills they can perform better than others, as well as some skills in which they are not so accomplished. With this setting teachers have a golden opportunity to set up the classroom so that all the children have chances to help others, as well as be helped by others, much as cooperative learning classrooms offer (Johnson et al., 1992). Considering the concerns of Young and Stone, mixed-aged classroom communities offer a much greater range of difference and less of a chance for an individual to feel "othered" (excluded).

Teachers often complain that the greater the variety of students (in terms of ages, skills, ethnic backgrounds, etc.) in their classroom, the more difficult their job is. How can they possibly meet the needs of all these different students? If they have the students in their classroom for 3 years, or more, they will have more opportunities, and if they see the other students in the classroom as potential resources and teachers, they will find the task of meeting everyone's needs is not so difficult. Having student diversity can add tremendously to the richness of the classroom curriculum, if teachers structure their classroom into a caring, democratic community.

People often ask, What happens to children who attended Summerhill or Montessori schools after they graduate? How do children who have attended a school which functions as a democratic community adjust to living in a larger world that is not so democratic? In *Summerhill School,* Albert Lamb, the editor and a former student, notes that in 1991, "the seventieth anniversary of the world's most famous progressive school, . . . there has never been a systematic study of Summerhill's actual mode of operation, its effect on pupils and its potential consequences for educational theory and practice in the larger context of the wide world" (Neill, 1992, p. xviii). Neill relates many stories of his students who had graduated and went on to be successes, as he defined success: "the ability to work joyfully and to live positively. Under that definition, most pupils in Summerhill turn out to be successes in life" (Neill, 1992, p. 125).

Neill (1992) also describes a survey published by Max Bernstein, an American, who interviewed former pupils living in the London area. These pupils complained about lack of protection from bullies, too-rapid turnovers of staff, and being overly influenced "by other children who were irresponsible with regards to academic work" (p. 128). "On the positive side, Bernstein found that the majority of past pupils felt good about their education" (p. 130). Neill notes that Bernstein's research is limited in numbers as well as by the fact that he ignores other factors such as home life. Neill reminds us he has students sent to Summerhill because their parents have raised their children in a democratic manner and want their children to continue to be educated in a similar manner, and he has students sent to Summerhill who have failed elsewhere and "thought Summerhill would undo the damage" (p. 130).

Thayer-Bacon's experience with children who left her Montessori classroom after attending a Montessori school from ages 3 to 12 is very similar to Neill's. The children leave feeling confident and assured about themselves. They have developed their own voices. They also leave still excited about learning, and they have acquired the skills and abilities necessary to continue life-long learning. They seem to be able to become members of other school communities and find ways to have those communities meet their needs as well as contribute to those communities. Those parents who enroll their children in a Montessori school for other reasons than agreement with the philosophy of education often do not continue their child's enrollment once the option of free, public education is available (Thayer-Bacon, 1987).

Although Dewey's criteria of **shared interests with full, free interaction among its members** are certainly necessary for a democratic community to have the opportunity to exist, they are not sufficient. Even Gutmann's principles of nonrepression and nondiscrimination are not enough. It is important for people to have the opportunity to be together and communicate with each other. But people must also take advantage of that opportunity and contribute to the community, and their contribution must be felt. People who feel cared for and valued as members will feel a desire and responsibility to contribute. People who are welcomed and attended to within a community discover they have many opportunities to develop ways to interact with others in the community and establish shared interests with other members. They find ways to make their contributions felt by the others in the community. **When people feel cared for and can make other people feel cared about, then the opportunity for a democratic community is more complete**.

Conclusion

We began by asking whether a form of community exists that does justice to individuals as well as groups. We brought out some of the concerns with 'community' as a concept through Lynda Stone's and Iris M. Young's work. We suggested that people desire community, even though they are aware 'community' is a concept fraught with problems and contradictions. We then defined 'community' as consisting of at least the two characteristics of involving more than one person and that these people have something in common, even if it is just the need for survival.

We examined two types of communities, individualistic and social constructivist, and found the individualistic models focus on the individual at the expense of the group, whereas the social constructivist models tend to emphasize the group at the expense of the individual. We suggested that the democratic community is a model that does justice to both the individual and the group by focusing on the interconnected, interdependent, interactive relationship that exists between the self and the community.

For democratic communities to be successful, they need to be caring and just, inclusive and affirming, balanced and harmonious, and allow for dissonance and discord, striving to meet the needs of the individual selves and the group. To meet these goals and teach these values, democratic classrooms need shared interests and free interaction, the opportunity to be together and learn how to communicate with each other. People also must have time to develop relationships with each other and feel a sense of responsibility to the community. People need the opportunity to find ways to contribute successfully to the community. Welcoming people, attending to them, and valuing them makes them feel cared for. People who feel cared for want to contribute to a community and feel a responsibility to do so. People who are cared for feel that they are significant members of their community and that what they contribute has meaning and importance and is noticed. We have argued that **caring** is a necessary ingredient for any community to be a democratic one, using Summerhill and the Montessori classroom to demonstrate the value of this important quality in a classroom setting.

Whereas others are discussing the importance of caring in our classrooms (Martin, 1992; Noddings, 1992), we are attempting to make the connection between caring and democracy as a unique contribution to this lively discussion. A teacher must focus on her or his students' interactions and encourage them to exchange ideas freely if she or he decides to encourage the classroom to function as a democratic community. The teacher must encourage the students (and the teachers) to develop their communication skills as well as their relational skills. She or he needs to create an environment that insists that each person has a valuable contribution to make to the community and ensures that each person's voice be heard. If schools are structured so that teachers and students have opportunities to spend more time with each other in manageably sized groups, and if schools ensure that these groups of people are varied in abilities and ages, they will find that opportunities for democratic communities to develop will increase. Teachers, students, and parents will have more of a chance to get to know each other under these conditions and more reasons to find ways to build healthy relationships with each other. The opportunities to learn how to communicate with each other, and therefore potentially increase their commonness and shared interests, will also improve.

We are not suggesting that these recommendations are a cure-all for all our problems. However, we do think reexamining our schools to find ways to help create caring democratic communities within them may go a long way to alleviate the loss of community or the harmful, destructive forms of community that many people experience today. Our children and their families are struggling in conditions that are not very reasonable or caring, where they feel excluded, made to be "the other." Schools are places filled with people who can help create a sense of belonging. Realizing that communities are dependent on individuals for their survival, just as individuals are dependent on communities for their survival, as the democratic model suggests, helps us see that we need to work together. We are each important contributing members whose needs must be met so that the needs of the community can also be met. Democratic communities must care for their individuals so their individuals can grow up caring about their communities.

In the Classroom

Activity 1

This exercise is intended to help you, as a student, see that you are members of a great many different communities and have varying degrees of involvement in each.

For some communities, you may feel an intense sense of involvement; for others, you may feel very little attachment. Nevertheless, each community to which a person belongs makes some contribution to who and what that person is, as well as the individual contributing to the community. This exercise allows you to recognize that your involvement in a community does not necessarily have to be on a face-to-face basis—you could be very much a part of a group that never meets in any formal way.

After listing the different communities in which you are a member, answer each of the following questions:

1. Which communities did you choose to join?
2. In which communities are you a member without joining?
3. Which of these communities do you meet with regularly?
4. Which communities never, or nearly never, meet (face-to-face)?

After making your list and answering the questions, meet with several of your classmates to talk about some of the ways in which you are members of different communities. Discussing your memberships with others should help you better understand the types of communities of which you may be a part and how these communities may make you members of even larger communities (i.e., membership in a particular Boy Scout troop means that the student is also a member of the larger organization of Boy Scouts).

This activity should conclude with a class discussion of how membership in communities helps individuals take care of their various needs. You should recognize that we deal with communities differently depending on how extensively we identify ourselves as members.

Activity 2

This activity is intended to help you appreciate how membership differs in each of the three types of communities described in the chapter.

In small groups—at least three groups (one for each type of community)—students should brainstorm ideas about what each of the three types of communities described in the chapter would be like from a student's perspective. Pay special attention to such details as these:

1. What would assignments be like for you?
2. How would you relate to your classmates?
3. What kinds of things are you likely to be doing each day in class?
4. How does your teacher interact with you?
5. How do you feel about being a member of this type of class?

You will want to include personal experiences in different types of classroom communities in your discussions.

After each small group has discussed the details of their type of community, focusing on student perspectives, they should present their ideas to the large group so that everyone has an opportunity to consider each of the three philosophical views. In the large group, each of the small-group communities can be a resource when discussing the particulars of their respective philosophical views.

Activity 3

This activity is intended to further help you understand the differences among the three types of communities described in the chapter by considering the issues teachers confront. Divide into small groups and choose which type of community you will present (or your instructor can assign these). Your group then picks a typical problem that teachers face fairly regularly. Some things you might want to consider are how would the teacher:

1. present lessons?
2. motivate students?
3. discipline students?
4. evaluate students?
5. relate to parents, colleagues, or supervisors?

You decide how to dramatize this problem to the larger class, without telling the class what perspective you are representing. Each group will need about 15 to 20 minutes to decide what they will dramatize, assign roles, and practice their skit; dramatization of the problem takes about 5 minutes per group to present. After each skit is presented, you should then be given the opportunity to say which type of community was enacted; after all skits are presented, you should then further discuss the problems enacted and how they are approached by teachers, depending on one's community/individual perspective.

Activity 4

In this chapter we discussed how communities have changed over time in an effort to define what a community is. We would like to challenge you to consider how communities will continue to change in the future. A good beginning focus is to look at how technology has changed communities in the past. Then discuss how these affect our communities right now and what changes we can foresee. Break into small groups and discuss how a specific technological development changed and continues to change communities.

Examples to choose for discussion are these:

■ Printing press
■ Television
■ Telephone
■ Computer

Do not forget to consider how technology has changed jobs, for example, and how these job changes have affected other aspects of community life, such as mobility and changes of job locations, which have then affected our family lives. This activity should help you, as students, consider the complexity of community life, and the dramatic ways in which one aspect, such as sources of communication or family structure, will affect communities at large.

Notes

This chapter began as a paper presented to the American Educational Research Association in 1993 titled "Selves in Relation: Reconstructing Community" by Thayer-Bacon (1993c). Different threads of thought within this chapter have been published as "Caring Democratic Communities" (Thayer-Bacon, 1995a), "Democratic Classroom Communities" (Thayer-Bacon, 1996b), and "Relational Qualities between Selves and Communities: Implications for Schools" (Thayer-Bacon, 1996c).

1. A recent discussion of Victor, the Wild Boy, can be found in Martin (1992).

2. Stone's definition is from Fox-Genovese (1991, p. 33).

3. See Martin (1992) for an excellent discussion on this topic.

4. We use the term *individualistic* to place the focus where it is for this type of view. There are many forms of individualistic communities. See Taylor (1989, 1992) for more discussion on this point. See also Betham (1977), Dewey (1935), and Steiner (1989).

5. John Stuart Mill's utilitarian slogan; see Mill (1859/1947, 1863/1950).

6. Sources on the notion of caring include Gilligan (1982), Noddings (1984, 1992), Thayer-Bacon (1993a), and Tronto (1987).

7. See Plato's discussion of the festivals for mating in Book 5 (cited in Cahn, 1970, pp. 460–462) of the *Republic*. Plato proposed a lottery system for procreation that was "fixed" so that gold people were allowed to procreate more than anyone else.

8. Other critical theorists who focus on schools include Apple (1986, 1996), Bowles and Gintis (1976), Brosio (1994), Giroux (1983, 1988), McLaren (1993, 1994), and Shapiro (1990).

9. We use the term *family* to define a group of people who care for each other and take care of each other, are responsible for each other's well-being, especially settings where there are mixed ages—for example, a baby and an adult person. A family need not be connected by blood or be of different sexes. A sense of care, concern, and connection—Martin's (1992) "3 C's"—is what helps bind a family together.

10. Samples of democratic theories: Barber (1984), Dewey (1916/1966, 1935), Fiskin (1991), Macpherson (1973, 1977), and Snauwaert (1992).

11. Gutmann (1987) discusses Dewey's Lab School in *Democratic Education* at p. 93. For a detailed description of the "Dewey School," see Mayhew and Edwards (1966). Dewey (1900/1956) describes it himself in *The Child and the Curriculum and the School and Society.*

12. Maria Montessori never actually wrote a detailed guide for how to set up a classroom like the ones she designed. Her books are general and broad and express much of her philosophical and religious beliefs, but a person had to attend one of Montessori's teacher training programs to learn how to establish a Montessori classroom successfully. Thayer-Bacon has attended such a program and was an elementary Montessori teacher for many years, so what we describe as a typical experience comes directly from her own experience in three American Montessori schools. Her four children have attended Montessori schools for a combined total of 25 years, the youngest child being in his first year as a Montessori elementary student. Sources for information on the Montessori method include Montessori (1972, 1977).

13. It is very difficult to find examples of Montessori secondary schools, at least in the United States. When Thayer-Bacon went through her training program in 1981–82, there were five secondary schools in the United States. A current listing could be obtained by contacting the American Montessori Society (281 Park Ave., New York, NY 10010) or the Association of Montessori International (1095 Market St., Suite 405, San Francisco, CA 94103).

2

The Nurturing of a Relational Epistemology

This book began with a discussion of sociopolitical concerns. We considered various types of associations and introduced classical theorists such as Plato, Rousseau, Marx, and Dewey. We also met current philosophers working in this area of study, such as Paulo Freire and Amy Gutmann. We hope you have begun to understand that how one thinks and feels about sociopolitical philosophical issues affects how one relates to students, students' families, and fellow educators. Assumptions we make concerning individuals and how we view them in relation to others shapes our behavior and decisions. Learning how others think about these issues helps all of us become clearer on what we believe and why, so that we can explain to others why we make the decisions and take the actions we do.

This chapter turns to a second field of study in philosophy, the study of knowledge, or **epistemology**. Teachers and would-be teachers may wonder, Why is it necessary to look at theories concerning knowledge, which philosophers label "epistemological theories"? The reason is that what we believe concerning how students obtain knowledge affects how we teach them. Actually, what happens for many teachers is they teach certain ways, not realizing that how they teach is based on certain assumptions about how students learn and what counts as knowledge. We want educators to have the opportunity in Chapter 2 to understand what theories of knowledge are and how they translate into classroom settings. We hope that with this understanding teachers will make conscious choices in how they teach, how they represent knowledge, and how they assess what their students know, based on their epistemological beliefs.

Richard Rorty (1989) describes philosophers as poets, prophets, and soothsayers. Theirs is the task of trying to envision the world in new ways and trying to redescribe the familiar through the use of imagination and metaphors. Philosophers do not have a "God's eye view" or an "inside line to truth." Their skills, the ability to reason and envision, are ones that are available to all, as are their tools, such as logic and critical thinking. With this in mind, we use the metaphor of "The Blind Men and the Elephant"[1] to take another look at knowledge.

After reviewing the distinctions and categories people have created to describe knowledge, we suggest that perhaps these past descriptions need revision. Defining and describing epistemology, a study of theories of knowledge, the way many others have described it, leads to a narrow representation of the world and creates serious problems. Is it possible that in defining knowledge we have excluded some essential qualities? Have we focused on parts of the elephant and lost sight of the larger animal? Is what we are each describing a part of something much larger and more comprehensive than any of its parts? We strive to soften distinctions and encourage a more interactive perspective among such categories as epistemology, metaphysics, and psychology—the knower and the known, and belief and knowledge, for example. Looking at school classrooms will help us understand problems we have created by defining knowledge in such a way that essential qualities are excluded.

The examination and redescription of epistemology, as a branch of philosophy, is necessary for us to be able to offer our own epistemological theory, what Thayer-Bacon describes as a relational epistemology.[2] This chapter begins by trying to motivate the need to develop an expanded conception of epistemology then moves on to further developing a relational epistemology. It will conclude by showing how a relational epistemology affects the way we understand education. We will look at others' contributions to epistemological theory along the way. In doing so, we hope to bring out some important issues and concerns, as well as others' attempts to address these concerns.

The democratic classroom community described in Chapter 1 is supported by a theory of knowledge we have labeled "relational." The relational epistemological theory we describe is one that assumes that people are social beings. As social beings, people grow and develop, learn a language and culture, and form a sense of self, all through their relationships with others. Who we are as individuals and how we think depend greatly on the social relationships we have with others, as well as the time, place, and culture into which we are born. Because of this necessary social beginning that all human beings have, which helps form who we are, we can never claim to know solely based on our own individual perspectives. What we come to believe are answers or solutions, our most trustworthy knowledge, which we derive through interactions with others. Given that we are social beings contingently placed in this world, affecting each other from the beginning, it is easy to understand that we need each other to be better thinkers. With such a model, knowledge takes on a very fluid image, always being redescribed as it changes and develops; the quality of the theories depends on people's ability to relate to each other and share their insights. A democratic classroom community offers a setting for all of this to occur.

The Elephant Poem in Relation to Past Theories

The Blind Men and the Elephant

There were six men from Industan
to learning much inclined
who went to see the elephant
though each of them was blind
so that by observation
each might satisfy his mind.

Many of us are probably familiar with this poem and laughed at the silly blind men who did not know they were feeling different parts of an elephant: one felt the tail and thought the elephant is like a rope, another felt a leg and thought the elephant is like a tree, one felt the ear and decided the elephant is like a fan, one felt the trunk and reported the elephant is like a snake, one felt the side of the elephant and suggested the elephant is like a wall, and the last man felt the elephant's tusk and announced the elephant is like a spear.

Imagine that the elephant poem is a metaphor for theories that explain what it is to know, epistemological theories. Maybe the six blind men from Industan are not so silly after all; maybe they represent all of us, as we struggle to make sense of a complex world.

We cannot do any of the important theories from our past justice in this space. However, highlighting some and comparing them with the elephant poem will hopefully convince us that we need to reexamine our conceptions of epistemology.

Plato (427–347 B.C.)

Plato[3] described knowledge as something Ideal, beyond the grasp of the world that we experience as reality. Even though we may each experience a different kind of elephant, we can all understand what an elephant is, because we each have an idea of Elephantness in its Ideal Form. According to Plato, our souls have all knowledge before they are born and inhabit a physical body. It is the inhabiting of a physical body that causes our souls to forget that knowledge. Learning is remembering what we already knew.

> The soul, then, as being immortal and having been born again many times, and having seen all things that exist, whether in this world or in the world below, has knowledge of them all; . . . for as all nature is akin, and the soul has learned all things, there is no difficulty in a man eliciting out of a single recollection all the rest . . . ; for all inquiry and all learning is but recollection. (*PFE, Meno,* p. 17)

It does not matter to Plato that each of us experiences the world in a different way; because we are souls inhabiting our bodies, we are blind to knowledge (what is true), just like the six blind men. We cannot trust our senses and be sure we really know what it is we are experiencing. We must tune in to what our souls know. Only by tuning in to the knowledge our soul already possesses can we hope to eventually realize the truth of what we experience. Others, such as teachers, may act like midwives and help guide the soul on its journey, but ultimately each soul must find the answers by itself. Finding the answers, realizing the Ideals, is to have knowledge of what is true, according to Plato.

"The Myth of the Cave," in Plato's *Republic*,[4] is a wonderful story that presents "reality" as something that is socially constructed. The people in the cave experience what they think is "reality," but what they are really experiencing are shadows on the wall, as they sit, chained and unable to move or turn their heads to see that there is a fire behind them and that those objects they thought were real are just shadows, the real objects being carried by people behind them. Like the blind men from Industan, their senses deceive them, and they cannot trust their experiences.

> [T]he prison-house is the world of sight, the light of the fire is the power of the sun, and you will not misapprehend me if you interpret the journey upwards to be the ascent of the soul into the intellectual world, . . . my opinion is that in the world of knowledge the Idea of good appears last of all, and it is seen only with effort. (*PFE*, "Republic," p. 85)

Many students who read Plato's *Republic* and "The Myth of the Cave" are struck by the profoundness of his description. He has escaped the problem of our experiences of "reality" being partial and flawed, by saying we should not trust our experiences anyway. We need to trust our souls. Plato points out one of the key tools available to any person striving to know truth: "divine contemplation." Divine contemplation is the tuning in to our soul in search of answers.

> Whereas our argument shows that the power and capacity of learning exists in the soul already; and that just as if it were not possible to turn the eye from darkness to light without the whole body, so too the instrument of knowledge can only by the movement of the whole soul be turned from the world of becoming to that of being, and learn by degrees to endure the sight of being, and of the brightness and best of being, or in other worlds, of the good. (*PFE*, "Republic," p. 86)

Aristotle (384–324 B.C.)

Aristotle[5] argued that knowledge was obtained through tuning in to the soul, to our ideas, and testing out those ideas through our experiences. He presented the case that ideas can be deceptive and misleading, just as our experiences can be deceiving. We know that six blind men can feel different parts of an animal, develop ideas of what they are experiencing, and never realize they are each feeling the same animal. If each of these six men never have an idea of elephant but rather have ideas of ropes, snakes, spears, fans, walls, and tree trunks, their ideas will not help them see the truth about what they are experiencing, either. Aristotle hoped that the use of both our ideas and our experiences would lead us to knowledge. "[R]easoning on matters of conduct employs premises of two forms . . . one universal is predicated of the man himself, the other of the thing" (*PFE, Nichomachean Ethics,* p. 117).

If our ideas and our experiences can both be flawed, then, as we understand the situation, Aristotle sent Western philosophers off on a task that still has not been resolved. Some philosophers have developed epistemological theories that have leaned in Plato's direction and favored ideas, such as René Descartes (1596–1650; see Descartes, 1641/1960); some have made suggestions that have leaned toward favoring experiences over ideas, such as John Locke (1632–1704; see Locke, 1690/1894). Descartes recommended that the blind men should use a doubting method in which everything they can doubt, they should dismiss, until they reach that which they take to be self-evident; what is beyond doubt is what they can be sure is true. This view says that what our minds believe to be self-evident we can trust to be a mirror of the world as it exists. Locke recommended that, because each of us came into this world as a blank slate (tabula rasa) with no knowledge before birth, we must rely on our experiences, along with our ability to reason.

Others have tried to find a balance between ideas and experience, as Aristotle recommended. Immanuel Kant (1724–1804) suggested that what we can know is not independent reality, "the thing in itself," but always reality as it appears to human beings. Our perceptions of the world are a result of our interaction with the external world and the active powers of our minds (Kant, 1781/1966). C. S. Peirce (1839–1914) suggested that because all of us are flawed individuals who cannot trust our ideas or experiences, we need to work with others, as a community of rational inquirers, to help further our knowledge and understanding.

Like Aristotle, Peirce (Wiener, 1958[6]) approached truth from a scientific perspective. We seek answers, new solutions, and therefore get closer to truth, as we run into problems with our current beliefs, and start to have doubts about what we thought was "truth." For Peirce, the only method out of *a priori* speculation (Plato's Ideals) is the "self-corrective" scientific method whose experimental results are always subject to revision by further evidence ("The Fixation of Belief," in Wiener, 1958, p. 92).

Truth, for Peirce, is absolute, but none of us will ever know absolute truth, because we are all limited beings. This is Peirce's theory of **fallibilism**. Truth is something we are emerging toward, for with each generation of inquirers we have more understanding. "The opinion which is fated to be ultimately agreed to by all who investigate is what we mean by the truth, and the object represented in this opinion is real. That is the way I would explain reality" ("How to Make Our Ideas Clear," p. 133). Truth is not something one person can find, all on his own; it is found through the collection of all rational inquirer's investigations; and because it takes all of us, the truth in the end will be the same for all of us. "[T])he method [for fixing beliefs] must be such that the ultimate conclusion of every man shall be the same, or would be the same if inquiry were sufficiently persisted in. Such is the method of science" ("The Fixation of Belief," p. 107). As Peirce described truth, it is something the last person on earth will know. "[T]rue opinion must be the one which they would ultimately come to" ("How to Make Our Ideas Clear," pp. 133–134).

Kant would tell the six blind men from Industan that they can never know the elephant as the-thing-in-itself, Elephant, but only the elephant as it is represented in relation to their experiences and their minds. Peirce would advise the six blind men to start talking to each other and share the information each of them has. Only by acting as a community of inquirers can they hope to gather a more complete understanding of elephants, one they can all agree on. But they had better be cautious and aware that, because they are limited human beings, they will likely not understand all there is to know about elephants, either, as the next generation will build on the knowledge they have gained through sharing with each other, and the next generation will reach an even better understanding of elephants than current inquirers can possibly reach.

Epistemological Theories in the Classroom

Let us look at the classic epistemological theories briefly presented here and try to consider how they translate into the classroom setting, the roles of the teacher and the student, and the method of instruction.

Plato's classroom could be described as being like a college seminar class, especially at the graduate level. If we looked at a high school classroom, it would resemble some honors and AP English classes and Critical Thinking or Contemporary Issues classes. We picture a small group of people involved in discussions and debates, in dialogue with each other. The teacher plays the role of a "Socratic midwife" attempting to help guide and direct students' efforts to answer their questions, but not trying to do the job for them. Plato's teacher does not try to give students the answers or even claim to know the answer. The teacher also encourages students to question what answers he or she might suggest. The teacher will represent viewpoints the students do not present and point to issues and concerns they are not addressing. Students are in a very active role, trying to find answers for themselves, for the belief is each of us have access to the Truth since each of our souls already knows Truth, the Forms. Because we already know the answers but just need to be reminded, we recognize answers when we discover (remember) them, and we do not need a teacher to verify this knowledge for us.

Aristotle's classroom is like a scientific laboratory. Students develop questions, suggest possible solutions and answers, and then must proceed to test out and judge for accuracy of prediction, much like the scientific method. Because teachers have more experiences than their students, they can serve as guides and resources, like a senior lab partner. Still, students are able to access their own ideas without a teacher's help, and they have a method for testing out their ideas to find out whether they are correct, so they should be able to judge their own solutions for accuracy and so forth. The proof in the accuracy of an experience is the experiment's ability to be duplicated and still come up with the same answer (reliability).

Descartes's epistemological theory draws forth the image of Rodin's "Thinker," a man sitting by himself, head leaning on one arm for support, obviously in deep thought. The teacher teaches students critical thinking skills and then steps back to let them each practice these skills individually. The setting we imagine is one of solitude and peace and quiet, like that in a library or study. The student is in the active role of using the doubting method to determine what is knowledge, that which no one can doubt.

Locke's (1823/1970) belief that students are like blank slates creates a much more active role for the teacher. If students are blank slates (empty vessels, or Freire's term of **depositees**), then teachers are the ones writing on those slates, filling those vessels, and depositing knowledge. We picture Locke's classroom looking very much like the individualistic classroom we described in Chapter 1. The teacher's role is to help shape the students and develop their habits of reason. The teacher does know more than students because of more experiences and has a responsibility to give them that knowledge. Students are being shaped and play a more passive, receptive role. Teachers, as the ones who know more, are able to assess what students know. This epistemological theory sets up the possibility of teachers using more direct methods such as lecturing and relying on such discipline techniques as behavior modification to shape students' actions as they strive for a managed classroom.

Kant's (1899/1960) classroom does not appear to be significantly different from the individualistic classrooms described in Chapter 1, either. Kant worries about how to solve the problem of teaching children to be disciplined, so that their animal nature is changed into human nature, while allowing children to exercise their free will, so that they will grow up to be free, autonomous individuals able to think for themselves. In Kant's classroom children are allowed liberty, as long as they do not interfere with anyone else's liberty. They learn that they can only attain what they want by allowing others to do the same as well. They learn that they are restrained and disciplined only so they will learn to cultivate and use their minds (1899/1960, p. 28). He recommends the teaching of an ordinary curriculum, instruction in the practical matters of life, and the training of the moral character (p. 30). The teacher needs to be a person of high moral character, who models this character for the students. Students are to be taught the importance of being steadfast and keeping to their purposes (p. 99). Teachers teach by examples and rules, and students learn common duties toward themselves and others (pp. 101–102). (See Chapter 3 for more discussion on Kant's views.)

As for Peirce, his classroom may look very similar to Aristotle's laboratory, as he also emphasizes a scientific methodological approach to inquiry.[7] Because of Peirce's idea of fallibilism, teachers must consider Truth to be something that is obtainable, but in a futuristic sense. The teacher's task is to teach students the skills they need to be good scientific inquirers by helping them "develop good habits of reasoning and conduct" (self-control) (Maccia, 1954, p. 212). They should foster the growth and development of reason by helping to "provide the experiences necessary for active learning" (p. 212). They should encourage students to "develop imagination which is rooted in experience" (p. 212). And they should help students "develop the concepts and techniques necessary for the communication of ideas" (p. 212). There is a tentativeness to whatever knowledge teachers have and also an awareness that students are in an active role of furthering awareness and understanding. The teacher and student roles are likely to change at times. As

Peirce talked about a community of inquirers working together to further knowledge, at the college level we picture people leaving their laboratories and classrooms to come together as a larger community to discuss their ideas and theories in a conference-type setting. In a high school or elementary class, it would be like students, as researchers, exploring and studying ideas individually or in small groups, and then coming together as an entire class or schoolwide student body to present and discuss their research. When they are off on their own or in small groups, they do not just remain in the classroom or library to study; they also go out into the world actively seeking experiences to help them learn.

The Elephant Poem in Relation to Current Theories

The issues and concerns about epistemology are still debated today as heatedly as they were in early Greece. If we look at the present debate, we can describe it this way: The in-flux world is a given (there is an ever-changing elephant), and any description of the world, the sense that is made of the world, is something people create; the meaning people give to the world derives, in part, from the descriptions people develop to explain the world: "reality." So the blind men of Industan offer descriptions of what they experience, each experiencing a different part an elephant or each experiencing the whole elephant in different ways; this feels this way, based on their past experiences and the meanings that have been attached to those experiences. When one man feels a snakelike shape, the trunk of the elephant, he describes the elephant as a snake, based on the meaning he has attached to an object having that particular shape. Attaching meaning to what each man describes helps each person make sense of the world he is experiencing, the part of the elephant or the whole elephant.

Sociologists have labeled this making sense of the world the **social construction of reality**.[8] People give meaning to the reality they experience, through language, and then pass that meaning on to their children through conversation and education. Children internalize their parents' socially constructed "reality" through the language they learn and what they are taught. "The child does not internalize the world of significant others as one of many possible worlds. [She or he] internalizes it as *the* world, the only existent and only conceivable world, the world *tout court*" (*SCR*, p. 134). One could imagine that each blind man from Industan had children whom he taught that an elephant is a fan, a snake, or a spear, because that is "reality" as he knows it. He has pieced together that "reality" and then passed it on as "reality" to his children. His children do not know this view of elephants is partial, flawed, or different from other views. They take it to be truth; the only way an elephant could possibly exist is in the shape of a fan, for example. Elephants as being like fans (or snakes, or walls) is all they conceive of Elephantness.

If descriptions of the world are created by people, then they are open to reexamination, criticism, and possible redescribing. For we know from the six blind men poem that people are fallible and flawed in their understandings; their experiences and insights are partial and limited, their views affected by their sur-roundings. This includes ourselves. Descriptions of the world and theories of why things are so are explanations that are socially constructed by people who are contextual beings. These people are in relation with other people,[9] and they are "embedded and embodied."[10] They are born into a setting, a certain time and place, surrounded by a certain culture, inhabiting a body that is uniquely their own, relating to at least one other person (even in utero), their mother.

All of this social context makes it necessary to assume that people have a past and have been affected by other peoples' views. They are not neutral, impar-tial, objective beings; their relationship with the world is transactive (as Dewey described it[11]), meaning people affect the world, and each other, individually and collectively, just as the world affects them. People are able to become reflective and critical of their context, but how that happens will need to be discussed (later in this chapter and also Chapters 4 and 5). Improving people's skills that are necessary for the development of knowledge—such as reasoning and cri-tiquing, imagining and intuiting, communicative and relational skills—is what makes it possible for knowledge to continue to grow and develop and for it to be redescribed and become more beautiful.[12]

Dividing Up the Elephant

Fields of study such as philosophy, psychology, sociology, and anthropology are examples of descriptive categories people have developed over time as a way of making sense of the world. (We are referring to the descriptive categories devel-oped by the Western world, as those are the ones of concern here.) Branches within those fields are further descriptive categories. For philosophy these branches are metaphysics, aesthetics, ethics, politics, and epistemology, for example. Epistemology, as philosophers have historically defined it, looks at questions about the **justification** of people's beliefs, not at how people come to believe certain things (those questions are for sociologists and psychologists). Philosophy is concerned with the normative status of knowledge claims (Are they good? Are they true? Based on what we know, what does this mean in terms of how we should act?) and what warrants those claims (involving an inquirer in questions such as what counts as evidence); psychology and sociology are con-cerned with causal questions concerning how beliefs are developed.

Epistemology is a branch of philosophy that considers theories of knowledge and truth as a necessary condition for knowledge. When we say we know some-thing, we are saying that something that we know is true; otherwise, it would not be called "knowledge" but instead a "belief." One cannot know something that is false. Beliefs are not necessarily true. There are different categories of beliefs, which depend on how close these beliefs are to being knowledge (true belief). **Mere beliefs**, or right opinions, are stated as "*S* believes that *p*," *S* being the subject and *p* being the object of the proposition; for example, Sarah believes that she is a good teacher. **Rational beliefs** are ones that are supported by compelling reasons ("*S* has good reason to believe that *p*"). Sarah believes she is a good teacher, and it is rational for her to believe this because students tell her how much they enjoy her classes, parents tell her they notice how much their children are learning, and her students score high on achievement tests. "*S* knows that *p*" means *S* has evidence for the truth of *p*, *S* believes that *p*, and that *p* is true.[13] Sarah knows she is a good teacher when she believes this claim, there is evidence to support her claim, and her teaching is in fact good.

If we compare what we just said with our elephant poem, we recognize that the blind men take their study of elephants (the world) and divide it up into more manageable categories. When they are trying to understand how they come to know about the elephant, they say they are studying psychology. When they are looking at themselves in relation to others studying the elephant, they say they are studying sociology. They say that, with either of these kinds of studies, the kinds of claims they will be making are causal ones.

When the blind men are trying to make universal claims of truth about elephants, they are studying philosophy. They say they offer evidence to support those claims. When they are trying to make universal claims about the beauty of elephants, the blind men say they are studying aesthetics. When they are looking at the essence of Elephantness and the necessary and sufficient qualities of elephants, the blind men say they are studying metaphysics. When they are trying to make claims about what they know about elephants, in a universal sense, they are studying epistemology. As the blind men define knowledge, they will only say they know something that is true. For something to be true, they say, they must believe that something is true, have compelling reasons to support their belief about such-and-such being true, and such-and-such must be true.

Let us consider these categories and distinctions, as the blind men have defined them, and see whether any problems emerge in dividing the world (elephants) in this way. Have we missed anything by focusing on elephants in parts? Once dividing up the elephant into parts to better handle the studying of it, have we stopped understanding the whole, or have we ever been able to understand the whole elephant? Are these categories the best way to consider elephants, or should we redesign our categories and redescribe our studies of elephants (the world)? In separating the study of the people who study the elephant from the elephant itself, have we created any problems or concerns? We will begin in the middle, with the field of epistemology, as commonly defined, then move to the distinctive studies within philosophy. We will look at the field of philosophy itself in relation to others, in hopes of teasing out some problems and concerns that dividing up the world in this way has maybe caused or overlooked. As we do so, we plan to add some "blind women's" perspectives into the discussion (Code, 1987, 1991, 1993; Flax, 1983, 1990; Jaggar, 1983, 1992).

Belief, Knowledge, and Truth

Because we want to offer an improved theory of knowledge, a relational epistemology, let us take a closer look at how epistemology has been defined. The way it has been defined since the days of the philosopher René Descartes, which philosophers have marked as the beginning of the modern age or the age of Enlightenment, assumes

> (1) that knowledge properly so-called is autonomous in that it is of no epistemological significance whose it is; (2) that knowledge acquisition may be of psychological interest but it is irrelevant to an epistemologist's quest for criteria of justification, validity, and verification; and (3) that knowledge is objective in the sense that discussion of the character and epistemic circumstances of subjects has nothing to contribute to the proper epistemological task of assessing the product. (Code, 1987, pp. 25–26)

Decisions about what counts as knowledge, what is unquestionably True, have been made based on these assumptions. If one wishes to question the wisdom of these decisions and the Truth claims on which they rest, then one must question these assumptions.

Let us translate these modern, Enlightenment assumptions using our elephant metaphor. The blind men are trying to gather knowledge of elephants. Who these blind people are or how they derive this knowledge is not important; from an epistemological perspective, what is of concern is the knowledge they derive. That derived knowledge is separate from the blind men who have derived it. If what they derive is in fact knowledge, it should be true for any of us, no matter who we are or what our perspective or situation is. From Enlightenment perspectives of epistemology's task, what the blind men need to be concerned about is what evidence they will have to find knowledge.

Remember, we said the blind men would only define as knowledge something that is true. And for something to be knowledge, the blind men (S) must believe that such-and-such (p) is true, they must have compelling reasons to support their belief that p is true, and p is true. The first requirement, the blind men must believe that p is true, does not help find knowledge very much, for we know it is possible for the blind men to believe that an elephant is a fan or a spear or a rope! (Just as we know it is possible for people to believe the world is flat.)

How about the second requirement? The blind men need "compelling reasons" to support their belief, but what counts as "compelling reasons"? This has been a heatedly discussed topic since the beginning of philosophy. Remember, Plato said we cannot trust our experiences to give us good reasons, and Aristotle said we cannot trust our ideas alone, either. The kinds of criteria philosophers have used to help judge reasons include clarity, consistency, coherency, cohesiveness, and comprehensiveness. Are the reasons clearly stated? Do they follow logically and not contradict each other? Do they make sense? Do they answer all the questions we can ask? Do the reasons fit together with other beliefs we consider knowledge? Our blind men might be very clever and give reasons to support their beliefs about elephants that are clear, consistent, coherent, cohesive, and comprehensive, and yet not true. (People certainly had good reasons to believe the world was flat.) Is it not possible that each blind man would have different interpretations of what he takes to be clear, consistent, coherent, and so forth? In other words, are not the criteria themselves subject to different interpretations?

This leads us to the final criterion for knowledge, that *p* is true. According to Enlightenment epistemological theories, the ultimate object of knowledge is reality itself. Even though one blind man may believe that the elephant is a fan, with compelling reasons to justify his belief, that still does not make the elephant a fan, unless it is true that it really is. But how is the blind man ever going to know whether what he believes is true or not? We seem to have ended up in a circular theory. Does this mean that there is nothing we can say for sure we know? Or is knowledge ultimately based on faith? Somehow such a theory of knowledge does not appear so helpful after all. What is the point of having a theory of knowledge about the world, when there is nothing we can say fits safely into that theory, for there is nothing that we can be sure to say we know?

Maybe we can find some help in understanding the value of epistemology as a category by turning to a current epistemologist. Harvey Siegel's (1987, 1992[14]) position is clearly an absolutist one coming from an Enlightenment perspective, and we will contrast it with a qualified relativist position embraced by many "blind women," feminist philosophers such as Flax, Code, Jaggar, and Thayer-Bacon.

Absolutism versus Qualified Relativism

Siegel has been complimented by philosophers, such as Burbules (1991, 1992), for moving epistemology away from vulgar absolutism to an absolutism that is less dogmatic, one that opens the door to fallibilism and pluralism. Siegel says that "[c]ontemporary epistemologists—absolutists and relativists alike—reject certainty, dogmatism, and all the other features of vulgar absolutism" (*RR,* p. 164). The sort of absolutism he recommends is a "non-dogmatic, non-certain, corrigible, fallible, non-unique absolutism" (*RR,* p. 164).

Translated to our elephant metaphor, Siegel is saying that all of us working in epistemology realize that we cannot be certain we understand all there is to know about elephants (the world, as reality, as truth). We all understand that people are limited, make mistakes, and have many different views and perspectives on elephants (as parts of elephants or as whole elephants).

Although such a description of absolute may not sound very absolute, for Siegel, "**absolutism is a necessary precondition of epistemological inquiry**" (our emphasis, *RR,* p. 165). What is absolute about a "non-dogmatic, non-certain, corrigible, fallible, non-unique absolutism" is "the possibility of objective, non-question begging evaluation of putative knowledge claims, in terms of criteria which admit of criticism and improvement" (*RR,* p. 162).

In other words, Siegel believes there must be some way to evaluate our different theories on elephants and judge that some are better then others. At the same time, he acknowledges that what we use as criteria for judging people's theories on elephants could also be flawed and must be open to criticism as well. So far, we agree with him completely.

However, Siegel goes on to say that a "relativist must regard epistemological debate as pointless, insofar as there is, for the relativist, no possibility of genuinely answering central epistemological questions" (*RR,* p. 165). By a relativist,

Siegel means someone who believes there is more than one way of looking at truth and more than one right answer. What is true depends on one's perspective. The relativist "gives up the absolutist conception of rightness" and therefore

> cannot assert that foundationalism (non-foundationalism), correspondence (coherence) theories of truth or justification, causal (reliabilist, defeasibility, etc.) theories of knowledge, or the like are non-relatively right. **But genuine epistemological debate does have as its aim the determination of the non-relatively right answers to these questions**. (our emphasis, *RR*, p. 166)

Because a relativist, according to Siegel, believes more than one right answer is possible, the relativist gives up the concept of "rightness" and the ability to say "I am right and you are wrong," therefore setting up the situation for any (**every**) view to be right.

We question how Siegel has defined a relativist perspective. Although he goes to great length in *Relativism Refuted* to distinguish absolutism from "vulgar absolutism," he is not so gracious with relativism. According to Siegel, only a "vulgar absolutist" believes that it does not matter what one's perspective is in relation to the elephant; one can still know the elephant in its entirety (truth). Vulgar absolutist epistemological orientations have been labeled by feminists, such as Lorraine Code and Donna Haraway, as "the view from nowhere." But is it the case that there is only one view of relativism, or is it possible that a "vulgar relativist" view exists, as well as a "qualified relativist" view? We think so. "Vulgar relativism," the belief that it does not matter what one's perspective is, in relation to the elephant, for all perspectives are right (true), has been labeled by Code and Haraway as "the view from everywhere." "Relativism is a way of being nowhere and claiming to be everywhere" but "absolutism is a way of being everywhere while pretending to be nowhere" (Code, 1993, p. 40).

Siegel does not argue that a knower can know the elephant in its entirety, no matter what the knower's perspective is, and the knower can be sure of being right (vulgar absolutism, the view from nowhere). We do not argue that all knowers are right and their knowledge is true, no matter what the knowers' perspective is (vulgar relativism, the view from everywhere). Although our positions sound like they are very similar, let us look closer.

From our earlier discussion on the way epistemology has been defined and the guidelines that have been given for helping find knowledge, we saw that indeed the guidelines seem rather circular and potentially pointless, from our qualified relativist perspective. They do not seem to help us find knowledge (what is true). At most, we can hope that Peirce is right and we are getting closer to truth. However, believing that we cannot find the truth about elephants does not mean we have to embrace all theories about elephants as being true. What it does mean is that we must acknowledge that we do not know the Truth about elephants, if what we mean by "know" **is find absolute truth**, what is right. We still try to describe elephants, seek to find out more information, and learn more about elephants. We continue to inquire, and we try to support our understandings about elephants with as much "evidence" as we can socially construct, qualified by the best criteria on which we can agree. Qualified relativists, such as Jaggar, Flax, Code, and Thayer-Bacon, ground their claims "in experiences and practices, in the efficacy of dialogical negotiation and of action" (Code, 1993, p. 39).

Although Siegel agrees with the need to reject a formal conception of rationality and to "regard rationality as a substantive epistemic notion, involving the contents of sentences rationally related" (*PES,* p. 228), he says that if rationality is determined by

> the actual activities, decisions, and judgments which people make, then I see a big problem: namely, there is no room on this view for actual activities, decisions, and judgments to be irrational, for there is no role for criteria to function in assessing specific activities, decisions, and judgments as rational (or not). (*PES,* p. 229)

Siegel wishes to argue that "rationality" (as a concept) is dependent on the idea of "absolutism," and "absolutism" is dependent on a criteria of "rightness" (truth), which must be objective and nonrelative, not something socially constructed. Yet, he has agreed that the criteria used to judge rival claims must be subject to critical assessment and improvement. Siegel says he is not claiming philosophers have a "God's eye view of truth" or he has found an Archimedian point where a philosopher can stand and judge the world. If the presently accepted criteria (the absolutist's belief system) can be critically assessed, Siegel suggests the criteria can be self-correcting and corrigible (capable of being improved).

> Principles embody rationality and define and assess reasons in a tradition at a time. As the tradition evolves, so do the principles which define and assess reasons. So what may count as good reason in a tradition may change over time; today's compelling reason may be seen as less compelling tomorrow. . . . Still, the principles which determine the compellingness of reasons at a time apply to all putative reasons impartially and universally. . . . [T]he principles which define reasons and determine their force may change, but rationality remains the same (Siegel, 1988, pp. 134–135, from *Burbules,* 1991, p. 251).

However, if we embrace fallibilism and pluralism, we have to admit that the criteria as presently accepted could be wrong, **right now**. A qualified relativist position such as the one we are proposing says that, given the presently accepted criteria, this is the best judgment we can make, but we are aware that our criteria may be limited and we could be wrong. Although this statement seems to be exactly what Siegel is saying with his definition of "absolute," it really is not, as Siegel believes he can say even more. Here is where we think epistemologists who embrace an Enlightenment conception of epistemology, as defined here, overestimate their abilities. Thayer-Bacon believes fallibilism and pluralism are theories that admit to the social construction of reality. Siegel does not agree with her. Though he admits that what he believes, right now, might be wrong (the possibility is there), that does not itself show that he **is** wrong, right now. If it did, then everything would in fact be wrong, because everything could possibly be wrong. If not wrong, Siegel says, than what he believes is right: **absolutely** right (right/wrong being understood as contradictories). And his reasons can also be absolute, as he has defined "absolute."[15]

We think Siegel's point is "As long as I believe *p* is true, and I have compelling reasons to believe *p* is true, I can claim to be right, because *p* is true, even though my claiming to be right is always subject to fallibilism. My being right, absolutely, is independent of my showing that I am." This is because there is a *p* that is true, independent of me and whether I can show that I am right or not. There is an elephant, that is an elephant, absolutely, independent of what any of us think about elephants and how any of us have defined elephants. Siegel is saying, "I am right, absolutely, if what I believe is right." Thayer-Bacon is saying, "I believe I am right, qualified by a socially constructed view of knowledge, so I cannot be sure I am right. In fact, I know I could be wrong, but knowing that does not entail that I *am* wrong."

Enlightenment philosophers have defined epistemology in such a way that **the concept of absolutism is built right into the definition of epistemology**. Siegel, who embraces this definition, helps us understand a central concern all epistemologists must address. The Enlightenment conception of epistemology implies that people must have something absolute that they can appeal to, true theories, or they cannot claim to know what is right. Unfortunately (or fortunately, depending on one's view), in the end, the criteria used to support theories are fallible themselves, which must be admitted. We cannot offer truth claims that are absolute any more then Siegel or anyone else can. We can offer new theory to try to explain what knowledge is and how it is we know. We can argue and debate with people as to why we think our description of reality is more inclusive or beneficial than others presented previously. That is all anyone can do.

Historically, epistemologists have assumed the value of absolutism in the very way they have defined the field of epistemology. Absolutist epistemologists have argued for the value of absolutism because it offers people the opportunity to judge what is right. Qualified relativists push for the inclusion of context because it forces people to open the door toward acknowledging that they could be wrong, that "right" is judged from a social perspective. We are all, as epistemologists, hoping to warrant our theories in reality and arrive at knowledge, but qualified relativists are acknowledging how extremely difficult that is to do, given that each of us is so embedded within our own socially constructed "realities."

Philosophers who embrace Enlightenment conceptions of epistemology not only overestimate their abilities; they also tend to act as gatekeepers to the field of epistemology. Absolutist epistemologists do not consider qualified relativists even to be epistemologists because qualified relativists have not embraced the field of epistemology as absolutist epistemologists have defined it, with an assumption of absolutism. Whereas some feminists, such as Lorraine Code, conclude there can be no feminist epistemology given Enlightenment conceptions of epistemology, we choose to try to broaden the definition of epistemology.

The way epistemology has been defined, in terms of distinguishing it from other branches, limits the possible questions and concerns an epistemologist can address to a dangerously thin level. Let us elaborate further.

Ontology and Epistemology

Philosophers have distinguished ontology as a branch of philosophy, separate from epistemology, since the days of the early Greek philosophers. By making such a distinction, philosophers have assumed that being can be separated from knowing, for ontology is the study of being (what is, the essence of things) and epistemology is the study of knowing (what is truth). These categorical distinctions separate knowers from knowledge/ideas. The distinctions treat knowledge as if it has a life of its own. This seems to be another central problem for philosophers. As Jane Flax (1983) observes, "[I]n philosophy, being (ontology) has been divorced from knowing (epistemology) and both have been separated from either ethics or politics" (p. 248).[16]

As we have discovered, philosophers have created categories, distinguished fields of study and branches within those fields, that are based on certain values and therefore biases. We learned in the discussion on belief, knowledge, and truth that those categories are based on an assumption of absolutism. Separating knowledge from being assumes philosophers are able to be neutral, objective seekers of truth. It does not matter which blind man is studying elephants, from which perspective, or that the blind man is from Industan. The character and circumstances of the knowers is not important; the assessing of the product, knowledge, is important. Yet, we know from the work of feminist scholars and scholars in cultural diversity that people's values and biases can be found in how they have defined what questions are worth considering, what methods for addressing those questions are considered valid, and what ideas and solutions are sound.[17] Like Flax (Code and Jaggar agree), we

> assume here that knowledge is the product of human beings. Thinking is a form of human activity which cannot be treated in isolation from other forms of human activity including the forms of human activity which in turn shape the humans who think. Consequently, philosophies will inevitably bear the imprint of the social relations out of which they and their creators arose. (Flax, 1983, p. 248)

As a naturalist, Gregory Bateson (1972) effectively describes the problem this way:

> In the natural history of living human being, ontology and epistemology cannot be separated. [One's] (commonly unconscious) beliefs about what sort of world it is will determine how [one] sees it and acts within it, and [one's] ways of perceiving and acting will determine [one's] beliefs about its nature. The living [human] is thus bound within a net of epistemological and ontological premises which—regardless of ultimate truth or falsity—become partially self-validating for [him or her]. (p. 314)

Let us give an example of this "net of epistemological and ontological premises" and how the premises become self-validating that can be related to the elephant poem. Historically, many epistemological theories have described knowers as autonomous rather than as individuals developed out of a community of other knowers, certainly affected by their environment and the people surrounding them. Peirce's view exemplifies an exception to this autonomous approach to knowers, as he recognized the influence we have on each other's opinions. But even Peirce argued that we each have "a critical self" within us that helps us persuade others and makes it possible for us to distinguish between absolute truth and what we do not doubt (Wiener, 1958, p. 191). That "critical self" within us is what separates us from others and helps us be able to think on our own. Peirce also favored a "scientific method" for approaching knowledge, one based on reason and logic rather than one that might acknowledge the value of imagination and intuition, for example.

If we assume a person can discover truth by him- or herself, then we will approach the study of elephants on an individual basis. Each of the six blind men from Industan will not worry about trying to discuss their individual theories with the others in hopes of gaining a better understanding. Instead, each blind man may even avoid contact with the others for fear they might bias his own inquiry or distract him. A person who believes knowers are autonomous will trust that he or she can critique, from an individual perspective, and find fault with what others have proposed. Yet we can understand, with our example of the blind men, how faulty one individual person's perspective can be. Alone, a person can decide that the elephant is like a snake or a spear! If we believe that knowers are autonomous, we are capable of believing we are right without necessarily testing our theory against others. Even when we test our theory against others, if we believe we can critique others' theories against our own, we will confidently dismiss others' theories (that the elephant is like a wall or a rope) as faulty.

If the blind men favor the scientific method, as Peirce and many other philosophers have throughout time, then they will try to collect data, likely based on their senses and ability to reason. Yet we can predict that with such an approach to knowledge the men may never arrive at any understanding of the whole elephant. They will need to be able to imagine a whole that is greater than the sum of its parts. They will need to be creative and use their intuitive skills, and they will find that if they rely on their emotional feelings as well as their mind, they will be more successful with their efforts to be creative and intuitive (we will discuss these points further in Chapter 4).

We question the assumption that knowers are autonomous, given the view that our "reality" is something that is socially constructed, and whether it is even valuable to view each of us as autonomous knowers. Accepting Peirce's view that we are all fallible beings and that truth is something we continue to get closer to as we work together and share our perspectives, why would we want to embrace a view of epistemology that encourages us to look at people as separate knowers? Why not embrace a description of epistemology that encourages us to see how interrelated and interconnected the world is, including the people in it? If Peirce is right, then our only hope of understanding the world, even partially, comes from our willingness to work together and welcome each other's contributions in an effort to understand them, before we critique and dismiss them.

We also question the assumption that the best approach to knowledge is through the use of one's reasoning ability at the exclusion of other potential skills.

We do not want to dismiss reasoning as a valuable capability, for certainly it is one we are relying on considerably in writing this chapter. However, we are also using a metaphor of six blind men from Industan and their study of the elephant to help us gain a better understanding of what knowledge is. The metaphor helps us imagine and intuitively make connections and understand how ideas are related. Thayer-Bacon did not think of this metaphor by methodically reviewing research articles and epistemological theories. It came to her as a flash of insight after struggling to find a helpful image. The metaphor did not come to her when she was using her logical reasoning skills but rather by not working at all. We suspect most of us make connections and understand the world in new ways, often "by accident" when we are **not** trying to figure things out. Acknowledging and valuing our "other" capacities to help us potentially know the world is something we hope to accomplish with a relational epistemological approach.

Philosophy and Psychology

We have discovered that the categories and distinctions concerning epistemology as a branch of philosophy are based on assumptions of absolutism and autonomy and favor methods for understanding that emphasize reason and the mind. What about the distinction that has been made between psychology and philosophy? Philosophers have described the epistemological task of assessing the quality of reasons as being quite separate from any discussion of the character and epistemic circumstances of subjects. Historically, epistemological theorists have argued that criteria for warranting knowledge claims can be found without having to consider the way human beings know. This view of knowledge treats it as a product quite separate from human beings, some "thing" that is "out there" or "in here." So, depending on one's perspective, any of the six blind men should be able to discover the truth about elephants, either by using their experiences and exploring elephants "out there" (remember Aristotle and Locke?) or by tuning in to their soul's awareness of elephants "inside" themselves (remember Plato and Descartes?).

If we view knowledge as something people contribute to, as something that people weave or quilt together, then the distinctions between knowers and knowledge are no longer so clear. In fact, knowers and knowledge become very intertwined and obviously interrelated. When we begin to understand the interactive connection between social beings and ideas, we realize it is necessary to look at the kinds of relationships people experience and which ones enhance the development of ideas and the quilting of knowledge. Ethical and political issues will need to be addressed in an epistemological theory that looks at knowledge as created by **people**, not just knowledge *per se,* for the quality of the social relationships people have will affect the ideas being constructed, especially in terms of whether the ideas even become expressed.

With such a view of knowledge, it becomes important to ask questions like, Why are these six people who are studying the elephant only men? Why are they all blind, and what effect does their blindness have on their theories about elephants? Where did these men come from—what are the contexts of their social situations? How is it they have no prior experience of elephants, and yet they are adults and live in a land where elephants are central to their social system?

Any attempt to look at knowledge claims, separate from any examination of how those claims were derived, is a serious mistake. "[A] theory of knowledge that lacks a reasonable understanding of how human beings can and do acquire and add to knowledge must be of dubious relevance. Sound psychological insights form an invaluable, *sine qua non* basis for any theory of knowledge that purports to explicate the way human beings know" (Code, 1987, p. 32). The historical distinctions epistemologists have made effectively remove epistemology as a field of study from the practical-political issues a feminist epistemology must address. As we are redescribing epistemology, any theory of knowledge is clearly affected by knowers and their circumstances. Like Lorraine Code, we will be arguing that "theories that transcend the specificities of gendered and otherwise situated subjectivities are impotent to come to terms with the politics of knowledge" (Code, 1991, p. 315).

Our writing on a relational epistemology is motivated by the desire to expand what epistemology means to include the qualities of knowing that have historically been viewed as detrimental or distracting to the obtaining of knowledge, qualities such as emotional feelings and intuitions that are usually linked to women rather than men. We attempt to redescribe knowledge, and the only capacities available to us are the same ones available to anyone else: our abilities to reason and think critically, our intuition, our relational and communication skills, our emotional feelings, and the fact that these are questions we care enough about to pursue. As with any other philosopher, all we can ever hope to do is "attempt to describe how understanding is possible in particular contexts; [philosophy] cannot create a universalizing theory of knowledge that can ground and account for all knowledge or test all truth claims because these are necessarily context dependent" (Flax, 1990, p. 38).

Are we trying to offer a universalizing theory of knowledge ourselves? We argue for the need to redescribe knowledge and present the case that what we are doing we consider to be epistemology. We cite evidence to support our claims that the field of epistemology has been too narrowly defined and based on assumptions such as absolutism, autonomy, and knowledge being a product separate from human beings as knowers. We do think it is possible to justify claims concerning reality, but we are also aware that it is hard to know whether what one considers "evidence" is real and not socially constructed.

However, the relational epistemological theory we describe is not one that we claim to be the best or truest theory, for we know many other theories will follow and others currently are being developed based on understandings we do not have. Although it is not the truest, best, most complete, or final explanation of knowledge, we do think a relational theory has important advantages over other epistemological theories. One advantage is that it is a more encompassing description of knowledge, because a relational epistemology includes vital aspects of knowledge that other theories tend to overlook or exclude from the discussion. Our attention to and valuing of such qualities as relationality and caring in an intersubjective world should make a relational epistemological theory more inclusive and less open to ideological abuse. Women, men, and children, from different ethnic backgrounds and ways of life, all should find that this theory applies to them. This must be the case if we are right at all in our claim that the theory we are developing is an improved description of how people know. We also hope that a relational epistemology opens the possibilities for valuing contributions from all people. We need each other to nurture the constructing/deconstructing of knowledge and help us in searching for knowledge that is sound, comprehensive, coherent, cohesive, as well as beneficial and beautiful. We also need each other to help problematize and unsettle knowledge that we take to be sound, therefore allowing for multiplicity, dissonance, and discord. Whether this theory meets these criteria (or other criteria deemed valuable and important) must be tested by all of us as contributors to knowledge.

Redescribing Epistemology: A Relational Epistemology

A relational epistemology begins with the assumption that all **people are social beings**.[18] We are all born relating to at least one other person, our biological mothers (even in utero), even if that relationship ends at our birth. Today a woman can have another woman's egg fertilized and implanted in her uterus, so that she may birth a child that is actually not genetically hers at all. Still, that woman is already in a relationship with that child, for what she does to care for herself and how she lives her life affects the child inside her. Many women and extended family members stroke, talk, sing, and read to their children before they are born.

If our relationship with our "biological" mother ends at birth, that does not end our lives as relational beings. None of us could survive to become potential knowers without the help of someone else relating to us, at least at a minimal level of offering food, clothing, shelter, and some form of physical contact. If not our biological mothers, someone else must take up the task of being our caregivers (Thayer-Bacon, 1993c). Our lives begin in and are lived in relationships with others. The quality of these relationships directly affects our abilities to become knowers. This is because **we develop a sense of "self" through our relationships with others, and we need a sense of self to become potential knowers**. We will discover that our ability to develop a sense of "self" is greatly enhanced if the relationships we experience are caring ones. Mothers must take care of themselves to give birth to live, healthy babies. Babies must be cared for to grow, develop a sense of self, learn a language, and begin to think ideas.

Given that we are social beings, the second assumption a relational epistemology makes is that **we are contextual social beings**. All of us are born into a particular setting—for example, as the youngest, oldest, or middle child. We are all born at a certain time and place. All of us are born into a setting that places us automatically within a certain culture. If you are born in a home that listens to Louie

Armstrong, the Beatles, or Bach, that is what you grow up listening to; if your family is vegetarian and grows their own vegetables, that is what you grow up eating.

All of us grow up experiencing our worlds through the filtering of a body that is uniquely our own. If you are a small child compared with others your age, the world you experience is different from your taller friends'. Each of us inherits a physical condition that affects how we experience the world. We may be fat or thin, have allergies and asthma, or wear glasses to see clearly; perhaps we need a wheelchair to get around or braces for our legs; we might have an extra X chromosome, diabetes, or HIV. How our bodies affect us also depends on our cultural context. In some cultures larger children are held in higher esteem; the heavier one's family members are, the greater your family wealth must be. Other cultures view fatter people as lazy and lacking self-discipline. Some families include physically challenged children in all activities; others exclude and isolate them. Most cultures treat boys differently from girls.

Because all of us are social beings with contexts that affect who we are and how we interpret the world, a relational epistemology must assume that **people have a past and have been affected by others' views**. The social practices that surround us promote us to believe certain beliefs and not others (Goldman, 1994). They may teach us that dreams, as experiences, are just as important as other experiences we have when awake. Or our social practices may teach us to pay no attention to our dreams, discounting them as experiences of any importance. Social practices, which are usually affected by the settings in which they take place, teach us the names and meanings for fifteen different types of snow, for example, or they may not attend to a variety of "types" and just teach us that what we experience as white, cold flakes is called "snow."

How people begin to make sense of the world is due to their contextuality, their social setting, and its past. This means that all knowledge is value-laden or interest-laden and that cognitive pursuits and their social organization are not independent entities (Fuller, 1988). Our culture teaches us that dreams are not important and ghosts do not exist. Therefore, when we have a dream, we do not pay attention to it and do not assign it any value or interest. When we think we hear sounds or see a phantom figure, we find some source for the noise that fits within our scheme of reasonableness ("Oh, it must have been branches brushing against the windowpane") or are told that a phantom is just our imagination.

All of us begin our relational lives in someone else's trusting arms. What they teach us we believe; we do not begin our lives as independent, self-reliant, autonomous knowers. We must trust others, for lack of trust impedes the growth of knowledge (Hardwig, 1991). Currently such social philosophers as John Hardwig, Steve Fuller, and Alvin Goldman describe the impact social and interpersonal practices have on modern knowledge. What seems to be missing from these social epistemologists' theories is the full impact of what it means to necessarily view knowledge as socially dependent.

Social epistemologists still assume knowers are autonomous and can find true beliefs through cognition. They still treat knowledge as a product quite separate from human beings. Consequently, at a substantive level, the insights of

social epistemology are not radically different from those of essentialist epistemology. It is not merely the case that modern knowers cannot be viewed as
autonomous and independent thinkers. From a relational epistemological perspective, that has always been the case and always will be. We are not
autonomous knowers sitting in a social setting struggling with whether we have
good reasons to believe that someone is an expert and we should believe what
she or he tells us. We do not just trust others because to do so quickens our
growth of knowledge. We really have no choice but to trust those others with
whom we are in social relation. We are social beings who learn from others (we
believe); because we are able to develop relationships based on such qualities as
trust, we begin to develop a sense of self and eventually learn to think more
autonomously (we can question our beliefs).

The relational epistemology being described here considers being (knowers)
as directly connected to knowing, which makes this theory pragmatic in a traditional philosophical sense. Like John Dewey, we view knowing as an activity, like
dancing, singing, or loving, that is done with others. Dewey (1934/1958)
described inquiry as a dialectical relationship between inquirers and their objects
of inquiry, a relationship that is dynamic, flexible, and reciprocal.

This pragmatic relational epistemology should not be confused with other
forms of pragmatism, such as Richard Rorty's form of pragmatism which calls for
the foregoing of experience in favor of language.[19] As Rorty (1991) describes experience, "[W]hat you experience yourself to be is largely a function of what it makes
sense to describe yourself as in the languages you are able to use" (p. 244). For
Rorty, each of us learns who we are because we have been given the language to
describe ourselves from others with whom we are in relation. If Rorty is right, this
means that experience is not directly accessible to us, because our language acts
as a filter, sifting and sorting through our experiences and helping us name and
give meaning to what we experience. Those experiences we do not have a language for fall through our filter and are lost as experiences. According to Rorty, we
may feel different types of snow, but if we live in a culture that has no language
for those feelings, we will have no way to directly access that experience and note
the sensations we have. Without the language to name what we are experiencing,
we will not be able to maintain that feeling and will lose it.

Kaufman-Osborn (1993) humorously points out in his discussion of Rorty's
work, using the metaphor of talking fish, that "Rorty effectively 'forgets' that language is always relationally implicated in palpable webs of immediate experience
that must be 'had' before anything caught up within them can be known' as a
determinate subject of discursive inquiry" (p. 128). The relational epistemological theory being described here assumes there is a direct relationship between
experience and meaning. True, the language we inherit from our social contexts
has a tremendous impact on our lives. Language affects how we view the world
and how we make sense of the experiences we have. But it is also true that much
of what we experience remains unnamed and cannot be reduced to its articulated
meanings. We urge people to be receptive and attentive to the inarticulate, too,
not just what is named. As Dewey (1981) explained, "[E]xperience warns us that

all intellectual terms are the products of discrimination and classification, and that we must, as philosophers, go back to the primitive situations of life that antecede and generate those reflective interpretations, so that we re-live former processes of interpretation in a wary manner" (p. 386).[20]

What will help us become aware of our social context and how it has affected who we are and how we view the world? What will help us be more receptive to the inarticulate experiences we have that our culture does not have a name for? We find that aside from pragmatic philosophers, feminist philosophers and post-modern philosophers also help us understand how it is possible for this under-standing and receptivity to occur. In Charlene Haddock Seigfried's (1991) discus-sion of the common grounds between pragmatism and feminism, she suggests, "Pragmatist philosophy . . . explains why the neglect of context is the besetting fallacy of philosophical thought. Feminism cogently and extensively shows how gender, race, class, and sexual preference are crucial parts of context that philos-ophy has traditionally neglected" (p. 16). Postmodernists such as Foucault have also taken seriously the fact that we are contextual social beings and drawn par-ticular attention to the power relations that exist in societies.[21]

Like other feminist (critical and postmodern) theories, this theory relies on the insights "that the personal is political, that there is direct relation, however complex it may be, between sociality and subjectivity, between language and consciousness, or between institutions and individuals" (de Lauretis, 1986, p. 5). However, this theory argues that it is possible for us to gain insights into the contexts of our lives. Liberal feminists believe along with their individualistic col-leagues (described in Chapter 1) that it is possible for knowers to look at the world as disinterested and detached spectators (the view from nowhere). Such a view denies the assumption we make that we are social beings who are embed-ded and embodied. Historical materialist feminists argue, like their social con-structivist colleagues (described in Chapter 1), that we can never gain insights to the contexts of our lives and so are forced to always view the world within a con-text on which we cannot gain a perspective (the view from everywhere).

We are describing ourselves as contextual beings, and we are acknowledging the dominancy of culture. Yet we are also describing ourselves as people who are able to begin to understand the setting we are born into and how it has affected and shaped us. We gain insights into our contextuality through our interactions with other people. As we begin to understand this contextuality, we begin to develop the ability to offer fresh, unique perspectives. We will discover that not only do we develop a sense of self because of the relationships we have, but we all become aware of that sense of self and how our social context has affected the way we view the world through our relationships with others. **Other people help us become aware of our own embeddedness**. We will find that our ability to improve our awareness as knowers is enhanced if we are able to experi-ence sustaining, caring relationships.

The relational epistemological theory being described here is a social femi-nist perspective, as labeled by Alison Jaggar (1983), and it provides a way out of the relativist/essentialist debate.

> Social feminist epistemology . . . is explicitly historical materialist and so is able to explain why culture is dominant and to link the anti-feminist consciousness of many women with the structure of their daily lives. At the same point, the socialist feminist account preserves the apparently contradictory claim that women occupy a distinctive epistemological standpoint that offers unique insight into certain aspects of reality. (pp. 377, 382)

This relational epistemology is a pragmatic social feminist perspective calling for active engagement, aiming at democratic inclusion, joining theory with praxis, striving for awareness of context and values, tolerating vagueness and ambiguities. Knowledge is something people develop as they have experiences with each other and the world around them. People improve the ideas that have been socially constructed and passed down to them by others. They do this improving by further developing their understandings and enlarging their perspectives. With enlarged perspectives, people are able to create new meanings for their experiences. In summation: **A relational epistemology views knowledge as something that is socially constructed by embedded, embodied people who are in relation with each other**.

Development of Self: The Importance of Nurturing

Let us now turn to a careful consideration of each assumption made earlier and what these assumptions entail. We begin with the assumption that all people are social beings. Knowledge is constructed by human beings who are in relation with each other. These human beings were once very young children, and when they were born, they were not born with a sense of self. Historically, epistemological theories have tended to treat people, when they come into the discussion, as if they are isolated beings who are born fully developed. These adults seem to have never gone through the process of being formed through their relationships with others. They also seem to be autonomous, individual adults who do not need others to be knowers. We present the case that relationships are indispensable for all people and in every area of their lives. It is because we are social beings that we develop a sense of self and are able to become potential knowers. Our ability to maintain relationships with others is what helps further enhance our development as knowers.

People are not born with the **ability** to think, speak, read, write, or even to relate to another. They are born with the **capacity** to do these marvelous things. They have to acquire and develop these skills. What forms the limits, the boundaries of knowledge, are peoples' experiences and their human capabilities (Flax, 1983, pp. 248–249). If we are right that the subjects of knowledge, selves, are actively involved and essential to any knowing, it is extremely important to take a closer look at selves and how they develop the skills necessary for furthering knowledge.

We have already found that people begin their lives in a relationship. This fact makes early infantile experiences and child rearing vital to the nurturing of knowledge.[22] People develop a sense of self through their relationships with others;

these relationships are internalized and interact with people's own innate constitutions. Relationships, first with one's mother, then with others, develop prior to as well as simultaneously with the development of language, thoughts, and ideas.

A healthy self, able to contribute to the furthering of knowledge is something most people take for granted. Healthy people have a hard time imagining what it would be like to not be healthy. Only when health is missing does it become noticeable. A healthy self has a sense of who it is and that it is something distinguishable from other objects and subjects in the world around it. A healthy self has what could be labeled a **voice**, meaning more than a perspective or point of view. A voice is the expression of a person's soul or spirit, what is unique about each person, the mind/body together. A person's voice is the "I," his or her feelings/thoughts/intuitions all rolled into one. It is the subjective, that which a person cannot lose or leave out of the thinking process (Thayer-Bacon, 1995b).

How does one develop a sense of "I"? As Piaget (1966) described this process, it is through interaction with others. A person must be in relationship with others, having the opportunity to respond to their attentions toward her- or himself, to learn that she or he is a self separate from others. As Jane Flax (1983) points out in her discussion of psychoanalytic theory, in particular, object relations theory, "the most basic tenet of object relations theory is that human beings are created in and through relations with other human beings" (p. 250). Flax sees psychoanalysis (especially object relations theory) as a crucial tool for feminist philosophy. "Its content represents a systematic attempt to understand human nature as the product of social relations in interaction with biology" (p. 249).

One can think of extreme examples of human beings raised by animals (e.g., Victor, the "Wild Boy" of Aveyron with whom Itard worked[23]) to remind us how important relationships with other human beings are for the development of self. But it is not enough to have relationships with others to develop a sense of self, a voice. A person must have the opportunity to relate to other human beings in a healthy way and be able to contribute that voice to the furthering of knowledge.

Healthy relationships are necessary to avoid a self that is in painful fragments. A healthy voice is something developed through caring relationships with others. Certainly one can think of children who have suffered, owing to harmful relationships they have with other people who abuse them and treat them like objects. Such children grow up, like Flax's (1990) patients suffering from "borderline syndrome," as people who "lack a core self without which the registering of and pleasure in a variety of experiencing of ourselves, others, and the outer world are simply not possible" (p. 218). These people suffer from psychosis.

Unfortunately, it is not necessary to think of people who suffer from extreme mental health problems to find examples that point to the value and importance of caring relationships. Belenky, Clinchy, Goldberger, and Tarule's (1986) famous study of women from different educational backgrounds and economic levels found women who were silent and unable to contribute to the construction of knowledge. A development of voice means a person has learned that she or he has a unique perspective to offer and that others will listen and are willing to hear her or his voice. A healthy self trusts that it has something of value to contribute. Babies born profoundly hard of hearing will stop babbling and developing their physical voice when they cannot hear it, having no environmental support for making sounds. So it is for people who are not listened to, who receive no environmental support for the development of an internal voice. They will think they have nothing to say and will become silent. All people are born with the possibility of developing a sense of self, but that possibility can only be realized through healthy, caring relationships with other human beings.

Flax (1983) points out in "Political Philosophy and the Patriarchal Unconscious" that a child, physically born in one day, after approximately 9 months of gestation, takes around 3 years to be "psychologically born" (p. 250). This birth is a complex process, which can only occur in and through social relations. "This long period of development is unique to the human species" (p. 254). Given that human beings are unique in the long period of psychological development that they must go through to develop a voice, a self, the importance of caring relationships becomes even clearer. Because people are social beings, dependent on each other for their formation of selfhood, they (we) must, necessarily, be able to relate to each other, at least to one other human being, in a caring way.

As teachers and future teachers, we will find that understanding more about healthy relationships will greatly improve our students' chances of being knowers in our own classrooms. We begin to understand that without the opportunity to develop a healthy sense of self, a person cannot become a knower/thinker able to contribute to the furthering of knowledge (Thayer-Bacon, 1989, 1991). Not only are people connected to knowledge, because they construct it; they are also connected to each other, for none of us could ever grow to adulthood without the help of others. And people cannot grow to adulthood able to contribute to knowing unless they have had the opportunity to participate in caring relationships with other people.

Healthy relationships are caring relationships that answer the call for life. They are nurturing and responsive. They offer the promise of existence and a future. Cultures have varying ways to care for their young. Some people place their babies in a crib or playpen so their child can play without being harmed; others strap their babies to a board or in some other form of a backpack, carrying their babies to keep them from harm. No one questions that these different approaches are all ways of caring and answering the call for life. How we care for each other varies according to our contextuality, but that we care for each other does not, if we are seeking to live.

Nel Noddings (1984) has written much about caring (as have others[24]), though not in an attempt to associate it with epistemology, as we are doing here. Her discussion of caring is from an ethical perspective, as we will see in Chapter 3. Noddings assumes that people's natural impulses are to care. That assumption is based on the same ideas we are presenting, that people are naturally in relation with others and that our individuality is defined in a set of relations. Noddings suggests, as we are, that people depend for their continued existence on the fact that others are a part of their lives in some relationship with them and that these others care about them. Caring about others is the glue that holds relationships together, and because it has been demonstrated that people are relational beings, it holds that people have at least the possibility to care. Noddings (1984) refers to this glue as "the caring attitude," and she discusses how this caring attitude is the fundamental universality of her ethic. "[T]hat attitude which expresses our earliest memories of being cared for and our growing store of memories of both caring and being cared for, is universally accessible" (p. 5).

Caring has been defined by Noddings (1984) as entailing "generous thinking" and "receptive rationality." By caring, we mean

> being receptive to what another has to say and open to possibly hearing the other's voice more completely and fairly. Caring about another person (other people's ideas, other life forms, or even inanimate objects) requires respecting the other as a separate, autonomous person, worthy of caring. It is an attitude that gives value to an other, by denoting that the other is worth attending to in a serious or close manner. Caring involves a 'feeling with' the other, and it stresses engrossment. All caring involves presence (being present), generosity, and acquaintance. An attitude of acceptance and trust, inclusion and openness, is important in all caring relationships. (Thayer-Bacon, 1993a, p. 325).[25]

Although Noddings and we agree that people are social beings who begin their lives in relations and have the capacity to care for others, we think it is important to examine carefully her assumption that caring comes naturally to people. Otherwise, how do we explain harmful, destructive, terrible parenting and the fact that children die in the hands of their parents? Although it may be the case that all people have the capacity to be caring, how *we* were cared for, or not cared for, will affect our actual ability to grow up able to care for others.

Sara Ruddick (1989) disagrees with Noddings on the assumption that caring comes naturally to people. In looking at caring from an adult perspective, Ruddick does not think caring is automatic; rather, she describes it as having an optional quality. For Ruddick, first is the fact of biological vulnerability and second is caring. We can certainly imagine people who are unwilling or unable to care for their young—the newspapers are full of such stories.

Ruddick (1989) also distinguishes 'caring' from 'mothering'. She does so to stress that all mothers (any "person who takes on responsibility for children's lives and for whom providing child care is a significant part of her working life"; p. 40) are "adoptive" (see Chapter 2 in *Maternal Thinking*). She also does so because she hopes to see mother and father roles combined. Ruddick's move to describe mothering as adoptive avoids the problem that has plagued women and men throughout history. It is a biological fact that women give birth to the continuing of the human race (at least until we are able to birth children in artificial wombs). Simone de Beauvoir (1952/1989) makes the case in *The Second Sex* that the fact of the ability to give birth (as well as physical strength) has affected women socially from the beginning of time. But a view around the world, and through time, shows that it is not true that only women care for the young or that only women are good at caring. Caring is not a feminine activity; anyone can be caring. It is important to make this clear because both men and women share a responsibility in caring for their young and helping them develop a sense of self, so they can grow up to be knowers contributing to our knowledge. Men *and* women are teachers who need to recognize the value of caring relationships with their students and how these caring relationships enhance their students' opportunities to learn. We, as a society, share in the responsibility of valuing and encouraging parents, child care providers, and teachers so that they feel supported in their efforts to be caring.

In *Philosophy and Feminist Thinking,* Jean Grimshaw (1986) shows very clearly how caring, if labeled feminine, can be used oppressively, made to be just the concern of women. What is considered 'feminine' has historically been devalued and considered inferior. Caring for other human beings has been considered the microcosm world of women and the macrocosm has been regarded as the world of men. "The devaluation of the feminine has not *only* worked against women, although of course it has done that, but . . . it has led to a distortion of values, concerns and priorities that [are] quite general human concern[s]" (p. 74). Grimshaw notes, "An assumption of separate male and female 'realities' is not a tenable one and does not do justice either to the extremely variegated nature of female experience or to the way in which this intersects with male experience" (p. 102). But she also warns that how Ruddick describes the mother/child relationship tends to treat it as an isolated self-contained unit. Mothering is embedded in other social relationships and institutions. "Insofar, then, as women give priority in their lives to the maintaining of relationships with others, and to attention to and care for others, such capacities should not be seen as 'maternal'" (p. 252). For Grimshaw, to care for another is to try to apprehend the reality of the other.

> The human self is 'embedded' in a network of relationships with others, both at very immediate and intimate and at wider levels. Human needs and interests arise in a context of relationships with other people, and human needs for relationships with other people cannot be understood as merely instrumental to isolable individual ends. (p. 175)

Noddings makes an important point concerning caring that answers another concern that often comes up in discussions on caring. Caring is not just an individual virtue; caring is relational and involves others (Noddings, 1992, pp. 17–18). One person may think she or he cares for another, but if the second person does not perceive that first person as caring, there is no caring. This helps us understand why people will insist that they "care" and yet are perceived as manipulative, overbearing, or dangerous. It explains how a parent can argue that they "cared" so much for their children when they encouraged them to drink poison (Jonestown massacre) or how a boyfriend/spouse can claim to "care" for a person he brutally beat up, when such acts of "care" result in the one "cared-for" dying. In these situations, we would quite reasonably say that the person who thinks she or he cares really does not.

Caring does not necessarily entail that one likes or loves the other, though certainly if one has an affection or fondness for someone else, he or she usually cares about that special someone. People are able to care without it involving friendship or romance. Caring is not sentimental or paternalistic, as described here. Caring for another person is life affirming. It acknowledges the other exists and is worth the effort of trying to perceive. Caring is an attitude of valuing and attending to another that tells the other person that she or he is a separate person worth attending to. Such acts of caring, where there is a bond and separateness, help each of us establish our own "core identity."[26] This kind of caring is the basis for a truly reciprocal relationship.

With this argument, we hope it is becoming clear that we need caring to help us be potential knowers, able to contribute to the furthering of knowledge. Knowing is dependent on the contributions of people. At a very basic level, only people who have had the opportunity to develop a healthy sense of self, meaning they are able to express their voices, will be able to contribute to knowing. People develop a voice they can express because of their ability to relate to others. People are able to relate to others because they have been cared for by others. A healthy self, which has been nurtured through caring relationships with others, is necessary for that self to know. Human beings are unique in terms of how long they are dependent, fragile beings in need of nurturing and protection. Because they are dependent on at least one other to take care of them for so long, they are vulnerable to much potential pain and disaster. Being a child's caregiver is an incredible responsibility, but without people willing to do this, none of us would ever grow up to be epistemic agents able to know anything.

Our Relationality Continues: Epistemic Agency

So far, we have discussed the first assumption, that all of us are social beings, and made a case for how it is each of us develops a sense of self: through our nurtured relationships with our caregivers, who can be male and/or female. We have discussed why it is necessary to have a sense of self to become potential knowers. What about our second assumption, that we are all contextual beings? Let us look now at how we begin to understand what our voice is and how it is different from others'. We need to consider how we learn that who we are is embedded within a cultural context. If potential contributors to knowledge are raised by their caregivers within a socially constructed view of "reality," how are they able to become reflective and critical about their own position within their relational context? How can people hope to learn about and understand how they have been affected by their relationships with others and shaped to make the choices they make? How can people hope to gain a perspective of their choices and contributions to knowing? And if we are all contextual social beings whose views of the world are partial and potentially flawed, how can any of us claim to know anything for sure? How can any of us claim what philosophers call "epistemic agency"?

Piaget (1966) explains in *Judgement and Reasoning in the Child* that the key concept to understanding children's reasoning is the concept of egocentricism. Piaget is not the only source on this topic, but he is such a major source for understanding this concept that we turn to him at this time. Egocentrism is a characteristic that prevails with children below the age of about 7 to 8 years, and, for Piaget, children do grow out of this characteristic by the time they enter elementary school. Egocentrism is not a trait one would expect to find in adults.

> Now, experiments show that the child's way of thinking occupies a place situated exactly between the "autistic" and the social. We have therefore given it the name ego-centric, which indicates that its interests tend not merely towards organic or "ludistic" satisfaction as in pure autism, [a state of emotional disturbance where one is abnormally withdrawn and subjective, accepting fantasy rather than reality] but towards intellectual adaption as in adult thought. (p. 204)

Piaget (1966) says that before age 7 to 8 years, children have trouble with introspection because they are not conscious of their own thought. "Ego-centricism of thought necessarily entails a certain degree of unconsciousness" (p. 137). What is important about this concept in terms of our discussion on self-awareness is that because children are unconscious of their own thought, they are also unaware that they have a point of view. They also do not realize that other people have points of view or that theirs may be different from others'. Piaget tells us that children at this age believe they are always understanding each other and have no suspicion of the egocentric character of their thought. For this reason, children at this age have no trouble finding answers to questions, though they cannot tell you how. Children just assume they are always understanding. The idea that someone means something different than what they understand has not occurred to them yet.

Piaget (1966) does not mean from his description on egocentrism that the child's view is personal and private. He does not think children are even aware that they have a separate point of view. They think theirs is just like everyone else's. They have the capacity to believe immediately in their own ideas, have complete assurance on all subjects, and are "impervious to experience." They do not seek verification for truth, because they do not even sense the need to do so. They do not doubt their own knowledge. As Piaget says, he uses the term *egocentricism* because of other works in psychology; he mentions Blondel's work on pathological thought (p. 204) and Freud's work on autism (p. 205). He is searching for a word that shows that thought is still autistic in its structure but that its interests tend toward intellectual adaption.

For Piaget (1966), this primary egocentrism for children is one we all grow out of as we come into contact with other people through social interaction. "We become conscious of ourselves to the extent that we are adapted to other people" (p. 210). The child does "not trouble himself about the reasons and motives which have guided his reasoning process. Only under pressure of argument and opposition will he seek to justify himself in the eyes of others and thus acquire the habit of watching himself think" (p. 137). We cannot use Piaget's model of how the child reasons and apply it to adult thinking, because only children can have this kind of egocentrism. As soon as children develop a sense of self and other selves, they have moved on in the thinking process, never to return.

Human beings have made tremendous strides in development at this point. They have learned they have a self! And they have learned this through their social interactions with others.

Let us look at perception in another way, to help clear up a criticism that has been issued at Piaget's description of egocentrism. We all agree that each of us perceives the world from a certain point of view. But does describing perception as involving a point of view commit us to the belief that each person's perception is necessarily private? As D. W. Hamlyn (1978) points out:

> [A] child's experience must be construed as an experience of a common world from the beginning, though not of course initially of this as a common world. It is to this that the child has to come, but there would be no possibility of doing so if the experience were necessarily concerned with private objects at first. It is only because the situation is other than this that a child can come to distinguish right and wrong ways of seeing things. Egocentricity cannot, therefore, be regarded as tantamount to privacy or subjectivity. (p. 120)

The egocentricity of people, to the extent that it exists, is simply one facet that is due to the fact that people necessarily have points of view.

> It is not a general characteristic of experience itself. Indeed [Lev] Vygotsky [the Russian psychologist] has claimed that it must succeed an initial socialisation as an internalisation of what is until then external. This is in effect to say that a private and personal point of view is possible only if given awareness of what is public and inter-subjective. (p. 120)

The concept of common experience is very important to a relational theory of knowledge, given that we do not believe that knowledge is innate (something we are born with, as Plato believed). Philosophers can argue that certain qualities of being human are innate (e.g., constitution, powers, tendencies), which is how we all come to perceive things in similar ways and can communicate with each other, without endorsing a theory that knowledge is innate. The social process, relations with other humans, is of utmost importance to such an argument, because we need a way for knowers to get things as right as they can, not just by accident. As Hamlyn (1978) says, "Getting things right means getting them right by public, inter-subjective and objective standards" (p. 90). Piaget would not disagree with this view of human knowledge and the importance of relating to other humans. The interrelating with other human beings is exactly what moves a child out of egocentric thought onto another level of reasoning, according to Piaget, and so it is very important.

Anything a young child can be aware of must initially be undifferentiated. But because children are human and born with a constitution that brings dispositions and ways of responding to things, children must inevitably have their attention fastened on some things rather than others. Relating to other humans helps children begin to differentiate, by drawing their attention in certain directions.

It is a fact of some importance that the child's upbringing is an initiation into a world as circumscribed by other human beings. It is part of the acquisition of what we call the objective view of the world that the child should enter into the human form of life. Relations with other human beings must therefore be of paramount importance. These, however, will not be possible unless he possesses already the potential for being human; that is to say unless he is a human child with a physical constitution that is capable of developing into an adult human one. What is important about this is that the child must be capable of responding to human attention of varying kinds in ways that are also human. (Hamlyn, 1978, p. 97)

As we found out earlier, we learn to differentiate, and we learn what is correct and incorrect (what is "real" in a socially constructed sense) from other humans. The concept of what is correct and incorrect, the concept of "truth" (in a fallibilist sense), is necessary for us to claim that we know anything. Because we learn what is "truth" from our interactions with others, knowledge can only exist in creatures capable of interrelationships that have something of the character of being personal. (A child must be a potential knower, in the position to accept "truth" as truth and to recognize correction as correction and must be capable of standing in relation to other humans to learn "truth," for knowledge to be possible. If a child lacks this possibility—that is, is profoundly mentally challenged—then the child will not be able to gain knowledge.)

All knowledge is perspectival, and we are all influenced by the community (or communities) into which we are born. But it is not possible for any of us, as potential knowers, to only see things from our own personal, private perspectives. As soon as we try to communicate orally with anyone else, we have to be able to translate our thoughts into words that will be understood by the other person. Otherwise, no oral communication will take place. To translate our thoughts into words that will be understood, we have to be able to understand what the other person's point of view might be. We have to try to attach our meaning to something they can associate with and therefore understand. In other words, none of us can remain only in our own point of view and orally communicate with anyone else. Even if we do not communicate orally but rather use sign language or gestures, we still need to be able to reach out to the other person and try to attach meaning to our gestures and signs so that the other can understand and meaning can be shared. If we would remain only in our own point of view, we would be labeled autistic, someone who is severely emotionally disturbed and only within his or her self.

Now that we have an understanding of our own perspectives within our cultural group, how do we gain further understandings of our contextuality as a cultural group? In other words, now that we know how our views differ from our siblings and neighbors, how do we learn more about the contextuality of our view in relation to others in different parts of the world and times in history?

Sandra Harding (1993, pp. 49–83) and other feminist standpoint epistemologists think they offer a possible answer to how we gain understanding of our contextuality.[27] Harding's feminist standpoint epistemology is a project of authorizing the speech of marginalized subjects. In "Rethinking Standpoint Epistemology: What Is 'Strong Objectivity'?" she presents the position that subjects who are not members of the community have views to offer, as outsiders, that will help community members become more aware of their own biases and prejudices. People from other cultures can help us understand our own culture. (And reading books written in earlier times help us understand past views in relation to our current cultural views.) So, for example, interviewing women and asking for their perspectives will help women and men see the world from other angles, or talking to women from the Third World will help women from developed nations see the assumptions they make about life as a woman.

Harding's (1993) method is to draw from the margins, "from marginalized lives" and to "take everyday life as problematic" (p. 50). She "sets the relationship between knowledge and politics at the center of (her) account" (p. 56). Harding argues that "the grounds for knowledge are fully saturated with history and social life rather than abstracted from it" (p. 57). Her perspective, like ours, emphasizes the social influence communities have on knowledge production. As she so aptly describes this social context, subjects/agents are not universal; they are "multiple, heterogeneous and contradictory or incoherent, not unitary, homogeneous, and coherent as they are for empiricist epistemology" (p. 65). All knowledge claims are socially situated; "all bear the fingerprints of the communities that produce them. All thoughts by humans start off from socially determinate lives" (p. 57).

Please note that although Harding and we agree that all knowledge is perspectival and each of us is influenced by the community (or communities) into which we are born, we do not agree about the level of effect this has on the individual or the community. We think the newborn child is fragile, dependent, and greatly influenced by the people he or she is in relation with, but we also think the newborn child influences the people in his or her life. We consider this social context to be interrelational and transactive, a dialectic relationship that is not just one-way and purely socially deterministic. As we discussed in Chapter 1, a child who is not even born yet can motivate a mother to change her eating and sleeping habits, even her work or companionships.

Although Harding (1993) presents feminist standpoint epistemology as relying on a logic that "refuses to essentialize its subjects of knowledge" (p. 66), she goes on to make the claim that some perspectives are more revealing than others. Now she is in trouble, for she has fallen into the same trap for which she has criticized other theorists. Several authors[28] have pointed out this problem for feminist standpoint theory. Harding is recommending that looking from the margins helps people see the dominant culture and its assumptions of superiority. The question that other feminists have asked, particularly Third World non-Western feminists, is, Why do you assume that marginalized perspectives have more agency than perspectives within the dominant culture? "Although the claim to epistemic privilege as a tool may seem to be a claim of the oppressed, due to some of its history, it nonetheless reveals itself also as a master's tool" (Bar On, 1993, p. 97). If it is wrong for men to assume they understand and can speak for women, is it not also wrong for (white, middle-class, heterosexual) women to assume they can speak for women who are poor, women who are black, women who are lesbians? "There are no tools that can replace it [the notion of epistemic privilege], nor are any needed, because when the oppressed feel a need to authorize speech, they are acting on feelings that are a function of their oppression. Speech needs to be authorized only when silence is the rule" (Bar On, 1993, p. 97).

If Harding and we are right in that all of us are influenced by the communities in which we grow up, will not a marginalized person who grows up in a world that excludes and mistreats him or her have a view that has been affected, tainted, by the situation in which he or she has grown up? In other words, if you and I have been told that we are stupid and have nothing of value to offer to the conversation and have been excluded from an education, even if researchers come along wanting to interview us, will they not find that we have nothing to say? That is what Belenky et al. (1986) found in their study, *Women's Ways of Knowing*. If we are embedded, embodied people, affected by our situations and social relationships, then all of us are affected by our contexts, not just people who are members of the dominant culture. This is one of Jane Flax's (1983, p. 270) points: women's experiences put them at some advantages for reinterpreting reality but also impose on them certain psychological difficulties. Women face the obstacle of having been raised with the typical feminine set of attitudes and modes of perception that have been imposed on women in a male-dominated society.

Uma Narayan (1989) reminds feminist standpoint epistemologists that being from a marginalized group and able to have access to the dominant culture "is not a guarantee that a critical stance on the part of the individual will result." The person can feel alienation, as "an outsider in both contexts," and, like many bilingual people, she can feel "a sense of clumsiness or lack of fluency" (p. 267). Narayan warns, "The thesis that oppression may bestow an epistemic advantage should not tempt us in the direction of idealizing or romanticizing oppression and blind us to its real material and psychic deprivations" (p. 264).

One last point of this issue of subjectivity and epistemic privilege: It would be a mistake to conclude, from the thesis we have been presenting—that knowledge is constructed by people who are socially constituted—"that those who are differently located can never attain some understanding of [one's] experience or some sympathy with [one's] cause" (Narayan, 1989, p. 264). To say that because we are not a Native American (Indigenous people, as many say they prefer to call themselves) we can never hope to understand at least some of the experiences and views of Indigenous people means there is no point in attempting communication. Such a view again falls back into the notion of social determinism and does not acknowledge the possibility of interaction.

Seyla Benhabib (1992) offers some insight that will help contributors to knowing gain perspective of their own context, as well as the contexts of the social beings around them, through her discussion of enlarged thinking and the generalized other and concrete other.[29] To attempt to understand a person's own subjectivity and other people's points of view, people need the possibility of interacting with others. Even if we have the willingness to reason from others' points of view and the sensitivity to hear their voices, "[n]either the concreteness nor the otherness of the 'concrete other' can be known in the absence of the voice of the other. The viewpoint of the concrete other emerges as a distinct one only as a result of self-definition. It is the other who makes us aware both of her concreteness and her otherness" (p. 168). As we try to believe and therefore hopefully assure ourselves of understanding what another thinks, we need to practice **enlarged thinking**, anticipating "communication with others with whom [we] know [we] must finally come to some agreement." Enlarged thinking does not imply consensus, just some agreement, and it cannot function in strict isolation—it needs the presence of others (pp. 8–10).

Considering that we are all social beings embedded in rich levels of context, what kinds of skills do we need to practice such methods as enlarged thinking? We are born with the capacity for enlarged thinking, but we need to practice and develop the skills that will help us be successful at understanding others and gaining further insight into our own perspectives. The kinds of skills we are alluding to are our relational and communication skills, the ability to tune into our intuitions and emotional feelings, the development of our imagination, and critical thinking skills. These skills will be discussed further in Chapter 4.

Given that we are practicing and developing the skills necessary for enlarged thinking and that we have attempted to understand others' perspectives and self-reflect on our own, in the end do we not have to choose an answer? How do we come to any agreement? How does one decide which ideas to leave in and use and which ones to dismiss?

We know people will be limited in their knowing by their environment, which includes their experiences with the world around them and each other, and their human capabilities. As Flax (1983) points out, "The boundaries of knowledge are our experiences and our human abilities" (p. 249). Because people are social beings formed in relationships, those relationships will cause people to be formed in certain ways and not in others and will limit the possibilities of constructed knowledge. Second, criteria for how to choose ideas will be fallible, as they are human constructions and therefore subject to change and improvement. As Harding (1993) describes this, "[T]he grounds for knowledge are fully saturated with history and social life rather than abstracted from it" (p. 57). Further discussion of criteria appears in Chapter 4.

In the past, philosophers have hoped to reach such lofty goals as Truth and Certainty, through the methods of inquiry they have proposed. More recently, philosophers have striven for less lofty aims such as trustworthy knowledge. Some have hoped for the possibility of arriving at a judgment that is a consensus/integration of others voices; others, like Benhabib, are striving for at least agreement. Noddings and Ruddick have pointed to harmony and peace as the goals for which we should be aiming. We will turn to goals and aims of knowledge in Chapter 5. As readers can probably anticipate, much work still needs to be done!

Implications for Education

Let us turn now to a discussion of how a relational epistemological theory affects our views on education and what kind of recommendations for schools such a theory implies. Most discussions on school improvement tend to focus on the knowledge students are supposed to obtain. Studies such as *A Nation at Risk, The Shopping Mall High School,* and *The Paideia Proposal* focus on the curriculum and requirements for graduation. Such studies are looking at the products of knowledge without considering the people who are doing the contributing to knowing: teachers and students. Exceptions to such a view of schools and knowledge can be found in Sizer's work (*Horace's Compromise* and *Horace's School*) as well as in Jane Roland Martin's (*The Schoolhome*) and Nel Noddings's (*The Challenge to Care in Schools*). These studies focus on the relationships that need to be fostered in schools. Given our argument for the interrelationship between people and knowledge, any recommendations we make must also have that focus. We must first be concerned with the conditions that make it possible for students to know before we can critique the results of knowledge students construct for such qualities as accuracy, clarity, usefulness, and beauty.

We begin by looking at teachers because we believe teachers have a tremendous opportunity to help their students develop skills so that they are able to contribute to the constructing of knowledge. Teachers, because they have survived and grown to the point that they are able to walk into a classroom and presume to teach others, must have already developed a sense of self. They must have already experienced caring relationships, at least to some degree, and they must have already had the opportunity to be knowers. We must ask, though, because we clearly are all affected by the context into which we are born and grow up, how aware is the teacher of her or his context? How much opportunity has the teacher had to become reflective and critical of this situatedness? These skills of self-awareness, self-reflection, and self-critique are ones that help contributors to knowledge become more able to perceive their limitations and mistakes and make it possible for them to grow and develop, as they learn how to construct knowledge and then deconstruct and reconstruct it.

Teachers learn the skills needed to be knowers just as students do, by interacting with others and practicing these skills. Therefore, the more likely teachers are provided teacher education programs that encourage the development and practice of such skills as communication, relational, and critical thinking skills, the more likely they will be aware of their own perspectives and the possible limits to these. Teachers and future teachers need the opportunity to interact with others different from themselves and to be supported and encouraged in their efforts, as they continue to learn and develop self-awareness. As discussed in this chapter, the way to learn about others' perspectives and experiences is to have the others inform us. We cannot presume to speak for others. Teachers need the opportunity to develop and enhance relationships with their professors, colleagues, administrators, students, students' families, and other potential teachers, so that they will have the greatest opportunity to gain perspectives on their contributions to knowing.

If these recommendations are followed, we can assume we will have teachers who have the opportunity to enhance the necessary skills to be knowers. These teachers will in turn be in a much better position to help their students develop and practice these necessary skills. Given that a relational epistemological theory focuses on people (educators and their students), viewing knowing as an activity with others means educators need to focus on the people in their classrooms as well as continue to reflect on themselves. In this focus, they need to continue to be aware and to help others become aware of the context all people bring to learning situations. Teachers and students cannot presume to speak for others. They need those others to speak for themselves, so teachers and students can learn about others' perspectives and experiences. This means a common language, with some shared meanings, needs to be established in the democratic classroom that we are proposing. With a common language available, people will have both the potential to speak and the potential to listen and learn. (We will discuss this further in Chapter 5.)

Having a common language is a necessary but not sufficient requirement for knowing to take place in a democratic classroom. A relational epistemological theory reminds us that the kinds of relationships students and teachers develop are also important. Teachers need to be aware of the reality that students will arrive in their classrooms having experienced different levels of caring relationships from their main caregivers (as have teachers). Also, students and teachers will walk in the door having grown up in different cultural settings. They will speak different languages and approach the activity of knowing in different ways. Most important, they will have different perceptions of what they have to offer, how they can contribute to knowing, or even whether they will be able to do so.

Democratic classrooms need to be supportive environments where students feel it is safe to risk speaking, so that they may have the opportunity to develop their own voices. Creating safe, friendly environments is something over which teachers and school administrators have direct control. Just as caring is vital to the development of voice in the home setting, so it is vital in any educational setting. In a classroom, people show they care by making an effort to understand each other's contexts. When people in the classroom communicate, through a shared language, they need to do so in a welcoming way. They need to show they are willing to attend to what others have to say, be receptive listeners, and practice generous thinking. People need to become aware of how each other's context will affect what goes on in their shared space. The possibility of knowing must be an activity available to all. Communication that generates the feeling all voices are welcome will help nurture a sense of community in the classroom, which will then enhance understanding and underscore the message that everyone needs the chance to learn and contribute to the constructing of knowledge. School personnel, administrators, and teachers have a unique opportunity to help students develop the necessary skills for knowing, as well as help students feel valued and appreciated. They need to do whatever they can to help make it possible for potential knowers, including themselves, to be successful contributors.

Much more can be said, and we hope to open up this topic for further discussion. Through dialogue with others we all learn. We have argued that the relational epistemological theory described here is a more encompassing description of knowing because it includes vital aspects of knowing that other theories tend to overlook or exclude. We have placed attention and value on such qualities as relationality and caring in an intersubjective world and argued that doing so makes this description of knowing more inclusive and less open to ideological abuse. Our hope is that people from different ethnic backgrounds and ways of life, women and men, should find this theory applies to them. We also hope that a relational epistemology opens possibilities for valuing contributions from all people. We need each other to further the nurturing of knowledge and help make it sound, comprehensive, coherent, cohesive, as well as beneficial and beautiful. Whether this theory meets these criteria or not (or other criteria deemed valuable and important) must be tested by all of us as contributing knowers.

Conclusion

We began this chapter by highlighting key classical epistemological theories that have been developed over time, using the metaphor of blind men trying to know an elephant to help us. We then compared the classical philosophical perspectives with current ones to examine how epistemology has been defined and various categories and distinctions used to separate epistemology from other fields within philosophy, such as ethics, and other subject areas, such as psychology and sociology.

We then began to redescribe epistemology from a more transactive perspective, by offering a relational epistemological theory. **A relational epistemology views knowledge as something that is socially constructed by embedded, embodied people who are in relation with each other**.

Because we are social beings in caring relations with each other, we develop a sense of self, our own voice; we learn our language and culture from each other, which then affects our thoughts/ideas. Knowledge is not created in isolation, and all of the theories that people develop will come into contact with these same social influences (culture, including language, gender, etc.). The self, once having developed its own perspective within its cultural group, learns to understand the contextuality of its own cultural group. This brought us to a discussion of feminist standpoint epistemology and the notion of enlarged thinking.

The relational epistemology presented here depends on an educated, equally respected, interactive community of thinkers/feelers actively participating and contributing to knowing. These people need to be caring and nurturing of others so they can benefit from those others' contributions to the discussions. They need to be able to hear ideas and try them on, making sure they understand them by trying to believe them before they dismiss them.

In the Classroom

Activity 1

This exercise is intended to help students project how the epistemological theories described in this chapter will translate into actual classrooms. Students should discuss in small groups what they think the following classrooms might look like (they may want to try drawing a diagram of the setting):

1. Socrates
2. Aristotle
3. Locke
4. Rousseau
5. a democratic classroom

Now reconvene as a large group and share the ideas discussed by each of the groups. If time is a potential problem, shorten this activity by assigning each small group one of the five philosophical perspectives.

You might want to discuss other perspectives also, such as Kant's, Peirce's, Freire's, or Dewey's. If students have not had the opportunity to read any of the philosophical writings of these famous teachers, you may want to review the descriptions offered in this chapter and Chapter 1 (for Freire and Dewey). Try to elaborate on the roles of teachers and students as well as the kinds of methods and curriculum an educator becomes committed to, if that person is being consistent with his or her epistemological perspective of how people acquire knowledge.

Activity 2

This activity is intended to help you, as a teacher or future teacher, think about what it is that you conceive of as knowledge and how you evaluate potential knowledge. This activity can be conducted with the whole class or in small groups. If small groups are used, each group may want to come up with potential answers for each question before moving on to the next one. Starting with some kind of definition of knowledge, such as a dictionary definition, will help start the discussion. After clarifying the definition of knowledge, consider the following three questions:

1. How do you know what you know? What are your sources of knowledge? From where do you derive the information that you interpret as being knowledge?
2. How do you know the information that you have acquired is knowledge? In other words, what are your criteria for judging and/or evaluating knowledge? How do you know that what you know is "right" or "true"?
3. Can we ever be certain that what we believe we know is in fact knowledge?

Activity 3

This activity will help you consider the ways that knowledge is socially constructed and the powerful forces it has on our lives. Depending on what our society views as valid sources of information, those sources are acknowledged as worthy of consideration. Sources not valued are considered nonsense, evil, or even insane.

1. Think of ways we have judged people of other cultures as being "unknowing" throughout time.
2. Think of ways we currently judge students as being "unknowing" in our classrooms.

Activity 4

This activity is probably best begun (as a homework assignment) by remembering as much as possible about a relationship with a special teacher from the past who was able to make students both willing and able to learn. You may want to list the qualities that defined that person as being a good teacher, then consider these questions:

1. How would you describe your relationship with that teacher?
2. How did you feel about your relationship with that teacher?
3. How did you feel about that teacher?

Now compare what you remember with others in the class. The objective is to get all students to look at the ways that special teachers in their lives have cared for them. Most of you should be able to come up with examples of teachers who were caring, even if you did not necessarily feel that way about the teacher at the time. We hope that this exercise will enable students to see that having teachers who care is something that helps them learn.

Notes

Different threads of thought in this chapter have been published by Thayer-Bacon: "Egocentrism in Critical Thinking Theory" (1991), "Navigating Epistemological Territories" (1996b), "An Examination and Redescription of Epistemology" (1997a), and "The Nurturing of a Relational Epistemology" (1997b).

1. "The Blind Men and the Elephant" is an old tale from India. A children's book version is retold by Lillian Quigley (1959), *The Blind Men and the Elephant* (New York: Scribner's). Reviewers have expressed two caveats about the elephant metaphor: (a) Does not the image of an elephant suggest a fixed world rather than one that is in flux? Our response is it can but it does not have to. Certainly elephants are as porous and changing as people and all living forms in our universe. (b) Does not the blind men "seeing" the elephant differently put a focus on our experiencing different parts of the whole rather than on the possibility that we can each experience the same whole and experience it differently? Again, our response is it can but it does not have to. Yes, the poem focuses on the blind men from Industan experiencing different parts of the elephant, but one can imagine that even if they experienced the whole elephant, they would likely experience the elephant in different ways. We will try to be careful that the elephant poem does not suggest assumptions that are not brought into question, and we urge readers to do the same. Be careful about what *you* read into this metaphor!

2. Thayer-Bacon cannot identify the exact source for this term; it occurred to her as she was reading a long list of feminist writers. But three philosophers who helped her see the need for a relational epistemology were Jean Grimshaw (1986), Nel Noddings (1984), and Sara Ruddick (1989). This relational epistemology could also be labeled a pragmatic social feminist epistemology.

3. Plato, *The Meno,* in Cahn (1970, p. 17), *The Philosophical Foundations of Education.* We will use *PFE* to symbolize this publication.

4. Plato, "The Myth of the Cave" (also known as "The Allegory of the Cave") is in Book VII of *The Republic,* in *PFE,* pp. 83–89.

5. Aristotle, *Nichomachaen Ethics,* in *PFE,* pp. 107–120.

6. All selections cited from Peirce are from this source.

7. Suggestions for Peirce's philosophy of education are from Maccia (1954, pp. 206–212).

8. Berger and Luckmann (1966), *The Social Construction of Reality.* We will use *SCR* to symbolize this publication. Berger and Luckmann begin their treatise by noting they are not claiming to answer the philosophical question "How is one to know?" The sociologist is forced to use quotation marks around "reality" and "knowledge." Sociologists cannot differentiate between valid and invalid assertions about the world, as a philosopher "is driven to decide" (*SCR,* p. 2).

9. The original sources for this idea are Mead (1934) and Dewey (1916/1966).

10. This is Seyla Benhabib's (1992) phrase, used in *Situating the Self: Gender, Community and Postmodernism.*

11. Dewey (1938/1965) discusses his transactive theory as the "principle of interaction" in *Experience and Education.*

12. We are suggesting that other than the typical criteria used by philosophers to justify theories as being based on compelling reasons, criteria such as clarity, coherence, and consistency, other criteria should be considered as well, such as beauty, elegance, harmony, inclusiveness, and beneficiality. We will say more on this in Chapter 4.

13. Harvey Siegel points out that this way of discussing knowledge is found in any introduction to epistemology text. Our source for this description was Hardwig (1991) and Siegel's direct correspondence to Thayer-Bacon. Burbules (1992) labels this description of epistemology "the Enlightenment conception."

14. Siegel (1987), *Relativism Refuted: A Critique of Contemporary Epistemological Relativism* (we will use *RR* to symbolize this publication); and Siegel (1992), "Two Perspectives on Reason as an Educational Aim: The Rationality of Reasonableness" (we will use *PES* to symbolize this publication).

15. Siegel, through personal correspondence, August 1994 and May 2, 1995.

16. Jane Flax discusses the psychological/philosophical distinction in "Political Philosophy and the Patriarchal Unconscious" and *Thinking Fragments.* She cites Hamlyn (1978), *Experience and the Growth of Understanding,* as a favorable source of the distinctions between the two fields. Flax offers Kant as an example in her footnote 8 in "Political Philosophy and the Patriarchal Unconscious."

17. See a related quote by Jaggar (1992) in "Love and Knowledge: Emotion in Feminist Epistemology," pp. 155–156.

18. Thayer-Bacon's sources for this social perspective have come from Berger and Luckmann (1966), Dewey (1916/1966), Mead (1934), and Peirce (1958).

19. In the following discussion concerning pragmatism and feminism, Thayer-Bacon wishes to point to three key articles that helped her in her understanding: Heldke (1987), Kaufman-Osborn (1993), and Haddock Seigfried (1991).

20. This quote came to our attention through Kaufman-Osborn (1993), "Teasing Feminist Sense from Experience," p. 132.

21. For examples of postmodern positions, see Derrida (1978), Foucault (1980), Lyotard (1984), and Rorty (1989).

22. Thayer-Bacon is not alone in drawing attention to the infant in discussions on epistemology. See Seyla Benhabib, Jane Flax, Nel Noddings, and Sara Ruddick. We will highlight some of their major contributions to her thoughts.

23. A recent citation/discussion of Victor can be found in Martin (1992).

24. Other sources on caring are Benhabib (1992), Flanagan and Jackson (1987), Gilligan (1982), Keller (1986), Offen (1988), and Ruddick (1989).

25. The source within this quote is Noddings (1984).

26. Flax (1983) points out that one of the basic tenets of objects relations theory is that in the first 3 years of life, the most important task we have is to establish a close relationship with our caregiver(s), so that we can establish a "core identity" (p. 251).

27. We use Harding to represent this perspective, but there are others, such as Nancy Harstock (1983).

28. Two that have helped Thayer-Bacon understand this point are Bat-Ami Bar On (1993), "Marginality and Epistemic Privilege," pp. 83-100; and Uma Narayan (1989), "The Project of Feminist Epistemology: Perspectives from a Nonwestern Feminist," pp. 256–269. See also work by Iris M. Young, Judith Butler, Anna Yeatman, Christine Di Stefano, and Lynn H. Nelson for discussions on difference and epistemological communities.

29. Thayer-Bacon believes Benhabib's enlarged thinking is very similar to Lorraine Code's notion of responsibility, in *Epistemic Responsibility*. Benhabib sites Hannah Arendt's "representative thinking" and traces that back to Kant's conception of reflective judgment. Peter Elbow (1986) has written about this idea in terms of "the believing game."

Justice and Care

Ethics in Education

In Chapter 1, we looked at social/political views of individuals in relation to others and presented the value of a redescribed democratic community perspective. In Chapter 2, we examined key epistemological theories of what counts as knowledge, arguing for the value of a relational perspective on knowing. Both of these chapters represent major fields of study in philosophy (social/political and epistemological). We now turn in Chapter 3 to another major field of philosophy, ethics, and examine it in relation to education.

What is ethics, and what does it have to do with teaching? Most, if not *all*, would-be teachers worry about ethical concerns before they even begin teaching. They do so in the form of *classroom management*. We hear their concerns in their questions: What will I do with a student who refuses to do the homework I assign or who regularly misses my class? How will I handle students who argue and fight with each other or are disrespectful to me? What is the right course of action to take if I catch a student cheating on a test? Ethics is a field of study that focuses on human behavior and tries to answer such questions as: What is right (good) behavior? What is a virtuous person? What is justice? Can virtue be taught to others? If so, how? If not, how does a person become virtuous?

Teachers spend much of their day dealing with human behavior, and many beginning teachers leave teaching in frustration because they have not learned how to manage their classrooms successfully in terms of behavior so that they can get on with the task of teaching students new information and skills (more than 50% of teachers leave teaching within 5 years; Goodlad, 1991). Such teachers say things like "I never had the opportunity to experience the intrinsic rewards of teaching, because I was so busy just trying to stay afloat and not drown. I seldom felt like I had reached a student or made a difference in someone's life. Instead, I faced students who didn't want to be in my classroom and were determined to spend their time diverting us from learning and sabotaging my efforts to teach them anything" (see Goodlad, 1984, for examples of what teachers say about teaching).

Successful teachers are aware that ethical concerns *must* be addressed for any teaching to take place. They develop an ethical philosophy and reflect on how to apply their ethical perspective to their own classroom situations. They may not be aware they have developed an ethical perspective, but if you ask them why they do such-and-such in their classrooms, they are able to tell you why. Having an ethical perspective means being able to give reasons for one's actions and show how those reasons relate to one's beliefs.

We have chosen a few case examples of the kinds of ethical situations teachers face in their classrooms that apply across ages, subject areas, and cultural/gender groups. We will refer to them throughout this chapter to help make the ethical theories we present more concrete and easier to understand. Then we will show how some key classic ethical perspectives relate to the case examples given here. Consider the following scenarios:

Situation 1: Assessment

All teachers face issues concerning assessment. Teachers have to find ways to determine what their students already know and what they need to be taught. Teachers need to know whether what they teach is being learned. Assessment can be accomplished in many different ways, and how teachers assess their students brings up ethical questions. Does a form of testing favor certain styles of learning over others? Is testing culturally or gender biased? What is being done with the information gained on students' skills? Are teachers using this information to track students and change their views of them as learners, including their expectations of what they can accomplish? Overall, the question is, How can assessment be fair?

Situation 2: Dishonesty

Most teachers face issues concerning setting rules for their classrooms and students breaking those rules. For example, students may not attend classes when attendance is required for a fair grade. Excused absence notes may be forged. Teachers assign homework that students may not turn in, or students may copy someone else's homework instead of doing their own. Students use cheat sheets to help them on exams or copy off each other's tests. Situations that involve lying and cheating are all forms of dishonesty and address ethical concerns. What is right behavior? How is a teacher to judge right behavior? What standards and criteria are the best ones to use? Are there general rules that apply to everyone, or should a teacher consider each situation on a case-by-case basis?

Situation 3: Exclusion

Most teachers face situations in which they witness their students being mean and treating each other disrespectfully. Many teachers experience unkind treatment toward themselves by their students, students' parents, or colleagues. Young children in kindergarten will exclude some children from their games, because they do not like them for whatever reason. Older children will bully children they dislike, physically pushing them around and intimidating them, or laughing at them and playing jokes on them. Lunchrooms are routinely places where some children eat by themselves because they are new to the school or do not have friends who want to eat with them. In classrooms, teachers will have students who interrupt others when they try to speak or laugh at each other. Some students exclude themselves from participation and remain silent, refusing to contribute to classroom activities. What should a teacher do in these kinds of situations? Is it right to step in and make rules like "You can't say you can't play" (Paley, 1992) and insist that everyone be included? How does a teacher teach children to be kind to each other? Can virtue be taught, or are some people naturally good whereas others are naturally evil?

Situation 4: Censorship

Teachers must decide what to leave in and what to leave out of their curriculum. All teachers, no matter what subject or age they teach, have only so much time to teach their students and only so much expertise themselves on the subjects they are teaching. The limits of time, number of students, background information, and so forth, force teachers to decide what they will teach and what they will not or cannot. These kinds of questions involve the issue of censorship. Countries, states, communities, and parents all develop rules concerning what information should be passed on to their future citizens, their children. How do teachers address concerns of indoctrination? How do they ensure that alternative views are included and ideas are represented fairly? How do teachers encourage students to think for themselves and critique even the lessons? Or what do teachers do if working in a setting where people want only certain ideas taught in certain ways and do not want students exposed to ideas that have been judged to be dangerous or harmful, for example?

Philosophers have been addressing these kinds of concerns for as long as we have records of their work. Now we turn to some of these people and see what they have had to say about ethical dilemmas that teachers face.

Principles and Rules

Plato (427–347 B.C.)

We begin with one of the most significant philosophers in the Western world, Plato. He is also our first systematic philosopher and the first to establish a university in the Western world. Plato's philosophy of education has had a significant impact in American education as he served as a model for one of our founding father's, Thomas Jefferson's, recommendations concerning education. Jefferson was actively involved in trying to establish an educational system in the

United States, as governor of Virginia, during his two terms as president of the United States, and as founder of the University of Virginia.

Plato wrote dialogues for the common citizens of Greece, with a focus on moral issues and Socrates, the Greek philosopher and Plato's teacher, served as the main discussant. Plato came from a wealthy, powerful, and well-respected family, and his older brothers and uncles were friends of Socrates. These family members are often other characters in Plato's dialogues. In these dialogues, Plato uses a dialectic method of questions and answers, and the other characters are the respondents to Socrates. In the *Meno* and *Protagoras* dialogues, Plato tackles these questions: What is virtue, and can it be taught to others? The order of dates when the dialogues were written is uncertain, but the *Protagoras* is classified as one of Plato's early dialogues and the *Meno* as one of his middle ones.

In Plato's *Protagoras* (Plato, cited in Cahn, 1970) the question "Can virtue be taught?" is addressed. Here Socrates seems to equate virtue with being a good citizen. The dialogue begins with Protagoras claiming that he is a teacher who teaches people to be virtuous ("You promise to make men good citizens"; p. 37). Socrates informs Protagoras that he used to think that virtue is not something that can be taught, but he does not know how to disclaim Protagoras's assertion that teaching virtue is his profession. Socrates asks Protagoras two questions as a way of trying to disclaim his ability to teach virtue: First, how is it we are all only knowledgeable of certain skills, yet we all claim to know what is good? Anyone can claim knowledge of the good; therefore, it cannot be taught. Second, why can we cite many examples of "persons who were good themselves, and never yet made any one else good, whether friend or stranger"? Why can we find many examples of good parents who have children who grow up to be bad? If virtue can be taught, why is it good parents cannot teach their children to be good?

In response to the first question, Protagoras offers a myth, which explains that while the gods gave people different gifts and talents, Zeus distributed a share of "justice and reverence among [people]" to all people, "for cities [countries] cannot exist if only a few share in the virtues" (p. 39). This is why we ask specific people who are talented in art or music, for example, for advice on those matters, but we ask any person for their advice on virtues. We think "that every [person] ought to share in this sort of virtue" (p. 39). According to Protagoras, we are all born with the capacity to be virtuous because it is a gift from Zeus.

A second proof offered by Protagoras is our belief that all people ought to profess honesty. We do not chastise people who are ugly or feeble, because these are works of nature, attributes with which people are born. However, we do chastise and punish people for committing a wrong because we think that by studying and learning virtue may be acquired. This further shows that we do believe everyone is capable of being virtuous, unless they are determined to be incapable of understanding right from wrong (p. 40).

What does Protagoras say in response to the second question suggesting virtue cannot be taught? Protagoras points out that we punish people for lying, stealing, and so forth, not because the evildoer has done wrong but because we hope the evildoer can be deterred from doing wrong again. We do not punish people for their past, so much as for the future, because we believe we can teach people how to live a good life. We believe people learn from their mistakes and punishment will deter future evils. People believe virtue can be taught.

So, how can adults be virtuous and their children grow up to be unvirtuous? Why do people behave wrongly? Because "they have no knowledge of virtue or encouragement toward it" (p. 41). Children who grow up to be unvirtuous do so because they have not been taught virtue. "Education and admonition commence in the first years of childhood, and last to the very end of life" (p. 41). Plato makes a strong case for the value of early childhood education as well as lifelong learning, as virtue is something we can begin to teach very young children and we continue to learn about our entire lives. Plato compares virtue to musical ability. Just because a parent is a good flute player does not mean that that parent's child will grow up to be a good flute player, for children grow up to be good flute players only if they have natural capacities as flute players. "[B]ut, at least they would all play the flute reasonably well in comparison of those who were ignorant and unacquainted with the art of flute-playing" (p. 42). It is the same for children growing up to be as good as their parents. Children grow up to be virtuous and good, or evil, not because their parents and other teachers do not try to teach them good but because of their own natural capacities. They will grow up to be at least somewhat good, because of their education, and will be better than people not educated at all (pp. 42–43). Who can teach children to be virtuous? "[A]ll [people] are teachers of virtue, each one according to his own ability" (p. 43). A good parent may not do a good job of teaching virtue to his or her child, which is why a good parent can have a child who is not as virtuous as the parent is. Plato's conclusion is that human care can make people good.

Please note that Plato suggests in the *Protagoras* that all of us have the capacity to be virtuous but apparently to different levels and degrees. Education is important for all of us to learn how to be virtuous, but even if we have the best teachers of good behavior, we may not necessarily grow up to be exceptionally good. Plato only suggests that with good teachers we will grow up to be "at least somewhat good." Some of what determines how good we become is based on our own "natural capacities."

"Situation 3: Exclusion" describes teachers struggling with what to do with students who are not being very virtuous. Plato suggests that children begin to be taught how to be virtuous at a very young age and that it is important that parents pay attention to their young child's education. Parents, as well as child care providers and teachers in schools, should be teaching children to be virtuous. All of us can teach children this, according to Plato; some of us are just better teachers of virtue than others. Is it right to make rules (e.g., "No hitting allowed") and punish children if they do not follow the rules? Yes, for it is through punishment that we hope to teach children how to behave better next time. But let us look further at Plato's idea that although all of us have the capacity to be good, some of us will be better behaved than others, not because of our education but because of our own "natural capacities."

In the *Meno* (Plato, in Cahn, 1970), Plato again struggles with questions concerning virtue and expands more on "natural capacities." The dialogue begins with Meno asking, Do we acquire virtue from teaching or by practice, or does it come by nature? Socrates believes no one knows what virtue is, including himself. The two proceed to try to define what virtue is, but for each definition Meno offers, Socrates shows problems with it, until Meno finally throws up his arms in exasperation and states he thought he knew what virtue was but now it appears he does not after all! He can cite examples of virtue such as just governing, courage, temperance, and wisdom, but he cannot find what is common to all of those different examples. Socrates seeks a universal definition, the essence of virtue that makes it possible to recognize virtue in any particular virtuous act.

When Meno and Socrates cannot universally define virtue, they decide to look at virtue from the angle of teaching, hoping to learn in the process what virtue is. If virtue is something we learn, through knowledge, then virtue can be taught. But, just as in the *Protagoras* dialogue, Socrates is not convinced there are any teachers of virtue. Again he says he has taken great pains to find them and has never succeeded. He doubts further that virtue can be taught because of many examples of good people who are not able to teach their children to be good. Socrates repeats the same challenge he asked Protagoras: If someone could teach virtue to others, then why is it we see virtuous parents who have children lacking in virtues? Would not parents teach their children to be virtuous if it were teachable? In this dialogue Socrates concludes that virtue cannot be taught, and if there are no teachers of virtue, then there are no students of virtue. He does not doubt that there are good people, though, so how do they become good? Virtue must be "right opinion" (p. 34), and by right opinion Socrates means "an instinct given by God to those to whom it is given" (p. 35).

Again, Plato suggests we are born with the capacity to be good, and some of us are born with more of this capacity or instinct than others. Plato does not believe only certain people desire good; he believes we all desire it. If any of us were to desire evil, then we would be desiring something that will harm us and make us miserable. Plato suggests that people mistakenly desire some things that are evil, because they think the evil is good (pp. 13–14). From the *Meno*, Plato seems to be telling teachers that they can help students understand the difference between evil and good and that their actions may seem to cause an immediate good but, from a larger perspective, will cause them harm. So, for example, if a child hits another child to get a toy, the child who hits may think that hitting is not evil—it brings the pleasure of getting to do what was desired: playing with the toy. The teacher's role is to help the child who hits understand that hitting is harmful because it hurts others, and if it is OK for one child to hit another, what would keep some other child from hitting that first child, too, and causing pain? For Plato, teachers must understand that children who hit are not bad people; they are just people who do not understand the fuller consequences of their actions, and they need help to see the harm in what they do. Perhaps they are people who have not been treated virtuously themselves.

Plato is also telling teachers that although they can help their students understand the consequences of their behavior, they cannot teach their students to be virtuous. Being a good person, having "right opinion," is a gift bestowed at birth, and some of us receive this instinct at greater levels than others. Some of us are destined to be good people no matter who our teachers are, apparently.

How do we find our most virtuous citizens, and how do we encourage all of our citizens to become as virtuous as they can? These are two of the questions Plato attempts to answer in his most famous work, the *Republic* (Plato, in Larson, 1979),[1] which is also written in dialogical style, applying the dialectical method. Plato continues to discuss ethical ideas in the *Republic*. Rather than trying to define *virtue* and determine whether it can be taught, Plato focuses on **justice**. We find out in Book 2 of the *Republic* that **justice is a type of good that is cherished for itself as well as for its consequences**. A problem for Plato, though, is how do we persuade people from an early age to value striving to be just (366c)? For it seems that an unjust person enjoys a better life than a just person (362d). Being a just person is no easy task!

In the *Republic,* Socrates and other participants try to define a just person but have trouble forming a definition. They adopt a plan to help them understand what justice is by trying to examine justice in a larger form than an individual person. They decide to examine justice in the larger form of "the just state" (which in modern days would be a "just country") (369). Such a move is similar to teachers deciding not to try determining what is good behavior for any individual child attending school, because that varies so much. Instead, they decide to look at what is a good school. If we can understand the qualities that make up a good school, then perhaps we will be able to apply those same qualities at the smaller level of individual students.

We find in the *Republic* that a country's educational system is very important for a just country. The educational system is what helps teach the future citizens of the country how to be virtuous citizens. The education system also has the role of encouraging young people to strive to be just. In Plato's ideal state, the most just people are the ones who will be the rulers and guide the country. The most just people are to be found, taught, and encouraged through the education system to become the guardians.[2] This educational system, which is to be free and available to all, is where students (future citizens) have the opportunity to discover that at which they are naturally good. In a just country with a national, public education system, all citizens find and develop their own natural talents and gifts, and then contribute those natural talents to their country. Thus, each of us is to do what we are best suited at doing, and what we each have to offer is equally valued by our country.

Being a guardian does not give a person higher status or greater wealth. Plato worries a great deal about the two corruptors, greed and excess, throughout the *Republic* and suggests that the guardians should have no private property beyond the bare necessities. The guardians' duty is to be responsible for the country's welfare, and the other citizens' duty is to supply the basic human needs for the guardians, such as food, clothing, and shelter. This way, the guardians will be able to avoid the temptations of greed, dishonesty, and so forth, and keep their minds on their important task of guiding the country (416d).

The problem of how to encourage students to strive to be just, when immediate goods are more appealing to them, is like our "Situation 2: Dishonesty." In this situation, teachers are concerned about how to get their students to come to class regularly, for example. They hope that students will understand and value the long-range reward of attaining an education. Appreciating the value or need of school education is especially a problem for poorer students, many of whom do not see a school education supplying their other family members with better jobs, for example. These students do not see others like themselves necessarily living a better life as a result of getting an education. What many poorer students learn is that the United States is not a just country, people do not all get a fair chance to contribute their talents, and their talents are not equally valued. Examples of the kinds of students who struggle to come to school can be found in Jonathan Kozol's (1991) *Savage Inequalities* and Samuel Freedman's (1990) *Small Victories*.

What would Plato suggest for students who are not interested in staying in school and learning? Likely he would suggest they have found out that studying is not their greatest gift, and they should find a job at which they are good, as a worker or craftsperson (Plato classified workers and craftspeople as bronze people in his "Metal Myth," in Larson, 1979, p. 415d). What would Plato suggest for students who want to stay in school but cannot because of more pressing needs, such as working and helping take care of their families? He would say the state has an obligation to help these students find ways to stay in school. These students who have the abilities and desire to learn are valuable national treasures in Plato's *Republic*, as they are the country's future leaders. For Plato it does not matter what one's parents do. All children must be judged fairly on their own and be given the chance to develop their own natural talents. All children have valuable contributions to make, and any child is a potential future leader. **In an ideal just state, individuals are valued for what they have to offer, and all citizens have the same fair opportunity to contribute their valued talents**.

Even for students who do attend school regularly, what motivates them to study and learn when doing so is hard work? In the United States grades are used to help motivate students to do their homework and study for tests. We give students who do well on tests A's and students who fail F's. We tend to reward students who do their own work and punish those who work with and help others. We call helping others "cheating." Yet, if we examine young children as learners, we find they are not motivated by grades. Grades are silly to preschoolers and even early elementary age children. Grades do not mean a lot to children with special needs, either. Through observation we learn that what matters to these children is the thrill of learning something and being able to accomplish a task successfully. The learning itself motivates students. Helping others learn, so they can experience the excitement that usually comes with learning, is also rewarding for these students. Plato suggests we use our schools to help find students who love to learn and are good at learning, offering them as much education as we can.

Could it be possible we have created situations in our schools where there is more good in cheating and lying than there is in actually learning? If so, we are not teaching children the value of striving to be good. Could it be possible we have created schools where we actually punish children for being virtuous, if we punish them for trying to help others? According to Plato, teachers need to be sure they are encouraging right behavior and helping students understand the value in being a moral person. Schools need to be structured so they encourage the right behavior that teachers should be teaching their students.

Plato's plan in the *Republic* to sift and sort citizens through use of the country's education system points out questions that were suggested in "Situation 1: Assessment." Remember, this situation asks how teachers are going to determine what their students know and what they need to be taught. No matter what form of assessment teachers use, a margin of error always exists. Certain forms of tests, for example, favor certain styles of learners. What are teachers and schools going to do with the information they gain on students, through whatever form of assessment they choose? Although it sounds very fair to develop an educational system that will help students find out what they are best suited to do, and then help students further develop their natural talents, we become pretty suspicious about how this will be enacted. How will we guarantee that the system for identifying students' talents is just?

Plato's plan, which at first glance supports ideas such as equality (women and men are both eligible to become guardians) and fairness (any child is considered a potential guardian, and all talents and gifts are to be valued by the country), in actuality this plan is not consistent with his expressed goals. Although he says the system is open and just, he explores the notion of mating festivals and a lottery system for procreation in which "commoners" are not allowed to procreate to ensure that "superior stock" (a "pure" gene pool) is used primarily for future citizens (457c–461e). Although the commoners will think the lottery system is fair, in actuality the lottery is "rigged," "so our worthless fellow will blame his luck and not the rulers every time he misses out on a get-together" (460). Plato even goes so far as to suggest that children born from the guardians will be raised in nurseries by child care providers, but inferior children born of any guardians, or from guardians mating with nonguardians, will be given to someone in the lower ranks of the community to raise. Defective children, children conceived outside the mating festivals, and children of any man or woman outside the breeding age will be left on the hillside to die (infanticide). Based on the criteria Plato plans to use for the selection of birthing of future citizens, this is certainly *not* an open, fair, just system. In fact, it sounds very similar to Hitler's plan in Germany in the 1930s.

In American schools, we begin testing students on their knowledge and talents at a very early age. Parents who suspect their children may be developmentally delayed are encouraged to bring their children in for testing as preschoolers. Our thinking is that the sooner we can start teaching our "slow" children, the more likely they will be able to progress. Most communities have children come in for testing before admission into kindergarten classrooms to determine their "readiness" for kindergarten. Kindergartners assessed as not being ready for first grade are often placed in "transition" classes or "reading readiness" classes. We begin to sift and sort children as soon as they come in contact with schools, a process usually called "tracking."

The problems with tracking and magnet schools/choice schools are many. The overall biggest concern most people have is, How do we make sure the assessing we are doing is fair? The move to have magnet elementary schools, where students have the opportunity to work more extensively with computers, in fine arts, or in drama and performance areas, is another example of a current adaption of Plato's idea to help students find what they very capable of doing and encourage those talents. Having magnet schools causes school districts to face moral issues concerning fairness as well. How do we make sure the choices we offer students are real and available to everyone? Is it possible for 6-year-olds to decide what kind of school they want to attend? The adults in children's lives are more likely to make that decision. What probably happens is that parents enroll their child in an elementary school that emphasizes music, because that is what they want to emphasize in their child's education. The parents are probably musicians—or wish they were. What else often happens in America's magnet school systems is that parents who have more awareness and knowledge of what is available for their children and what their rights are as parents have a better chance of getting their children placed in the "best" magnet programs. Also, parents who have political influence and use their political clout often have greater success getting their children enrolled in the most popular schools of choice. Although it appears that any child enrolled in a school district has an equal chance to go to the best magnet schools, the reality is that some children have better chances, because their parents know how to get them into their choice programs.

Plato does not suggest there should be different schools that offer different curricula; he suggests all students should be enrolled in public, state-run schools that offer the same broad, general liberal arts curriculum. (Plato and Aristotle, Plato's student, are responsible for suggesting the liberal arts curriculum after which most American schools are modeled. We will discuss moral issues concerning a liberal arts curriculum further through Aristotle's ideas.) As the children get older and their talents and interests become known, the curriculum begins to vary: some branch off into trades; others continue with an academic curriculum of science, math, and philosophy. However, for all children, Plato suggests that the country is responsible for ensuring their children are only exposed to "the good" within the subjects they are taught. Plato is a strong advocate of censorship.

Plato suggests in the *Republic* that education forms a child's character and mind and teachers need to make sure children are exposed "to the opinions we think they should have when they grow up" (377b). The impressions children receive when they are young "shape their souls" (377c). Also, what we expose children to when they are young becomes the criteria they use to judge what is moral and aesthetic, so we need to expose them to the best, so they will be able to judge what is good and beautiful when they are later exposed to crude lies and seemly, poor-quality works. "A child can't distinguish allegory from fact, and early impressions are hard to wash out. For this reason, perhaps, we must make sure that the first stories he hears are well composed for the purpose of teaching excellence" (378e).

Plato suggests that if we expose children only to what is beautiful, we will teach children to love grace and beauty. Children will be able to recognize and value good and beautiful things because they have a lasting and good effect on character. If we expose children to only excellence while they are young, we will allow them the opportunity to establish good character before being exposed to evil. The evil will then have less effect on children, if they are exposed to it later, because good character has been established.

Certainly most parents do not want their children exposed to evil. They do not want their children to witness murder, rape, or brutal beatings, for example. They rightly fear that such exposure will harm their children, scarring their psyche for potentially a lifetime. Most of us are in favor of some form of censorship in a young child's education. Yet, Plato's recommendations force us to face serious ethical questions, if we take his suggestions to heart. These are the kinds of questions suggested in "Situation 4: Censorship." Many of us disagree on what should be included and what should be excluded from a student's education.

For some of us, we differ on what age is appropriate to teach students a topic. For example, many believe schools should teach students about sexual activity and procreation before the age students might be sexually active and risking disease or pregnancy. Others think the topic of sex education is appropriate when students are more mature and better able to use the information. Others feel the public schools have no business teaching sex education at all; that responsibility belongs with parents and churches. Another example: Socrates believed students should be taught and encouraged to use critical thinking skills. He encouraged youths to question and critique beliefs. Many today agree with him. The sooner students learn critical thinking skills, and the more opportunities they have to practice them, the more likely they will use them in their own lives and become better thinkers. Plato believed students should *not* be taught critical thinking skills until they were 30 (e.g., as graduate students), at an age where students are more mature and better able to judge when and how to use their critical thinking skills. Plato's view was affected by watching his beloved teacher, Socrates, placed on trial for inciting the youth of Athens, found guilty, and sentenced to die. Socrates' students used their critical thinking skills to question everything, including society's norms, and were viewed as rebellious and dangerous to Greek society.

People disagree not only on age appropriateness for curriculum but also on perspectives that should be taught. Plato did not believe the Greek gods should be portrayed as quarreling or plotting against each other (378c) or responsible for any evil, rather only responsible for good (379c). The gods should remain simple and always in their own form (not changing shapes or represented as sorcerers or liars) (381d, 382e). Children should be told stories that lessen their fear of death (386b), and the characters in the stories should be temperate models, not people who laugh or carry on too much (388d). Consequently, Plato recommended Homer's writing should be censored, which many people today consider classic and very beautiful.

The standards of what is considered good behavior and what is considered beautiful vary. These qualities are not universal, as Plato assumes. People from different worldviews (which includes their religious beliefs, family, community, and cultural beliefs, all part of the context that affects who they are) vary on what they believe their children should be taught. What one family would want its children exposed to, another wants censored. We see these issues debated today in terms of multicultural curriculum (what ethnic groups should be included, and who decides how they should be represented?) and religious curriculum (is it possible to separate church from state, and do we teach certain values in our public schools that others oppose for religious reasons?). In the United States, many have solved these concerns by forming their own private schools where they can have more direct control over the curriculum taught to their children, and others have opted to home-school their children.

No matter what subject a teacher teaches, what age students, supporting what institutional belief systems (church, family, or government, e.g.), ethical issues come up concerning what to leave in and what to leave out of the curriculum. As we pointed out in situation 4, all teachers have only so much time to teach their students and only so much expertise themselves on their subjects. The limits of time, number of students, background information, and so forth, force teachers to decide what they will teach and what they will not or cannot. These kinds of questions involve issues of censorship.

Plato answered questions described in our four situations by focusing on principles and rules for the ideal country and ideal citizens. His aim for education was to teach people to be good citizens, which we find is the same as being virtuous people in his *Republic*. Others argue for the value of unique individuals over an ideal state or that individuals and states be considered on equal par, viewing Plato's proposals as potentially elitist and unjust.[3]

We will continue to discuss a principled approach to ethics, finding advantages and disadvantages with it. At this point, we hope it is becoming clear why teachers and would-be teachers need to be aware of the decisions they make, either directly on their own or by supporting decisions others have made for them about what they will teach. Without that awareness, teachers are in danger of indoctrinating students to embrace certain beliefs on faith. Fairness and justice are certainly issues of concern here.

Aristotle (384–322 B.C.)

If Plato is considered the Western world's first systematic philosopher, Aristotle, Plato's student, is considered the second. Aristotle is often called the "father of science" because he developed a system of logic and worked to classify the world around him. He attended Plato's university and then branched off from Plato to form his own university. He apparently wrote dialogues, as Plato did, but these have all been lost. Much of what we know about Aristotle's ideas comes from notes his students took of his university lectures. Although Aristotle did go off in his own direction, he still shares much in common with Plato. For example, Aristotle was the teacher of Alexander the Great, following Plato's idea of trying to teach a leader of a country to be a guardian. Aristotle's ideal-state proposals in *The Politics* are very similar to Plato's theory in the *Republic*.

Two works by Aristotle that directly address the kind of ethical questions raised in this chapter are the *Nichomachean Ethics* and *The Politics* (Aristotle, in

Cahn, 1970). Let us begin with a discussion of the *Nichomachean Ethics*. Aristotle's discussion of ethics seems to begin from a different angle than Plato's, yet it is similar in that he looks for what is the Supreme Good in a universal sense, just as Plato did.[4] Plato looked for the Supreme Good through his discussions concerning what is the essence of virtue and justice; Aristotle looks for the Supreme Good through his discussions of virtue and happiness. Both assume there is a common Good to which all people ascribe. This universality is built right into their methods of argumentation, for we saw Plato, through Socrates, searching for not specific examples of virtue but what is common to all examples of virtue. Aristotle does the same thing by searching for "that at which all things aim." He reasons that "a thing pursued as an end in itself is more final than one pursued as a means to something else" (p. 107). What is the Supreme Good that is final and self-sufficient, the End at which all actions aim? The answer for Aristotle is **Happiness**. "Happiness, therefore, being found to be something final and self-sufficient, is the End at which all actions aim" (p. 108).

What does Aristotle mean by Happiness? He begins to define Happiness by ascertaining what an individual's function is, for "the good of man resides in the function of man" (p. 108).[5] What is it that makes people unique from other beings, what is it we do that other life forms do not? Aristotle argues that what is unique to human beings is our ability to reason, "the exercise of the soul's faculties and activities in association with rational principle" (p. 109). After declaring that what humans do best is reason, Aristotle steps back and defines Happiness as "an activity of the soul in conformity with perfect virtue" (p. 109) to reargue the case that Happiness is "perfect virtue." In the end of the *Nichomachean Ethics,* he comes back to reason, and we find that if Happiness consists in activity in accordance with virtue, then Happiness is activity with the highest virtue, which is intellectual virtue. However, first Aristotle leads us through a discussion of "perfect virtue."

Aristotle's answer to Plato's questions "What is virtue?" and "Can virtue be taught?" is to describe virtue as being of two different kinds. First, Aristotle separates the soul from the body. Then he describes the soul as consisting of two parts, one rational and one irrational, to support his argument that there are two kinds of virtue, one intellectual and the other moral. "Wisdom, Understanding, and Prudence are intellectual [virtues], Liberality and Temperance are moral virtues" (p. 110).

Can virtue be taught? For Aristotle the answer is yes, but not taught in the same way. He has distinguished two kinds of virtues, which leads to two different methods of instruction. Moral virtues are virtues of character. Theses virtues are of the nonrational part of the psyche, such as courage, temperance, generosity, and so forth. We acquire none of the moral virtues by nature, but nature gives us the capacity to receive them (p. 111). So none of us are born courageous, but we are all born with the capacity to be brave. We learn how to be brave (and the other moral virtues) by practicing being brave. The more we practice and act as a courageous person would act, the more we have a chance to establish the habit of being courageous. According to Aristotle, "[W]e become just by doing just acts, temperate by doing temperate acts, brave by doing brave acts. . . . In a word, our moral dispositions are formed as a result of the corresponding activities" (p. 111).

Let us turn to one of our situations to help us understand Aristotle's position and advice to teachers. "Situation 3: Exclusion" describes students who are making fun of each other and excluding some of their classmates from group activities—for example, 7-year-olds at recess who are playing a ball game and will not let other 7-year-olds play, or college students who laugh at a question a student asks, so that the student feels uncomfortable asking other questions. Aristotle's advice is to have teachers teach students manners of politeness, by modeling it and correcting the students, and getting them to practice their skills until the skills become automatic. Seven-year-olds should practice social skills such as how to ask whether they can join games and how to contribute to the games so that others will want them to play. Students need to also be taught the value of inclusion and not hurting others' feelings. Teachers need to help students develop their abilities to communicate with each other and practice their social grace skills. Teachers can even help all the 7-year-olds practice their ball-playing skills so they will be able to contribute to the games. In the college seminar setting, teachers need to set the ground rules for conversation in the classroom and then be sure to follow through on these rules consistently, so the students will practice discussion skills. If a student is being excluded from the discussion, the teacher could call on students or go around the room and make sure each person talks as a way of getting everyone in the habit of contributing to the discussion. If students were being rude and laughing at others' questions, perhaps the teacher would need to admonish them to help break them of their impolite habits.

Aristotle claims that it is very important that we develop good habits, beginning in early childhood. Like Plato, Aristotle makes the case that early childhood education is very important, because this is when each of us begins to establish our habits of behavior. Aristotle suggests that if we examine moral virtues carefully, we discover they are usually a mean between defects and excesses. In learning moral virtues, the goal is to find the middle ground between two extreme vices. Take courage as an example again. People with no courage will hide and avoid engaging in potentially dangerous experiences, therefore removing themselves from living an active life. People with too much courage will seek dangerous situations and embrace experiences that can end their lives. Neither of these extremes is good. Moral virtue is a mean, which is "why it is a hard task to be good, for it is hard to find the middle point in anything" (p. 114).

Are all moral virtues means? No. Aristotle gives some examples of actions or feelings that denote evil by their very names: malice, shamelessness, envy, adultery, theft, and murder. "All these and similar actions and feelings are blamed as being bad in themselves; it is not the excess or deficiency of them that we blame . . . the mere commission of any of them is wrong" (p. 114). So, a little murder is not good, a little robbery is not the mean we should be aiming for, any murder or robbery is evil, and none should be committed. Still, *most* moral virtues can be found by finding the mean between two extremes.

Aristotle also explains that all moral virtues must be acts done by a person who is of a certain state of mind. The person being brave, for example, "must act with knowledge" (it does not count if a person is brave by accident, without awareness of what she or he was doing and the dangers involved); the person "must deliberately choose the act, and choose it for its own sake" (it does not count if a person does a brave act to gain fame and fortune or because someone else forced that person to be brave); and "the act must spring from a fixed and permanent disposition of character" (until a person does brave acts again and again, we cannot be sure he or she is brave, because the person could have just been brave by accident). "**[V]irtue results from the repeated performance of just and temperate actions**" (p. 113, our emphasis).

In the *Nichomachean Ethics,* Aristotle gives suggestions for how to establish the mean in moral virtues. First, "avoid that extreme which is the more opposed to the mean" (p. 114). So, if a person is trying to establish the temperate habit of getting enough exercise, one extreme is to get too much exercise, and the other extreme is to get none. We imagine the extreme more opposed to the mean would be getting no exercise, so that is the one to avoid. Second, "notice what are the errors to which we are most prone . . . then we must drag ourselves away in the opposite direction, for by steering wide of our besetting error we shall make a middle course" (p. 115). If we know we are most prone to try to do too much exercise and thus become sore or injure ourselves, then we should begin by doing a little exercise rather than too much. Third, "we must in everything be most of all on our guard against what is pleasant and against pleasure; for when pleasure is on her trial we are not impartial judges" (p. 115). If we have set up a routine to walk to and from school as a way of getting exercise, and then wake up to find it is raining or cold outside, we still must not ride in a car because to do so will be more pleasurable. We must stick to our original plan. If we choose to do the more pleasurable activity, before we know it we will not be walking to school and not getting exercise.

How do these rules help teachers in their moral dilemmas? Let us look at "Situation 2: Dishonesty." Here we have a teacher who has a student, say, Daraka, in the habit of not turning in homework assignments on time and making up excuses for why things are late or not turned in. The homework assignments do not come in, in spite of Daraka's ability and opportunity to complete these assignments. He could be involved in many activities and too overstretched to complete what he begins, because of lack of time. Or, maybe Daraka is a procrastinator and lazy, having established the habit of avoiding what he perceives to be the boring, mundane practice of skills. He only likes the challenge of new activities and does not see the value in doing homework. No matter what the reason is for Daraka not turning in homework assignments, the teacher is faced with holding him to the same standards all other students are held to, to remain consistent and fair in grading.

Teachers can encourage students to use Aristotle's rules to help them break their bad habits so they can meet the course requirements. If the student is doing too much, rule 1 is to avoid the extreme that is more opposed to the mean, so the student should begin doing fewer activities. According to rule 2, the student should notice when she or he has a tendency to get overcommitted and avoid those situations. For college students, perhaps they become overcommitted at the beginning of the semester, when their work load is lightest in classes, and then become overwhelmed when the work load increases. They should be especially leery of their start-of-semester commitments. For high school students, maybe the extra hours at their after-school job brings them immediate monetary rewards that are hard to resist, so they overcommit to working after school but do not have time to finish their homework. Aristotle's advice to these high school students would be that they should decide how many hours they can reasonably work after school, before they start working and receiving wages. Rule 3 says to be on guard against what is pleasurable about our bad habits, for we are not good judges in the moment of pleasure. Maybe the overcommitted college students receive pleasure from their social interaction. Helping and being with other people are fun. Aristotle would advise these students to avoid getting into pleasurable situations where it is easy to lose track of time and once again not get their homework done. According to Aristotle, if we follow his advice, we will learn to break our bad habits and help us establish good ones, so that we will develop good moral virtues as character traits, which will become fixed and permanent dispositions. By practicing being organized and making reasonable time commitments, students will be able to finish their tasks on time and turn in their homework assignments when they are due, completed to the best of their abilities.

Does Aristotle's advice pose any problems? Imagine our fictional student Daraka, who seems to be lazy and a procrastinator. He may not turn in homework assignments for many reasons. Maybe he is bored with the assignments because he already understands the concepts and does not need further practice. However, Daraka must take the class because of state requirements for attendance or graduation or certification requirements. What if Daraka really is incapable of doing the homework assignment on his own but cannot articulate what the confusion is? Or maybe he faces other issues at home that make it impossible to concentrate and complete the assignments. In the 1988 movie *Stand and Deliver,* one of Jaime Escalantes's students has to fix dinner for her father, baby-sit her siblings until her mother comes home, and then when her mother comes home the mother is exhausted and wants the student to turn out the light so the mother can sleep. Another student works after school in her father's restaurant to help the family business. A third is in a gang and cannot be seen with a book for fear of rejection and repudiation. All of these students are capable of doing the work and have the interest in the subject area they want to learn. However, other social issues affect their ability to get their homework done. Do they have bad habits and basic moral character flaws, or are their problems more complex? Although Aristotle's principled ethics is helpful in broad general terms, in unique, specific situations it may not always be so helpful.

Now that we have examined moral virtues, what about intellectual virtues? How are these taught? Whereas moral virtues must be practiced and established as habits, intellectual virtues are not practical reasons that can be treated through action (they are not means-ends relations). Nor are intellectual virtues theoretical reasons that can be treated as Universals (what Plato called The Forms). Intellectual virtues are "for the most part both produced and increased by instruction, and therefore require experience and time" (pp. 110–111). Wisdom, understanding, and prudence are all intellectual virtues that can be taught, and we can gain understanding of them through our experiences, over time.

Aristotle offers no more advice on how these intellectual virtues are to be taught in the *Nichomachean Ethics*. He does, however, go on to support his claim that the intellectual virtues are higher than the moral virtues, based on what he assumes is unique to human beings. Remember, what is unique to human beings and what we do best is reason, according to Aristotle. As reason is what we do best, the function of humans is to reason. Because reasoning or contemplation is the highest form of activity human beings can do, and intellectual virtues all involve contemplation, it therefore follows that intellectual virtues are the highest form of activity for human beings.

Aristotle further explains why the intellectual virtues are the highest:

> [T]he intellect is the highest thing in us, and the objects with which the intellect deals are the highest things that can be known; and also it is the most continuous. . . . [A]ctivity in accordance with wisdom is admittedly the most pleasant of the activities in accordance with virtue, . . . and it is reasonable to suppose that the enjoyment of knowledge is a still pleasanter occupation than the pursuit of it. (p. 119)

The activity of contemplation is self-sufficient, needing others less than other virtues such as justice and bravery. "Also the activity of contemplation may be held to be the only activity that is loved for its own sake: it produces no result beyond the actual act of contemplation" (p. 119). The activity of the intellect is also leisurely and offers "such freedom from fatigue as is possible for man. . . . [I]t follows that it is the activity of the intellect that constitutes complete happiness—provided it be granted a complete span of life, for nothing that belongs to happiness can be incomplete" (p. 120).

Happiness is therefore the activity of contemplation, or one could say Happiness means living a contemplative life, developing one's reason to its fullest extent, which takes a lifetime to achieve.

In the United States, we can see that Aristotle's value on reason and contemplation has been translated into a value on receiving an education, in general, and especially an academic college education. Students are encouraged to develop their intellect, and high school students have a higher status in our country if they take college preparatory classes. Honors high school students are encouraged to take 4 years of math, science, and English; at least 3 years of history/government; and usually at least 2 years of a foreign language. Students who are talented in academic subjects are praised and rewarded for their intelligence. We do not tend to view students who are gifted in music, the arts, or sports as the most intelligent. Students who opt for vocational education programs also are usually viewed as less intelligent. If money is tight in our public school system, the programs that are always threatened with cutbacks and possible extinction are art, music, and foreign language programs, thus continually giving students and parents the message that these programs are not as valuable and important as math, science, English, and history programs, which are very seldom cut.

Valuing academic subjects such as math and science over art and music can be said to be based on a value of intellect over emotional feelings, the mind over the body, and a view of reason as the highest faculty of human beings, separate from and more valued than emotions, intuition and imagination, for example. Many philosophers have criticized the Greek distinction between mind and body, calling it false and dangerous. They argue it is false because we cannot separate the mind from the body[6] and dangerous because to view the world so that we see our selves separate from our bodies and the world around us objectifies and distances us from each other and our world.[7] In Chapter 4, we will look at emotions, intuition, and imagination as possible tools to help us be good thinkers and improve our reasoning skills. For now, the point is that Aristotle's philosophy of education assumes a valuing of reason and the mind, and that valuing has affected how many people in the United States regard intelligence. The view of intelligence as contemplation (which is the road to happiness) potentially places many students at a disadvantage.

In "Situation 1: Assessment," one of the ethical dilemmas teachers face is how to assess students' abilities fairly. Much research concerning testing and how classes are taught has shown that our schools favor a certain style of learning, a certain gender, and a certain cultural background.[8] It should not be surprising to find the research suggests that males from a European cultural background who have a decontextualized, field-independent style of learning have historically and consistently scored better on the multiple-choice, true/false tests and continue to do so, despite an awareness of test biases and efforts to change these trends. White, European-American males, who can trace their roots of knowledge and what counts as intelligence back to the ancient Greek philosophers, are generally assessed as being the most intelligent people in the country.

Nel Noddings (1992, pp. 44–62)) has taken up this topic in her book *The Challenge to Care in Schools*. She presents the case for a need for greater respect for a large range of human capabilities, using Howard Gardner's (1983) work on multiple intelligences to support her case. Gardner has made the case that there are at least seven different intelligences: logical-mathematical, linguistic, musical, spatial, bodily-kinesthetic, interpersonal, and intrapersonal. Others are currently discussing the idea of "emotional intelligence" (e.g., Goleman, 1995). We do not wish to make a case for how many intelligences there are; we only want to suggest that there is more than intellectual intelligence and that whether reason is the highest form of intelligence is debatable. Noddings hopes that if we learn to respect multiple forms of intelligence, all of our children will feel welcomed and valued in our schools for their contributions. She develops the metaphor of a large heterogeneous family to help us see how we need to change our schools so they meet all children's needs. These changes hinge on us, as a society, valuing more than reason as a form of intelligence. We will look further at these issues from a multicultural perspective in Chapter 5.

Many scholars have questioned Aristotle's assumption that what is unique to human beings is our ability to reason. Scientists have demonstrated that other animals are able to reason. Margaret Mead (1970) presents the case in *Culture and Commitment* that what is unique about human beings is our ability to educate our young and pass on our culture to the next generation:

> Today, as we are coming to understand better the circular processes through which culture is developed and transmitted, we recognize that man's most human characteristic is not his ability to learn, which he shares with many other species, but his ability to teach and store what others have developed and taught him. (p. 72)

Noddings (1984) argues that it is not our ability to reason that makes human beings unique but our ability to sustain caring relationships over long periods of time. Both authors point out that even though we human beings are able to educate our young and able to maintain long-term caring relationships with others, we are not consistently good at these abilities.

In *The Politics,* Aristotle defends the value of a liberal arts education. His recommendations for education have served as the model for Western civilization, and so it is important that we understand clearly what he suggests before we look at how his recommendations have been translated into our current schools and consider ethical issues concerning curriculum ("Situation 4: Censorship") that his model creates.

Aristotle divides the soul into two parts, rational and irrational. Then he divides reason into two parts, practical and speculative reason. The whole of life is also divided into two parts, business and leisure. He recommends that all should be educated as to which of these are better: "For men must engage in business and go to war, but leisure and peace are better; they must do what is necessary and useful, but what is honourable is better" (p. 124).

Like Plato, Aristotle recommends young children should be raised by caregivers who help them establish good habits, through amusements and play, and expose them to nature's harshness, gradually, so they can learn to endure. Censorship should be employed so that young children are only exposed to what is decent and good, "kept strangers to all that is bad" (p. 125). The state should control the education of the youth, so as to mold citizens for the state's needs. For citizens do not belong to themselves; they all belong to the state. Because the state "has one end, it is manifest that education should be one and the same for all, and that it should be public, and not private" (p. 126). Embedded in Aristotle's recommendations are issues on censorship that we have already explored through our discussion of Plato's philosophy of education.

What is it that all citizens should be taught in these state-run, public schools? According to Aristotle:

> There can be no doubt that children should be taught those useful things which are really necessary, but not all things; for occupations are divided into liberal and illiberal; and to young children should be imparted only such kinds of knowledge as will be useful to them without vulgarizing them. (p. 126)

How does he define vulgarizing occupations? "[A]ny occupation, art, or science, which makes the body or soul or mind of the freeman less fit for the practice or exercise of virtue" (p. 126). Liberal is defined as "free," illiberal as "menial and servile" (p. 126). A liberal education is a balanced education, one that is harmonious and enhances mental, physical, and spiritual aspects of people. In a liberal education, the focus is on the blending together of all of these needs and the education of whole people. A liberal education helps people nurture and enhance all aspects of human potential and therefore increases the chance for people to reach their full potential and find happiness. The curriculum includes

- reading and writing (which he viewed as "useful for the purposes of life in a variety of ways"),
- gymnastic exercises (which are also useful in developing the body, giving health and strength, and infusing courage),
- drawing, and
- music (the latter two being "useful for a more correct judgment of the work of artists" and for attaining "true pleasure") (pp. 127–129).

Aristotle defends his choice of music as having a power of forming the character, being what citizens need for relaxation, and providing intellectual enjoyment in leisure.

Now that we understand what Aristotle means by a liberal education, let us look at some of the ethical issues that have developed owing to this notion of liberal education. They can be easily seen in American schools. First, and probably most important, is the fact that a liberal education is one Aristotle recommended for "freemen." Only the future citizens of the state receive this balanced, harmonious education. Whereas they are free to study and develop their full potential, others (women and slaves, who were *not* citizens of the state) are not to receive a liberal education at all. Aristotle's curriculum recommendations count on a racist, sexist, class system in which others are illiberal, performing menial tasks, so that freemen are able to concentrate on how to spend their leisure. The women and slaves of Greece did not have any leisure time, so they had no need to worry about what to do with it!

We can see how this view of liberal education was translated, in that in colonial America the people who received an education were "freemen." Girls and slaves were not educated.[9] In the 1700s, academies were established that were more secular and practical, and they were open to girls as well (not slaves). Our early education system began with elementary schools, to teach reading and writing, and even after those elementary schools were open to girls, only boys of European decent went on to Latin grammar schools, which were the schools that prepared students for colleges.

As girls and other minorities have been allowed to attend schools, they have not been offered access to the same curriculum that Euro-Western boys have received. Girls were taught graces and homemaking skills (even in the 1960s and 1970s, these were the focus at many single-sex women's colleges). The aim was to help girls be good wives and marry to the highest social class level they could obtain. Minorities were funneled into vocational education classes and trained for manual labor and factory jobs. Many argue this is still what we do with poor minorities in the United States. We do not expect or encourage them to receive a liberal education. Poor students are not viewed as having the leisure to enhance themselves, as Aristotle described. They must work and take care of their basic needs.

Mortimer Adler (1982), in *The Paideia Proposal,* has argued that the United States needs to guarantee all of its students an equal education to ensure that it is a democracy. He says the only way we can make sure all students receive the same quality education is to have a one-track school system in which every child is educated to her or his full capacity, through the same objectives for all. He wants schools to be general and liberal, nonspecialized and nonvocational, for he describes our current multitracked system as not guaranteeing all students the same quality of education. Even offering electives opens the possibility of students poorly selecting what courses they take and therefore not graduating with the same level of education and the same chances of competing in the job markets. Adler makes the case that a liberal education is good because it is a general education focusing on general skills that can be applied everywhere and anywhere. These skills are ones such as reading, writing, understanding of mathematical concepts, knowing the historical background of this culture and others, understanding the basic needs of people, how to think critically, and how to use leisure time. The knowledge of these basic skills allows people the opportunity to be self-reliant, adaptive to changes in society, and therefore able to be autonomous. Autonomy is a necessary requirement for achieving happiness.

Adler makes the case for everyone taking the same courses and being exposed to the same curriculum, much as Aristotle did, only Adler includes women and minorities in his recommendations and argues that the same curriculum will ensure equality. Taking the same curriculum means we will all receive the same, equal education. Of course, this argument assumes that all students attend schools of equal quality, with the same quality of supplies and teachers, for example. A quick glance through Jonathan Kozol's (1991) *Savage Inequalities* will convince even the most skeptical reader that American children do *not* attend schools of the same quality. Many children in urban (and rural) schools cannot even count on whether a teacher will be assigned to their room for the day. Several children find that they have no desk or chair, let alone books and supplies such as lab equipment or computers.

Noddings (1992) considers the topic of liberal education in Chapter 3 of her book *The Challenge to Care in Schools*. She agrees with Adler's description of American schools—power structures and forms of discrimination do exist. She then suggests that insisting that everyone take the same courses will not rid us of the inequality. Noddings predicts that Adler's attempt to remove privilege from the curriculum by insisting all students take the same courses will probably not work because we will just change the forms of privilege. (One can see this in private schools where students all wear the same uniform to remove signs of privilege, and then re-create signs of privilege through their accessories, shoes, etc.)

Noddings (1992) does not question the value of a liberal education but suggests it "is a false ideal for universal education" (p. 28). We have learned, though, that Aristotle did not propose a liberal education as an ideal for universal education; he only proposed it for the privileged citizens class of Greece. Only in the 20th century has a liberal education been proposed as an ideal for all people. Adler suggested all should receive a liberal education to make the U.S. educational system more democratic, equal, and available to all students.

What about the value of a liberal education? We learned that Aristotle's liberal education proposal included music, art, and physical activity, which is more well rounded than the current model of liberal education in high schools and colleges. Using Howard Gardner's list of seven intelligences, described earlier, we can see that Aristotle's liberal education allows for the opportunity of many different intelligences to develop, even though we learned that his philosophy of education favors intellectual intelligence. His program includes art and music, allowing for musical and spatial forms of intelligence. Because his model includes reading and writing and what has become science/math, his model allows for logical-mathematical and linguistic forms of intelligence, too. With gymnastics in his liberal education model, room exists for people to develop their bodily-kinesthetic intelligences. We do not see him emphasizing interpersonal and intrapersonal intelligences.

What about American schools today? Our schools currently insist that students take many more academic classes, math and science, for example, than arts. Most high school students take 4 years of English and 3 years each of history, math, and science and are required to take only 1 year of the arts (and within that 1-year requirement, one might take art or music, so that one becomes somewhat proficient in one area and not proficient at all in the other). Remember, Aristotle recommended that students take enough art *and* music that they would be able to appreciate good forms of these and adequately critique performances. Students should be exposed to enough art and music that the arts help shape their character. And students should be able to practice the arts well enough to enjoy them in their leisure time. What about physical education? Many schools require only one or two semesters of physical education. This is certainly *not* enough to ensure students have a sound body, as Aristotle recommended. Our schools seem to focus on the logical-mathematical and linguistic intelligences, and they are actually less well rounded than Aristotle proposed.

Noddings (1992) criticizes liberal education because, first, "it draws on only a narrow set of human capacities"; second, current proposals such as Adler's are misguided in that "in any case, educational programs need *educational* rationales as well as political ones"; third, not all children need the content of a liberal education curriculum (p. 28). We discussed Noddings's criticism concerning a narrow set of human capacities in our discussion of Aristotle's valuing of reason and the intellect over emotions, intuition, and imagination, for example. However, Noddings does not distinguish what Aristotle proposed from what currently exists in our schools. Aristotle's proposal does allow for a greater range of human capacity, though certainly not a complete range.

Noddings's second criticism, that Adler argues for a general liberal education for political reasons (equality and fair access to all) but does not support the value of a liberal education on educational grounds, is false. Adler does offer educational reasons for a liberal education. He says a liberal education gives people a general education with general skills that can be applied for any job and adapted as society changes. A liberal education helps people develop their abilities to reason well, communicate to others through writing and speaking skills, and understand general calculation knowledge. He suggests a liberal education is what allows people to be autonomous and free.

Let us look at Noddings's (1992) third criticism of a liberal education: not all children need the content of a liberal education curriculum. Noddings points out that we all agree with Adler that "true democracy demands equal education for all children" and that all children should have access to whatever forms of education are available (p. 29). But why should all students be made to take the same courses? Should not the school curriculum be tailored to students' needs and interests? The liberal education curriculum, according to Noddings, is geared toward certain styles of learning, highlighting certain talents and devaluing others. "Forcing all students through a curriculum designed for the capacities of a few cannot be done in the service of equality" (p. 31). The liberal education today favors "those whose talents are primarily linguistic and/or mathematical" (p. 31). Noddings worries, When do students who are not good at linguistic and/or mathematical forms of knowledge "have opportunities to develop and demonstrate their own strengths and, thereby, to choose a suitable occupation"? (p. 33). Success comes in many forms and depends on many different capacities. Noddings suggests society needs to change its values and value all human capabilities. Adler seems to say, because we as a society value a liberal education over other forms of education, we should make sure all students receive an education that is valued. He does not question the valuing of only a liberal education, but Noddings does.

Aside from the issues of liberal education being available to all students (which it still is not) and whether it is balanced or favors certain forms of knowledge over others (apparently it is less balanced with our modern version of a liberal education than with what Aristotle recommended), other important questions need to be addressed concerning the idea of a liberal education being a well-rounded education. Taking a few classes in many subject areas does not necessarily make people well rounded. Most college students take foreign language courses in high school so they can be admitted to college. After completing their foreign language requirements, many students promptly forget what they learned. Unless they have an interest in their courses and a need to use the skills they are taught, those skills are quickly lost. How many remember their French, Spanish, or German? How many remember what they learned in geometry or calculus? If we do not remember what we learned in our liberal arts curriculum because we had no interest or need to learn the subject or did not understand how this knowledge related to our lives, how well rounded are we, really?

Insisting that all students take the same courses seems to be based on a lack of trust that students will choose wisely. In fact, students who are given the opportunity to choose what they will study and when, as we can see with Summerhill and Montessori schools, usually end up with a well-rounded, balanced education. They may start out only interested in geography, but through that interest they will learn more than just the names of all the countries on all the continents and the capitals of all those countries. Likely they will go on to learn about what types of animals and plants live on different continents (biology), what kinds of climates exist and how weather affects people's clothing and homes (social needs), how to calculate the distance from one city to another (math), and further their basic reading, writing, and reasoning skills.

Most of us, if given the opportunity, do not study just one field of knowledge. Rather than treating subjects as isolated and separate from each other, through our own interests we discover that following one interest leads us on to other interests: drama leads to reading plays, which leads to reading short stories, which leads to reading novels. Learning that is based on interest and need is the type of learning we remember. When we move to Europe and live in Germany, we learn how to speak German and remember it. When we start dating someone who speaks Spanish, we are motivated to learn Spanish, too. When we find out we have to teach U.S. history to students, we finally learn it ourselves. Although a liberal education may be designed to be comprehensive and connected, as Adler argues, if it is not relevant to students and does not relate to their backgrounds and experiences, it will not be meaningful. It may be learned to pass a test, but it will be promptly forgotten. Many current philosophers of education and school reformers believe schools need a curriculum that is more relevant to students' lives.

Does a liberal education curriculum leave out anything important? As Aristotle described his model, women and minorities were not to be offered a liberal education, so it is safe to assume that skills and knowledge forms often attributed to them were left out or devalued. We saw, using Howard Gardner's list of intelligences, that Aristotle did not include interpersonal and intrapersonal forms of intelligence, which have been traditionally associated with women. Emotional intelligence and spiritual intelligence are often associated with women and Indigenous people living off the land.

Jane Roland Martin (1984, 1985, 1992) suggests that the ideal of a liberal education must be revised to include what has been not worthy of consideration. These include a valuing of relational skills such as care, concern, and connection. Martin discusses these "three C's" in her book *The Schoolhome*, and we find in her Chapter 2, "Culture and Curriculum," a discussion of problems with a liberal education curriculum in terms of what is left out. The familiar liberal education curriculum does not reflect or include Asian, Latino, African, and Indigenous peoples' cultures so much as it includes European male cultures. When students do not find themselves reflected in the curriculum, they feel alienated and denigrated. What we choose to teach, what we call "education," is given our seal of approval. Whatever a culture chooses to pass on to its children is considered important and worthwhile (Martin, 1992, p. 80). What we leave out has great significance for the students we diminish.

Martin (1992) points out that "children do not have to learn the same things at the same time in order to feel connected to one another." They also do not have to learn by the same methods. "People process what they are taught in different ways" (p. 81). We all bring our own unique contexts to our learning situations, as discussed in our Chapter 2. Dewey (1938/1965) reminded us long ago, through his principles of interaction and connection, that we build our current learning on our past experiences, and it is only by connecting with our past experiences that we can make any sense of what we are currently experiencing. We each contribute our own personal perspectives to what we are exposed to, curriculum-wise.

Martin (1992) concludes, "If there is no guarantee that mandating the same knowledge for all of us will give us identical repertoires, if in fact the likelihood of this happening in a society as diverse and individualistic as ours is slight, then the argument that a unified people must study an identical curriculum collapses" (p. 82). Rather than attempting to teach "bits or bodies of knowledge," Martin recommends that a common core curriculum be "composed mainly of attitudes, skills, and values" (p. 84). These attitudes, skills, and values should be ones that help us feel at home and encourage us in our efforts to get along with each other and live together in peace and harmony.

We wish to encourage all teachers and would-be teachers to consider carefully what they assume should be the mandatory curriculum. Choices concerning curriculum place teachers in moral dilemmas concerning what to leave in and leave out, what to consider valuable and important and what to treat as expendable. All of us must face these choices, but we wonder how many of us do so without considering the consequences of our decisions. The consequences are great.

Kant (1724–1804)

We present Immanuel Kant as our final example of a moral philosopher who approached morality in a principled way, based on rules, or what Kant called "maxims." Kant said that he was woken from his dogmatic slumber by another philosopher, the British empiricist David Hume. At age 57, Kant published his first famous critique, *Critique of Pure Reason*. From 1781 until he died, he went on to have a very productive philosophical career (1781/1966, 1783/1950, 1785/1949, 1788/1956, 1790/1951).

Kant represents for the Euro-Western world our last systematic philosopher, as most since him have not attempted to write a complete systematic philosophy, assuming such a task is impossible. Kant tried to account for the necessary and universal knowledge of science and mathematics by arguing that because the structure of human sensibility and understanding is constant, objects will always appear to us in certain ways—as subject to certain *a priori* conditions. (Postmodern philosophers have raised serious questions concerning the certainty of *a priori* conditions for science.) Kant also asked, What can we know apart from experience, and answered that the mind can determine only objects given in experience, and that is all we can know. (Postmodernists have brought into serious question that we can "know" what we experience.) Kant argued that metaphysical knowledge of concepts such as God, freedom, and immortality can only proceed from the categorical imperative.

What is the categorical imperative? It is the principle of morality, or the law that proceeds from reason. Ethical knowledge is possible, according to Kant, because there are *a priori* principles of morality and thus ethical objectivity. (Postmodernists have raised serious questions concerning the whole concept of "objectivity," given that we are all contextual, fallible human beings.) This categorical imperative is what Kant is probably most famous for, and it is what has survived and become his greatest contribution to moral philosophy, despite others' criticisms. Kant's categorical imperative provides a moral basis for a democratic society based on reason. One could say the categorical imperative is a philosophical attempt to replace the Bible and other religious sources of laws for good, moral behavior. Religious beliefs have supplied people with moral codes of ethical behavior throughout time. The categorical imperative can be stated as the principle of universality:

> Act only on the maxim whereby thou canst at the same time will that it should become a universal law;

the principle of humanity:

> So act as to treat humanity, whether in thine own person or in that of any other in every case as an end withal never as a means only;

or the principle of autonomy:

> [So] act that the will could at the same time regard itself as giving in its maxims universal laws.

These general rules command people to act a certain way, regardless of any desired ends, including happiness. People are morally bound to follow these rules, according to Kant, because it is the most reasonable thing to do, whether they want to or not and without regard to whether what they do fulfills their own self-interests. Kant's maxims are not based on what result the immediate action(s) might bring about. They are based on the overall results, at a universal level.

For example, the principle of universality says that people should not choose in terms of what benefits themselves but rather in terms of what is reasonable for normal people to do. Take "Situation 2: Dishonesty." Kant's maxim suggests that students should not lie to their teachers because they would not want their teachers to lie to them. What would the world be like if it were OK for people to lie to each other? No one would know when someone was telling the truth or not, so people would have to assume that probably whatever someone tells them is a lie, and nothing could be believed. When a person finds out a friend has lied, he or she begins to doubt everything the other person says and whether the so-called friend can be trusted.

According to Kant, it is reasonable to tell the truth to teachers, even if it means students may be punished for not completing an assignment on time. This is because in the larger picture, if students can turn in their assignments late by lying about their tardiness, then everyone can do that, and having a deadline for an assignment no longer has any meaning. If students can lie about late assignments and get away with it, it becomes unreasonable for students to turn things in on time. They might as well take as much time as they can get away with, to do their best effort on the assignment. According to Kant, it is reasonable for students not to cheat on their exams, even if doing so helps them get a better grade. This is because saying it is OK to cheat opens the door for everyone to cheat, and therefore students' grades would no longer have any meaning. Tests, which were designed to measure how much knowledge the students have achieved, would no longer serve that function. Instead, the tests would show who are the most resourceful students or the best at cheating.

Kant's universal rule expresses a core rule found in all of our great religions, the golden rule: Do unto others as you would have them do unto you. What about his principle of autonomy? This principle makes clear, again, Kant's belief that reason should rule our decisions, not what we desire. We can examine this principle more clearly through the example of "Situation 1: Assessment." In assessment decisions, teachers must find ways to determine what students know. One of teachers' moral dilemmas is how their means of assessment can actually further support the aims of education toward which they are striving. In other words, teachers may have the goal of trying to teach their students to help and cooperate with each other. Yet, they never grade their students on how well they work together or give their students the opportunity to do group projects for a group grade. In this example, the means of assessment contradicts the actual aim of education that teachers profess to have. When teachers who are trying to teach cooperation punish students for helping each other by accusing them of cheating, the teachers are contradicting their own aim.

Another example is if teachers are trying to teach their students to be critical thinkers but only assess their students' knowledge through multiple-choice and true/false exams. Their means of assessment contradict their professed aim. When teachers hoping to teach critical thinking punish their students for questioning the teachers' ideas, are they not teaching their students not to think critically when it concerns the teachers' ideas? Teachers need to consider whether their forms of assessment support their aims of education.

Kant's (1899/1960) aim of education was to help students form moral characters. We learn in *Education* that a person has good moral character if "[he] keeps steadfast to his purpose" (p. 99) and is "ready to act in accordance with 'maxims'" (p. 84). Kant explains that one of the biggest problems facing his aim is that the methods necessary to teach moral character undermine the qualities needed to be a moral person. Children have to learn how to control their desires through discipline, so that they can become moral agents who transcend discipline. This is what Kant called "the pedagogical antimony." "One of the greatest problems of education is how to unite submission to the necessary *restraint* with the child's capability of exercising his *freewill*—for restraint is necessary" (p. 27).

What Kant acknowledges as a problem is the very issue we can see in situation 1. If we need to use discipline to teach students how to master their "animal nature," how do we get beyond discipline so they can learn how to be moral agents? For Kant, we want children to learn how to be moral agents, make reasonable decisions, and follow the categorical imperative without use of restraint, but we have to use restraint to help them get to the point where they can make moral decisions. "Moral culture must be based upon 'maxims,' not upon discipline; the one prevents evil habits, the other trains the mind to think" (p. 83).

Kant's solution is to place before the child as much as possible examples and rules for living moral lives. Teachers must model moral character themselves and:

> allow the child from his earliest childhood perfect liberty in every respect . . . provided that in acting so he does not interfere with the liberty of others. . . . Secondly, he must be shown that he can only attain his own ends by allowing others to attain theirs. . . . Thirdly, we must prove to him that restraint is only laid upon him that he may learn in time to use his liberty aright, and that his mind is being cultivated so that one day he may be free. (p. 28)

Kant's third maxim, the principle of humanity, is suggested as part of his advice on how to teach moral character. Recall that the principle of humanity reminds us never to treat others as means to an end but only as ends. We must treat others as we would want to be treated, as people who are free and autonomous, able to think and make decisions for ourselves, and deserving to be treated with dignity. When we treat people as means to an end, we treat them as objects, as instruments for our use, as others (they's) rather than as persons (I's, and we's).

Looking at "Situation 3: Exclusion," we find Kant's third maxim is easy to understand. What should teachers do in a situation in which some of their students are being mean to another child? What if Lynn does not really like Sarah but is only nice to her because she wants the teacher to think she is good, so the teacher will reward her by letting her choose the game the class plays today or lead the students out to recess? What if Miguel is friendly to Chris because he wants to meet Chris's sister and ask her out on a date?

Both of these are examples of students using another student as a means to an end, not as ends. Neither Lynn or Miguel are being friendly with Sarah or Chris because they like them and want to be their friends. They are being friendly to achieve some alternative goal, therefore treating them as objects of their desires, not as people worthy of being treated with dignity. Kant's advice to teachers is, Ask students how they would want to be treated. Would you like it if others excluded you and did not allow you to play? Would you like it if someone acted like she or he were your friend but really were not? You should always treat your fellow classmates as you would want them to treat you. Everyone deserves to be treated with dignity, for it is only when we are treated freely with dignity that we can become moral people.

What are some problems with Kant's "maxims" approach to moral education? Kant has been accused of not acknowledging the required historical context for his moral maxims to make sense. Yet, Kant's moral point of view only makes sense in the light of the revolutions of modernity and the establishment of freedom as a principle of the modern world. As Hegel (1802, 1803/1975) describes the problem, Kant presupposed his philosophy to be ahistorical, not dependent on the context of his times and what had preceded him. However, taken out of the context of his times, Kant's maxim "Act only on that maxim through which you can at the same time will that it should become a universal law" is at best inconsistent and at worst empty.

For example, not cheating on tests only makes sense in a world in which grades matter. Young students who have not learned the value or meaning of grades will help each other willingly and not think twice of doing so. Students who come to American schools from other countries where their culture values and encourages students to work together will help each other with assignments, not worried about their grades. Students who do not think they have a chance of getting a good grade and have decided that therefore good grades are meaningless will purposely cheat, possibly out of rebellion, as a means of protestation, or out of sheer frustration as an expression of hopelessness.

Kant has been accused of privileging the institutions and principles of secular, Western democratic societies and representing them as the universally moral point of view. Although many point to the valuable contributions modernity has made for human rights and dignity, modernity certainly has not benefited all people. Modern times are marked as starting in the 16th century. What supposedly distinguishes modernity from premodernity, according to philosophers such as Seyla Benhabib (1992, pp. 23–67), is that modernity marks the beginning of recognition that all beings capable of speech and action make up the moral community. However, never in the history of the human race have all people had equal rights and all people been treated with dignity, even during modern times. Since the 16th century, we have witnessed racism and sexism of many forms and genocide of the Jewish population as well as Native Americans and other Indigenous people. Children are yet to be treated as part of the moral community in many "reasonable" communities.

Kant assumes reason is the highest tool available to help guide us in all of our decisions. Many philosophers, such as Martha Nussbaum, Alison Jaggar, Sara Ruddick, Jane Roland Martin, and Nel Noddings, have pointed to Kant's theory as an example of a narrow view of "rationalism" and as therefore neglecting the affective and emotive bases of ethics. Why are reasonable judgments that remove feelings and desires the best? Is it even possible to do this? Are not ethical judgments based on many qualities, including reason, emotional feelings, and intuitions?

Here is another example to help understand potential problems that Kant's moral philosophy creates. Teachers behave reasonably when they design a course so that it has certain objectives that students must meet to pass the course. And teachers behave reasonably when they require certain assignments and determine certain forms of assessment that will be consistent with the goals and objectives of the course. Following Kant's maxims, teachers must follow the principles and rules they establish consistently for them to be fair for all students participating in the course. But what if students are unable to complete an assignment on time, because they become sick or their parents are in an accident and need them to come home and help out? Or what if some students have a learning disability and cannot complete the assignments in the time allotted but could if given a time extension? Are teachers behaving reasonably when they tell students they should withdraw from the course and retake it when they are able to meet its requirements? Following Kant's advice, a teacher would be unfair in allowing students to get credit for a course if they did not attend every class when others did. Kant would say it is unfair for some students to get extensions on deadlines and not give extensions to everyone. For the sick student or the student who must go home, retaking a class may not be possible. For the students with learning disabilities, they may never be able to meet the requirements of the course.

Kant's universal maxims, though acting as reasonable guides, do not allow for the differences that make up each of our own unique lives. His principles do not allow teachers room to consider the contextuality of individual students' situations and be adaptive and flexible to their students' needs. Basing decisions on what is the most reasonable thing to do, for all of us, washes out all that distinguishes each of us and makes us different. None of us are exactly alike, and how can any one of us feel confident that we can make right decisions for all of us? And how is it we can decide based on reason without taking into consideration, for example, our affective feelings as well as those of our students? If as teachers we decide to make exceptions for students who have family responsibilities that conflict with our classroom objectives, are we being unreasonable, or are we being caring?

In *A Theory of Justice*, John Rawls (1971) tries to answer Kant's critics on the issue of individual needs by adding two maxims to Kant's suggested three.

First Principle

Each person is to have an equal right to the most extensive total system of equal basic liberalities compatible with a similar system of liberty for all.

Second Principle

Social and economic inequalities are to be arranged so that they are both (a) reasonably expected to be to everyone's advantage, and (b) attached to positions and offices open to all.

Second Principle restated as a Principle of Equality of Opportunity

Social and economic inequalities are to be arranged so that they are both (a) to the greatest benefit of the least advantages and (b) attached to offices and positions open to all under conditions of fair equality of opportunity. (p. 302)

Rawls acknowledges that we do not all start out in this world with the same biological assets or social circumstances. Each of us is unique and different, and some of our differences put us at a social advantage (e.g., being born with athletic ability), whereas others put us at a disadvantage (e.g., being born with cerebral palsy). Rawls's principles do not require society to redress an individual and try to compensate for inequalities. The principles require that all moral people should agree to share in the benefits of the natural talents of everyone. Like Noddings, Rawls makes the case that we as a society need to value all people's contributions to society and consider whatever they have to offer as special gifts.

Rawls's advice to teachers who have students in their classes with special needs or circumstances is this: It is essential that we ensure all students who enroll in this class have the same opportunity to complete the course successfully. If a teacher's standards and criteria privilege many students at the expense of a few, then the teacher needs to address the disadvantaged and arrange the course so that the standards are to the greatest benefit of those who would have been disadvantaged. Students with learning disabilities will need the opportunity to show their knowledge gained through alternative methods besides written tests, so all should be offered the opportunity to be assessed with alternative methods such as oral exams or take-home tests. If nontraditional students are disadvantaged in a college setting because classes are offered at times when they cannot attend and still work to support themselves and their families, we need to offer night and weekend classes that they as well as anyone else can attend.

Benhabib (1992) tries to answer Kant's critics through her theory of "communicative ethics" (formulated by Karl-Otto Apel and Jürgen Habermas).

> Instead of asking what I as a single rational moral agent can intend or will to be a universal maxim for all without contradiction, the communicative ethicist asks: what principles of action can we all recognize or agree to as being valid if we engage in practical discourse or a mutual search for justification? (p. 28)

The search is for what would be acceptable for all. Benhabib shifts the focus of ethics from **rational agreement** to the **process** whereby we can sustain practices and relationships in which reasoned agreement can flourish and continue **as a way of life** (p. 38). Others have asked her, Are you not just pushing the problem from Kant's conception of coherence to your definition of the conversation situation? How are you avoiding Hegel's criticism of being inconsistent or trivial?

Benhabib suggests the way out of this dilemma is to understand that communicative agreement counts on strong ethical assumptions. These ethical assumptions commit us to making sure everyone is included in the moral conversation and has the same rights in the moral conversation.

> They require of us: (1) that we recognize the right of all beings capable of speech and action to be participants in the moral conversation—I will call this *the principle of universal moral respect*; (2) these conditions further stipulate that within such conversations each has the same symmetrical rights to various speech acts, to initiate new topics, to ask for reflection about presuppositions of the conversation, etc. Let me call this *the principle of egalitarian reciprocity*. (p. 29)

Do Benhabib's ethical principles avoid the charges of circularity and dogmatism that Kant has faced? She thinks she is able to avoid these by pleading for a "self-consciously historical universalism" (p. 30). Benhabib believes the communicative ethics theory is capable of avoiding these charges because she allows the presuppositions of the moral conversation, her ethical principles of respect and reciprocity, to be continually questioned and critiqued from within the conversation itself. She allows for "comprehensive reflexivity" (p. 42). This is the same position Harvey Siegel takes concerning essentialist epistemology and critical thinking, which we discussed in Chapter 2. "Precisely because such a framework can challenge all its presuppositions, and precisely because it is ready to submit its fundamental principles to debate, it can provide the bases for the public philosophy of a pluralist, tolerant, democratic-liberal polity" (p. 44). However, to question Benhabib's principles from within the conversation, a person must already have accepted them as true.

To truly question the ethical principles Benhabib proposes, a person must step outside the moral conversation as communicative ethics defines it and consider the possibility that these criteria and standards themselves might be wrong. The definition of what is a moral conversation, itself, must be questioned. If one can only do questioning and critiquing from **within** the very framework one is trying to question, the questioning and critiquing are limited. It is like telling students they are welcome to question what you say, as a teacher, but they must do so by being able to submit to your rules for what counts as good reasons. Close examination of Benhabib's argument reveals she is vulnerable to the same criticisms that were used in Chapter 2 against essentialist epistemological theories. Communicative ethics is not philosophically neutral, nor is it morally neutral. Benhabib's communicative ethics only makes sense within the context of modernity and does not appear to have avoided the same charges of circularity and dogmatism that Kant's theory has faced.

All of the principled ethical theories we have described have some weaknesses as well as some strengths. They function as guides to help educators make decisions, but they are also vulnerable to limiting options and possibilities, narrowing what is considered "good" in ways that can be discriminating and dangerous to people. In the name of what is ethical and good, harm to individuals occurs. Let us now look at an ethical theory that takes the opposite approach from principled ethics, considering what is good first from an individual perspective and relying on human affective response to help define ethical behavior. This ethical theory has been labeled **caring**.

Care

Nel Noddings

Nel Noddings is a former math teacher and a parent in a large, heterogenous family, which she uses for her model in *The Challenge to Care in Schools* (see our prior discussion on a liberal arts curriculum). She is known particularly for her contribution to ethics with *Caring* (1984). Noddings suggests that "ethics has been discussed largely in the language of the father: in principles and propositions, in terms such as *justification, fairness, justice*. The mother's voice has been silent" (p. 1). Noddings rejects ethics of principle "as ambiguous and unstable. Whenever there is a principle, there is implied its exception and, too often, principles function to separate us from each other" (p. 5). She also rejects the "notion of universalizability," that what is fair and just for one person is fair for all people and for all times.

Noddings has run into the same problem in ethics that we described in Chapter 2 concerning epistemology.

> Many of those writing and thinking about ethics insist that any ethical judgment—by virtue of its *being* an ethical judgment—must be universalizable; that is, it must be the case that, if under condition X you are required to do A, then under sufficiently similar conditions, I too am required to do A. I shall reject this emphatically. (p. 5)

In rejecting the principled rules of ethics, Noddings does exactly what we suggested a person must do to really bring principled ethics into question. The critique must come from outside the rules of the moral conversation.

How does Benhabib respond to Noddings's challenge of principled ethics? Benhabib (1992, p. 180; p. 199, footnote 8) dismisses Noddings's contribution in a footnote as being too dichotomous and inadequate. She thinks the oppositions "between universalism and historicity, between an ethics of principle and one of contextual judgment . . . are no longer compelling" (p. 26): "[p]recisely because I do not think that a moral theory adequate to the life of complex modern societies can be formulated without some universalist specification of impartiality and the moral point of view" (p. 180). We can see that the criticism concerning the ability to critique principled ethics from within the conversation is accurate, in that it is not possible to do so from within the defined moral conversation without contradicting oneself, and if one moves outside the confines of the moral conversation, one is dismissed as unworthy of debate because one's theory is inadequate. Contrary to Benhabib, we think Noddings's relational ethics is worth serious consideration.

Noddings's attention is to human relations, on "how we meet the other morally . . . , not on judgment and not on the particular acts we perform" (p. 5). Her ethic of caring is founded in *relation*. As she describes this, "I am not naturally alone. . . . My very individuality is defined in a set of relations" (p. 51). Human caring and being cared for forms the foundation of an ethical response, according to Noddings. Because we want to be viewed as one-caring and we need to be cared-for, caring serves as an ethical ideal.

Benhabib's communicative ethics is also founded in relationships, in particular the need to sustain relationships through a process of dialogue, conversation, and mutual understanding. Through relationships Benhabib (1992) focuses on communication and connects this to ethics:

> To know how to sustain an ongoing human relationship means to know what it means to be an "I" and a "me", to know that I am an "other" to you and that, likewise, you are an "I" to yourself but an "other" to me. . . . Communicative actions are actions through which we sustain such human relationships and through which we practice the reversibility of perspectives implicit in adult human relationships. (p. 52)

Whereas Benhabib begins with relationships to argue for an ethic based on communication, Noddings begins with relationships to argue for an ethic of care. For Noddings it is not that we know "I" and "other" to be able to communicate with each other and therefore sustain relationships with each other; it is that we begin our lives in relationships with others, at least one other, and that other is the one who cares for us. Because that other, the one-caring, is willing to care for us, the cared-for, we develop a sense of "I" and "you." Noddings says, "We want to be moral in order to remain in the caring relation and to enhance the ideal of ourselves as one-caring" (p. 5). Her attention is to how we meet the other morally and nurture in ourselves a sense of ourselves as ethical, as one-caring and cared-for. Her concern is with a desire to "preserve the uniqueness of human encounters" (p. 5). Because caring is an ethical ideal, her theory depends on an emphasis on moral education. "The primary aim of all education must be nurturance of the ethical ideal" (p. 6).

Even though Noddings rejects the model of principled ethics and its focus on universal rules for us to live by, she does base her caring ethic on one fundamental universality, "the caring attitude" (p. 5). For Noddings the caring attitude is "that attitude which expresses our earliest memories of being cared for, and our growing store of memories of both caring and being cared for" (p. 5). The caring attitude is universally accessible (much like Plato's view that being virtuous is a capacity with which we are all born). Thus, caring is able to function as a universal ethical ideal in that caring is accessible for all, even though each of us may express caring at a personal level in a variety of ways and to a variety of levels and degrees. Contrary to Benhabib's criticism, Noddings does not make a wholesale rejection of universalism; rather, she places universalism in a much more humble position, within the context of individual people's lives. Her position is a qualified relativist one, similar to what we argued for from an epistemological perspective in Chapter 2.

Let us look for more clarification in terms of how Noddings defines caring. Caring involves a "feeling with" the other, a receptive mode. She does not say caring involves "empathy" if by empathy one means projecting oneself onto the other. "I do not project; I receive the other into myself, and I see and feel with the other" (p. 30). I respond; I communicate with; I work with. "We do not begin by formulating or solving a problem but by sharing a feeling" (p. 31). Contrary to existentialism and its identification of *anguish* as the basic human affect, caring "identifies *joy* as a basic human affect" (p. 6). Existentialism is a philosophy rooted in the individual rather than in relations. "It is the recognition of and longing for relatedness that form the foundation of our ethic, and the joy that accompanies fulfillment of our caring enhances our commitment to the ethical ideal that sustains us as one-caring" (p. 6).

How does caring work as an ethical ideal? Because we know that for Noddings caring is *relational*, we can understand the importance of both parties contributing to the relationship. It is not enough for a person to say "I care about you." Even though I may think I care, if the one I care-for does not recognize and respond to my caring attitude, we cannot say caring is taking place. The one cared-for "contributes to the relation by recognizing and responding to the caring. . . . To participate genuinely as care-for in a relation requires discernment and receptivity" (Witherell & Noddings, 1991, p. 166).

Noddings's ethic of care begins with a moral attitude of longing for goodness, not with moral reasoning. She suggests that what we as human beings do best is care, not reason, as Aristotle argued. In "Stories in Dialogue: Caring and Interpersonal Reasoning" (Witherell & Noddings, 1991), Noddings discusses **interpersonal reasoning** as the form of moral reasoning we should encourage in our students. What is interpersonal reasoning? It is "open, flexible, and responsive"; "[i]t is guided by an attitude that values the relationships of the reasoners over any particular outcome"; it stresses attachment and connection (p. 158). What are its components? An attitude of care, as defined earlier. How does interpersonal reasoning develop? "It requires sustained interpersonal contact" (p. 164), practicing by engaging in activities of care (p. 165). "To participate genuinely as cared-for in a relation requires discernment and receptivity," yet Noddings suspects "we cannot teach the skill of discernment directly. It develops in close relationships over time" (p. 166).

Implications of Caring for Teachers and Students

The idea that caring, as an ethical ideal, is relational has significant impact for teachers. Principled models of justice and virtue allow teachers the opportunity to stand back from specific situations and pass judgment from a distance. As the enforcer of the rules, teachers are encouraged to try to take an objective, neutral position and use their moral reasoning to decide what is fair. Having the opportunity to get to know their students and develop a trusting relationship with them is not the focus of principled ethical models, but it is emphasized in a caring ethical approach. In a caring approach, teachers must begin by trying to establish relationships with their students. They can do this in many ways: by beginning their classes with introductory activities, by opening up opportunities for students to regularly share events in their lives, by creating a safe environment where people feel they can express themselves and effort will be made by others to receive what they communicate and understand, as generously as is possible. After establishing caring relationships with their students, teachers make moral decisions based on the contextuality of those relationships.

We interviewed six professors identified as caring in a pilot study, "Caring in the College/University Classroom" (see note 1) to help us further define just what caring means to educators. Those six professors defined caring in terms of

- trying to be approachable and welcoming to their students,
- placing their emphasis on the learning process and on learning conceptually,
- offering students a say in what they are learning so they can experience engaged learning, and

■ being concerned with making their classrooms safe, supportive environments where engaged learning can take place.

We analyzed what these teachers had to say from a philosophical perspective in "Caring Professors: A Model" (Thayer-Bacon & Bacon, 1996b). We have found that a caring ethic is based on certain philosophical assumptions. We said earlier that Benhabib's communicative ethics is not philosophically neutral or morally neutral, but neither is Noddings's caring ethics.

What does a caring ethical approach mean for teachers and others who work in our schools? How does a caring model of ethics translate into our four situations? And are there any problems with this relational approach to ethics? Let us look at each of the four situations for education that we have been using throughout this chapter to help us understand the ramifications of a caring ethical approach for education.

"Situation 4: Censorship" focuses on teachers' ethical dilemmas concerning what to teach and what not to teach their students. Caring teachers whom we interviewed say they focus on the learning process and are concerned that their methods of instruction be student centered. They believe people learn in many different ways, and teachers must help students find the avenues that work for them. They also assume that all of us, as learners, bring our own unique experiences to our current situations, which affects our learning today. These teachers design their curriculum from their students' experiences, using those experiences as bridges to what they are trying to teach. Designing a curriculum around students' experiences means teachers must find ways to get to know their students and what their experiences are, so they can take them into consideration in their curriculum. Being student centered commits caring teachers again to trying to establish relationships with their students.

With caring as one's focus, "Situation 2: Dishonesty" takes on a different emphasis. We find that caring educators believe their students must take responsibility for their own learning for them to be engaged learners. This is partly because they believe students know what their strengths and weaknesses are and how they learn better than anyone else. An assumption is also made that students need to be actively involved if they are going to have any meaningful learning. Caring teachers believe we do not really learn something until we make it our own. Thus, caring educators design activities, lessons, and exams where cheating is no longer an issue (e.g., take-home exams, journals). Instead, the activities' focus is what students actively contribute.

In terms of evaluating what their students know ("Situation 1: Assessment"), caring teachers try to be coaches and guides as well as observers. Students decide how well they will do, based on how much time and effort they are able or willing to put into tasks. These educators give their students opportunities to suggest what they will attempt to accomplish while in their class because they believe learning is enhanced when the student feels a sense of ownership. Students who have an opportunity to take control of their own learning are more likely to be intrinsically motivated as learners. Several issues seem to promote intrinsic motivation, but control and challenge are clearly two essential qualities. The student who has some control over his or her learning is able to use that control to create challenges (Bacon, 1988; Deci, 1975, 1980; Deci & Ryan, 1985).

Given the assumption that none of us can ever be impartial, neutral, and objective, caring teachers struggle with concepts such as fairness and impartiality in grading students. The people we interviewed feel very uncomfortable with trying to be objective and think impartiality is an impossible task. They also express concern that in being consistent, they may become oppressively discriminatory, for they believe no two students are the same. They assume students all have contexts, which they have come to know and feel a need to acknowledge in evaluating their work. They are consistent and fair in that they do this for all of their students. All students are all allowed to do such things as rewrite and resubmit work or, if time runs out during a course, take an incomplete and finish it later.

What about "Situation 3: Exclusion"? Caring educators aim to encourage their students to develop their skills and help them continue learning. They express a desire to challenge their students intellectually, seeing themselves as facilitators and resources, or conduits. They try to help their students develop critical thinking skills as traditionally described (Ennis, 1962, 1987). They also worry that their students gain greater understanding of themselves and their perspectives. They encourage students' awareness of their own contingent situatedness and how it has affected their views. They say these skills are just as important as reasoning skills, because they assume that self-knowledge becomes a foundation on which all other knowledge is built and, again, that we are all partial, flawed, social beings.

Caring educators place an emphasis on students having the opportunity to engage in conversation with each other because they assume that it is through conversation with others that we learn more about ourselves and others. They encourage students to share and listen attentively, with sympathy, openness, and caring and thus learn "enlarged thinking" (Benhabib's term). Caring professors do not presume to speak for their students and do not allow their students to speak for each other. They assume we each must attend to others in a serious and close manner. We need to attempt to be receptive to what others are saying, trying to "feel with" the speaker(s) and understand in a generous, good-faith manner. We have to value what others have to say and attempt to believe the other(s) to make sure understanding has taken place, before using our critical thinking skills to doubt and critique. The judging and assessing are a vital part of enlarged thinking, but so are caring and the awareness of one's personal voice (Thayer-Bacon, 1995b). Just as in Benhabib's communicative ethics, the aim in a caring ethic is not necessarily for students to agree with each other or reach a consensus but to try to ensure students and teachers understand each other.

Implications for Education

In thinking about a caring ethical approach to teaching and its ramifications, we turn to our own lives. One of us is a man, interested in clarifying the affective issues of teaching and learning, and one of us is a woman, developing a theory for how it is we know based on relationships and caring. While we will use our own experiences here to help make the issues and concerns related to a caring model more concrete, we are not trying to hold ourselves up as wonderful, caring teachers. We are two people who focus on affective issues as part of our own research and in our own classroom teaching.

We are struck by how hard it is to care, encouraging personal and expert knowledge growth, allowing for feelings as well as thoughts, treating students as concrete, unique subjects rather than disembedded and disembodied generalized others. Caring is time-consuming and wrenching to the self. We suspect it also causes much more personal growth, because of the pain and doubt it triggers. We think it offers greater intrinsic reward for the educator, for your chances of being a successful teacher able to effect change and further knowledge with students are greatly enhanced. The teacher definitely develops a strong sense of relationship and connection to people and the world.

We believe we can support the claim that caring teachers are more likely to be successful in teaching their students. This is the most serious ramification of the type of teaching we are describing, and so we turn to it first. The task of educating requires making connections between what students already know and what they need to learn, which requires teachers to know something about their students and their lives (Dewey, 1938/1965). The reason that caring educators are more likely to be successful is because they are attempting to relate to their students as subjects, on a personal level. By relating to students on a more personal level, teachers learn more about their students' lives. This knowledge increases teachers' chances to do their work effectively. They know more about the students and their past experiences; therefore, they can make connections for the students and further their understanding. Distancing themselves from students decreases the number of opportunities for teachers to know students. Not knowing their students limits their ability to bridge new ideas with the old. A caring approach assumes the students are willing to relate to their teachers. For students who are unwilling to be in a relationship, caring teachers are limited in what they can do, potentially limiting students' learning.

Caring teachers give students the message that what they have to say is valuable and important and will be attended to. Caring teachers receive student contributions in a generous, serious, and close manner. These teachers acknowledge, rather than ignore, what goes on outside the classroom as being relevant for learning. Each student is treated as a unique and whole person who is respected, accepted, and perceived as being worthy of caring. In a setting full of these messages, students are more likely to feel safe and trust that they can open up and expose their thoughts and ideas. That trust must not be violated by the teacher or other students. With a willingness to open up and risk, the student's opportunities for actively engaging in the learning process are greatly enhanced. With more opportunities for learning, more actual learning will take place. This is why we are confident that teachers who are more caring are more likely to be successful at helping their students learn. The teachers who taught us the most were the ones who made us feel both welcomed and acknowledged in their classrooms. They were willing to put aside the day's lesson to talk about what was on our minds—such issues as racism, sexism, poverty, crime, and war.

What are some of the issues caring teachers face? One is the sheer amount of work. The amount of difficult work involved in being a caring teacher is unavoidable, we believe. If one is going to be a successful educator, then working hard is a given. In our six interviews with caring professors, they discussed a number of other concerns: students, personal, institutional, and societal. We face these same concerns. Are the problems because of an ethic of care itself, or do they stem from other factors?

For example, we find that students sometimes do not respond positively because they feel that the caring educator wastes their time. Many students prefer (or are at least accustomed to) being told what they are supposed to know and then having to demonstrate that learning on a test. We also have students who, when given the opportunity to express their feelings, use our class as an opportunity to gripe about other teachers. Many students seem compelled to work through their bad experiences, silenced feelings, and unattended needs before they can take advantage of what a caring professor offers them. Many students will have to go through a process of relearning how to be active, engaged learners, responsible for their own learning. We often experience resistance about what we ask students to do, partly because it is just as hard for them to be caring as it is for the teacher and because it requires so much from them as students.

One of us has had colleagues who see caring as "unprofessional" because he treats students as equals and develops relationships with them. The other has had colleagues who felt she lacked rigor as a teacher, in spite of successful learning experiences for her students. Colleagues may see the behaviors of caring as excessively "touchy-feely" and therefore an undesirable throwback to the sixties. Giving students the opportunity to rewrite papers raises some people's concerns that we may potentially give too many A's, resulting in grade inflation.

Some colleagues worry, Is the caring educator setting an undesirable precedent for everyone else on the faculty? In other words, if one cares about students in the ways we are describing, does it mean that all teachers will have to engage in such caring? The fact that a caring teacher is likely to become popular among students at the school may also be perceived as threatening to some colleagues.

One of us was hired to teach an Introduction to Teaching class of 200 students, in an auditorium, as an efficient way to pass on knowledge to large numbers of students. How does a professor model caring as a way of teaching with that many students? In general, we do not find many opportunities to meet with students in comfortable surroundings where people would naturally want to spend time and be together. One of us has taught in a room that was too small to create discussion groups or move about. One has also taught in a building that was being remodeled and had to endure the consequent excessive noise and many interruptions.

There are ways to work around these problems and persevere in trying to be caring educators. We are concerned, though. Since we began our interviews of caring professors, two of our original six interviewees have opted to leave college/university teaching. One of us chose to leave also but returns periodically. We believe that much could be done to create a more supportive environment for caring in the university setting. In the following subsections, we discuss some of the techniques that have worked for us.

Students

We have found it well worth our while to explain to students what we are doing and why at the beginning of class. Choosing books that stimulate discussion and support a caring approach is also helpful. Building time into the classroom for discussion—small-group, large-group, and one-on-one—helps students get to know each other and feel supported in their efforts to understand. Setting ground rules in the classroom that do not allow gossip, making fun, or just general gripe sessions and insisting that people conduct themselves as professionals (e.g. protecting others' rights to privacy) are important. Making yourself available to help students is helpful, by setting aside time outside the classroom when you are available and students can find you. Making the classroom a warm, friendly place to be is a good idea—for example, displaying students' work, decorating so that your room reflects your interests as well as your students', or having an open door policy. Making comments/suggestions on students' assignments to coach them along, as well as getting their papers graded and back to them in a timely fashion so they can exercise their option to rewrite, encourage them to work more. Asking them about their lives and how they are doing and bringing what is going on around them into the classroom (e.g., current news events) make them feel that you care. Being willing to share with them the things that are happening in your life, too, reminds them that you are also a person with a life outside the classroom. Tell your students when your car broke down on the way to work, or an article was accepted for publication, or your toddler spoke her first words.

Colleagues

Getting to know your colleagues, engaging in conversations, and sharing what you are doing all go a long way toward encouraging acceptance and avoiding being perceived as a threat. To build feelings of respect and trust, good communication is essential. Being interested in others' work and sharing knowledge gained from workshops and conferences, new ideas and books, for example, makes others feel validated and cared about.

The System

Breaking down a large class size so that students meet in small discussion groups with their teacher, or discussion leaders, helps them feel more cared for. Taking desks out of rows, looking for spaces to use that allow for movement of furniture, or placing tables so that people can face each other help a room feel more welcoming. Allowing for breaks or refreshments or even meeting in other settings, such as a lounge area or outdoors, helps get out from under a rigid clock and setting. Sending students off to work in pairs (e.g. study teams) and giving them the opportunity to meet at a time other than class time and report to you is another method.

Many have made suggestions of ways that the education system and structure could be changed to make it more feasible for a teacher to be caring. We have talked about things educators can do to be more caring and discussed the importance of being more aware of students' needs and experiences and allowing students more input and the opportunity to interact with each other as well as the teacher. But what about the teachers themselves? What can the school do to make caring educators feel that what they are doing is important and that their hard work is appreciated? Caring educators need to feel cared for by the school.

For example, some urban schools offer classes off-campus and at unusual time slots to try to reach nontraditional students. They meet early in the morning and on weekends. They offer child care facilities for young parents to be able to finish their education. Many schools also offer before- and after-school child care.

Knowing that school systems are capable of these kinds of changes, we have reason to believe they could be more flexible with scheduling and location to fit teachers' needs too. They could at least reserve certain rooms in the school building, ones with moveable furniture, for example, for those who need them. Showing teachers that the school is aware of their professional needs and trying to accommodate them is an affirming experience. Acknowledging good teachers and the work they put into their classes is important, as well as showing interest in classroom projects on which they are working, even possibly offering assistance. Schools can encourage faculty collaboration efforts—team teaching, for example. Schools can ask more experienced faculty to act as mentors for newer faculty. Knowing the faculty and acknowledging events, situations, accomplishments in their lives (births, deaths, birthdays, other accomplishments in the community, etc.) makes faculty members feel attended to. Having an open door, being available for lunch or meetings, holding receptions or occasional parties give faculty the opportunity to know their administrators as well as each other.

Conclusion

Seyla Benhabib (1992) talks about "generalized others" and "concrete others." When we view what we, as human beings, share in common, we are relying on the concept of generalized others. The concept of concrete others acknowledges that each of us is a unique human being with our own specific context and different, individual gifts and talents as well as needs and limitations.

Principled ethics focuses on generalized others, and a caring ethic focuses on concrete others. Ethical approaches based on principles and rules do not allow for the unique differences that exist in particular situations, and ethics based on particularities of individuals focus on local, specific situations that are framed within the context of situations as well as on each of our own capacities as finite human beings. There is a limit to how many students each individual teacher can care for and how much each individual person can care, as well as extenuating factors due to the ones cared-for, the students' willingness to be in a caring relationship with their teachers. Limits also arise from the context of the situations the caring relationship takes place in and the restraints schools, parents, communities, and society at large place on caring.

Benhabib wonders whether we cannot rely on justice *and* caring for our ethical model. Why not use both to help us? Caring helps encourage us to be willing to reason from others' points of view and develop the sensitivity to hear their voices. Caring encourages us to acknowledge people's subjectivity and reminds us we cannot assume to speak for others but must create a space for others to speak for themselves. But Benhabib does not trust just "the sentiments of empathy and benevolence" to sustain us when we face moral dilemmas (1992, p. 168). She wants to keep impartiality and the moral point of view ("what is morally good is what is best for those like me"; p. 187) and admits that of the two, she trusts justice to help us be moral more than caring. She does not think the caring perspective amounts to a moral theory.

> My goal is to situate reason and the moral self more decisively in contexts of gender and community, while insisting upon the discursive power of individuals to challenge such situatedness in the name of universalistic principles, future identities and as yet undiscovered communities. (p. 8)

We are not so convinced that a particularized, relativized caring model is less powerful than a universalized justice model. Most parents develop rules to help guide them in child rearing, but as they have more than one child, they quickly learn how unique and different children can be and that rules that work for one child do not work for another. The same goes for teachers, only even more so as they have more students to work with.

Teachers are continually asked to implement rules that are passed on to them from well-meaning administrators, school boards, and legislators. Proficiency exams, for example, were not teachers' ideas; they were others' ideas of how to make sure students are learning what schools say they are teaching and that teachers are doing their job. They were designed with the hopes of raising the standards and quality of teaching, by serving as a means of objectively accounting for knowledge gained or not. For students who are succeeding in school and receiving a quality education, proficiency exams are easy and reaffirming to the students and their teachers. For students who are enrolled in most of our city schools, proficiency exams become one more message of failure. For those teachers and administrators in our urban schools who find that their jobs, as well as federal funding for resources for their school, are determined by student test scores, the proficiency exams become a form of blackmail. Either I teach to this test, or my students will fail. If I teach to the test, I will be teaching a curriculum that is deadly dull to students who are already struggling to find meaning and a reason for attending school. Proficiency exams are meant to serve as a means of supplying justice, but they end up being unjust to the very students they intend to help, because they are not able to take into consideration the con-textuality of these individual, unique students' lives. For these very reasons, we trust the value of a caring approach over a principled justice approach, unlike Benhabib. However, like Benhabib, we would like to suggest that teachers consider how they can use both.

If we return to the examples of Summerhill and Montessori schools to understand how justice *and* caring fare in a democratic classroom, we see that Summerhill does not begin with rules, other than the health/safety ones they must maintain to keep their school licensed and open for enrollment. The school supplies the structure for the development of general rules through its democratic process of weekly town meetings. Everyone attending the school that year is involved in the voting that establishes the general rules and consequences if rules are broken. Then the rules apply to all the students attending. Yet the rules are flexible and able to adapt to the needs of particular students, because the town meetings continue to be held each week all year, and every single student in Summerhill has the right and opportunity to bring up for question any of the rules. If a rule is not what it was designed to do, it can be changed. Through the students' use of "interactive rationality" (Benhabib's term), in dialogical form in the town meetings, room is made for caring as well as for justice.

In Montessori classrooms, rules are supplied so that students have a framework in which to function freely in the room. No one may take another child's work or join in on another's activities without asking the child who was doing the work. Children have the right to say no when someone asks and choose to work by themselves. Usually limits are placed on how many children can work together, so things do not get too noisy in the classroom and the noise level does not break the concentration of other students trying to work. Yet, it is possible to create a democratic community within this kind of setting, where students have a great deal of say concerning the rules, and the classroom holds regular meetings to allow students to adjust and adapt the rules to fit their individual needs. Teachers also reserve the right to make exceptions to rules, for example, as acts of care for individuals with special needs.

Going back to the example of proficiency exams, Summerhill offers teacher assistance to students interested in taking qualifying exams, so they can learn the required knowledge and practice the necessary skills to be able to pass the tests. Students not interested in taking the exams are not required to do so. Montessori schools often offer proficiency exams of some form or other, because it is required by the state in which they reside. But they do not teach to the exams other than to teach their students how to fill in test answer sheets and take timed tests. They trust that the students have learned the necessary skills by learning to apply their knowledge actively gained in the Montessori curriculum to varied situations. Thayer-Bacon's students with severe learning disabilities who were only going to learn from a proficiency exam that they are failures at taking timed tests were not given the tests. Refusing to administer the tests seemed the only moral act she could do, as a teacher who knew her students very well and had established caring relationships with them.

Caring, as an ethical approach, allows a teacher to take into account the student as a whole person. Such a relational approach also suggests serious ethical questions worth pursuing. How personal should the relationship be? What are the differences between caring relationships that are not friendships and friendships or love? Do people of certain ages or cultural backgrounds approach caring in different ways?

In addition to being known by their students as caring, for the most part, the people we interviewed are known as superb teachers at their respective institutions. However, they are also suffering for being caring. They face many problems and challenges that wear them down and frustrate their efforts. How do they cope? Do they also have caring relationships with their colleagues and administrators? What about our society at large? Do we as a society value caring? One of the people we interviewed expressed his views on this question this way:

> I think it's caring teachers that do a lot of good for our society, but there's very little recognition and certainly then the pay is not commensurate with what we do. Our society is pretty screwed up in terms of our priorities, education being way down the list, entertainment and escapism being way up on the list.

If our goal, as teachers, is to encourage students' growth and stimulate their enthusiasm for learning, as well as to teach them the skills that they will need to be lifelong learners, able to effect change, we need to make serious, critical studies of what we do in schools and how schools can be more supportive of caring efforts. We turn in Chapter 4 to a closer examination of the skills students (and teachers) need to practice and develop so they can function in a democratic classroom successfully.

In the Classroom

Activity 1

In collaboration with one or more classmates, write a skit that will allow you to act out each of the four problem situations described in the chapter. You should look at each of the four situations first from a principled ethics perspective and then from a caring ethical perspective. The object is to give you an opportunity to see how each of these two ethics will manifest themselves in classroom situations.

After playing the scenes, talk as a group about how each of the problem scenarios might be perceived and understood from both a teacher's and a student's point of view. For each of the two ethical perspectives, consider advantages and disadvantages, feelings about students and the teacher (and the class), and potential short- and long-term effects.

Note to instructor: Because we have offered four problem situations in the chapter, this activity has the potential to be built around as many as eight groups, four presenting each of the problems from a principled ethics approach and four presenting each of the problems from a caring ethic perspective. If your classes are smaller or you merely want to shorten or simplify the activity, you may configure the class in other ways, such as having one group do two, or even all four, of the problem situations for one of the ethical perspectives.

Activity 2

What follows is a micro-ethnography of sorts. Your instructor should have discussed the two ethical approaches as presented in the chapter and have given you the opportunity to ask questions and receive clarification about the meanings and implications of each approach. This activity will work best if the class collaborates, as a group, to create a set of survey questions to interview classroom teachers about how they handle ethical issues. These questions serve to create a common ground for the interviews and will help you stay focused on the task of finding out how teachers think about ethics.

Using the survey questions as a starting point, you will then conduct an interview with a classroom teacher. The problem situations from the chapter may be used to give interviewees a better understanding of your questions. The interviews may be recorded and transcribed, but you might also take copious notes during the interview and then flesh them out immediately afterward. Recording interviews has the advantage of creating a record that is superior to memory alone and may be listened to repeatedly.

Along with the interview, observe the teacher as she or he teaches. We hope that in your observations you will see how the teacher deals with ethical situations in the moment, as opposed to in theory or some obscure ideal. A teacher may hold a certain ethical perspective intellectually but not always act on it.

Once the interview and observation(s) are complete, you should analyze what the teacher said and what you observed, attempting to determine which ethical perspective the teacher is using. Back in class, you can compare and contrast your findings with those of your classmates. By examining the group data, the class should be able to get an idea of the extent to which the teachers interviewed are using a principled ethic, a caring ethic, or both. These findings will potentially open up a discussion of how common it is to find teachers using an ethic of care and what some of the implications of using that ethical approach may be.

Activity 3

Think back to your own experiences in school, and remember times when you were involved in a moral dilemma. Try to remember what happened, developing as many details of the situation as you can, and then try to explain how the situation was resolved. You should write out as much of the experience as needed to assure that you represent the event accurately. Once you are confident that you have a reasonable portrayal of the experience, you should answer the following questions:

1. What was the ethical approach that was used in resolving the dilemma?
2. How did you feel about the resolution?
3. What would have been your ideal resolution of the dilemma?
4. Did any long-term repercussions ensue as a result of this experience? If so, what were they?

We hope that you will come to recognize that how you interpret and use ethics will have an impact on the experiences that your students will have in your classroom.

Notes

Threads of this chapter have been published by Thayer-Bacon as "Caring and Its Relationship to Critical Thinking" (1993a) and by Thayer-Bacon and Bacon as "Caring in the College/University Classroom" (1996a) and "Caring Professors: A Model" (1996b).

1. All translations of the *Republic* use a numbering system that makes it easy to refer to passages. The numbering system is printed in the margins of the text and refers to the Stephanus edition, where the paragraphs were numbered and lettered rather than the pages of the text. We follow the universal Stephanus system in referring to specific passages in the Larson translated version of the *Republic*.

2. Some translations call the guardians the "philosopher-kings," and more recent feminist discussions call them the "philosopher-queens." Because Plato makes an elaborate argument for the equality of men and women and presents the case that both men and women are capable of being the wisest and most just, and therefore future leaders of the state, we choose to use the neutral term of "guardian" to signify the rulers Plato describes.

3. John Dewey (1916/1966) discusses Plato's *Republic* in *Democracy and Education,* Chapter 7, "The Democratic Conception in Education."

4. Following Aristotle's lead, we are using capitalized words to symbolize the concept when it is discussed in universalized terms. For example, eating good food and receiving a gift are events that can cause a person to feel happiness, but they are not Happiness as a Supreme Good—they are concrete specific examples of temporary happiness.

5. Aristotle uses *man* throughout his writings without any attempt to argue for women being considered as equal. In fact, he is very sexist in his comments about women. We will use his word *man* as a reminder of his political position and because this position is in direct contradiction to his assumption that what he presents is universal to all human beings.

6. Dewey (1916/1966), in *Democracy and Education*, offers excellent arguments against the mind/body distinction, especially in the later chapters. Richard Rorty (1979) also discusses these false distinctions at length in *Philosophy and the Mirror of Nature.*

7. Eastern philosophers, Indigenous people, and philosophers with a holistic, ecological perspective criticize the separation of mind/body, selves/others from this perspective. See, for example, writings by Madhu Suri Prakash (1990, 1994), Wendell Berry (1977, 1981), and Ivan Illich (1973).

8. Feminist scholars, multicultural scholars, and critical theorists have all presented and supported these claims. See, for example, Bennett deMarrais and LeCompte (1995), Freire (1985), Giroux (1981), McLaren (1994), Sadker and Sadker (1991), Sleeter and Grant (1994), and Spring (1994).

9. For the history of American education in terms of girls and African Americans, see Sadker and Sadker (1991); Tozer, Violas, and Senese (1993); and Tyack and Hansot (1990).

Constructive Thinking

In Chapter 1, we made the case for looking at students and teachers in classrooms as democratic communities. These communities are dependent on certain conditions and skills to thrive. We know that communities involve at least **more than one person** and these people have **something in common**. We also know that for these people to establish that they have something in common, some form of communication must take place, based on some form of **common language**. One of the skills vital to democratic community members is **communication skills**.

Democratic communities are different from other forms of communities in that they have **shared interests** and **full interaction within the group as well as with other groups**. Democratic communities need to be **flexible** and **able to adjust** to their members' needs. Not only do community members need to be able to communicate with each other (able to listen and express themselves); they also need to be able to relate to each other. Democratic communities are dependent on their members having **relational skills**. Teachers in democratic classrooms need to work on creating an environment in which their students feel **safe** to contribute, so they can practice their communication and relational skills.

In Chapter 2, we described what knowledge is in terms of relationality. It is important for students to develop their abilities to **reason**, to learn and practice **critical thinking skills**. But as vital as critical thinking skills are, they are not enough. Prior to and simultaneous with developing critical thinking skills, people need to evolve a sense of who they are, their own **personal voice**. We learn about our own worldviews by relating with others. The relating with others helps us better understand our own voices, which are greatly affected by our unique social contexts, and how they differ from others. We also need healthy relationships to help us continue to grow and learn. We all need to feel **cared-for** as well as be able to experience what it is like to be **one-caring** for others. Not only do we learn about ourselves by relating to others, but we also learn how to understand others' perspectives by relating with others. We use our ability to communicate, relate, reason, and care, with the aid of our capacities to **intuit**, **imagine** and **emotionally feel** to help us learn how to be enlarged thinkers, able to understand other worldviews.

Finally, when we have to make decisions on what seems to be the best course of action to take, what is the best solution to our problem, and so forth, we use all of these skills to help us, in what we call **constructive thinking**. In Chapter 3, we concluded by suggesting that the best course of action may be to rely on **reason** as well as **caring** and, again, to use all the tools we have to help us be more reasonable and caring. In this chapter, we explore others' views as a way of attempting to define and understand the concepts highlighted in this introduction. We also want to consider the implications these concepts have for education. We begin by defining the chapter title, "Constructive Thinking."

The term *constructive thinking* is adopted from "constructive knowing" in Belenky, Clinchy, Goldberger, and Tarule's (1986) *Women's Ways of Knowing*. Both terms acknowledge that one's personal voice is contributing to the conversation (as well as one's expert, reasoning voice) and allow that feelings such as caring for the other are necessary and present (not just thoughts). Constructive thinking views knowledge as personal and public. As a model for knowledge, it stresses the impossibility of separating the self from the object, the knower from the known. **A constructive thinker attempts to integrate personal knowledge with expert knowledge, to integrate the inner voice (the subjective, intuitive, believing voice) and the voice of reason (the objective, critical, doubtful voice)**. This description of thinking allows for an interaction between subjectivity and objectivity and "assigns equal rights to both factors in experience—objective and internal conditions" (Dewey, 1938/1965, pp. 38–39).[1]

A Quilting Bee

Imagine a democratic classroom community being like a large quilting bee.[2] People of different religions and genders (as well as sexual orientation); different ethnic and social class backgrounds; different talents, kinds of intelligence, and levels and abilities are present. If the students spend more than 1 year in this classroom and are of mixed ages, as we recommended in Chapter 1, then people of different ages are also participating. These people are getting to know each other by relating to each other, trying to communicate and establish a common language. They all share the common interests of being together to work on a quilt (or quilts). The quilts they are working on we will call "knowledge."

Quilts of knowledge are being quilted within frames. The frames that hold our quilts stand for reality, our shifting, changing, in-flux, live world. We, as constructive thinkers, cannot go beyond the frames—they set our boundaries—but within the ever-changing frames, we can create whatever kinds of quilts we want. The different varieties of patterns and styles that will develop in our quilts depend on many factors—for example, the number of contributors we have; what these contributors bring to the quilting bee in terms of their own contexts, knowledge, and skills; and the tools and supplies we have available for our use.

How do quilters usually begin a quilt? There does not seem to be a "usual" to this process. Many begin by drawing a scaled picture of what they hope to end up with, after much discussion and a survey of supplies. Many decide what kind of quilt they will make based on the quilt's intended use. Others just begin with what they have and keep working and putting together different pieces of fabric until they decide the quilt is done. We may all begin on the quilt together, or we may all decide to go off on our own or in smaller groups and begin by making our own smaller pieces first, which will then be added to the others to form the quilt.

What about the roles different participants play in the quilting bee? Does everyone have to participate by sewing a patterned shape? Not necessarily—again, this depends on the participants and what they decide. At some quilting bees, everyone sews, but everyone does not necessarily sew at the same time. People may take turns working at the large frame, while others are taking a break or cutting more material to use. At some quilting bees, some participants may not actually sew at all; instead, their talents will be used in other supportive ways: as cooks and servers of food and drinks for everyone, as child care providers so others can work, as gatherers and organizers of the supplies, as responsible scouts for the location of the quilting bee, as people making sure participants help set up and clean up, or maybe as people supplying music to help keep the quilters entertained. A quilting bee might be somber and quiet, with little interaction taking place, but most of us probably think of quilting bees as being lively, noisy places, with lots of conversation going on and a real sense of warmth and friendship. Quilting bees are certainly places where people can practice their communication and relational skills.

The materials used to create the quilts include the batting or "filler" used inside quilts and the lining material, and the covering material we see on the outside. These materials stand for our ideas, thoughts, and beliefs in this quilting bee metaphor. These materials are often leftover scraps of material from other sewing projects or old recycled clothes and blankets, but they can come from any possible source. It is the same for us as inquirers. We learn from movies and television programs, books, newspapers, magazines, journals, and computer programs. We also learn from our friends, family, neighbors, and fellow citizens. Every experience we have is a potential source for our ideas and thoughts.

The tools used to help quilters are usually items such as tape measures, scissors, straight pins and needles, thread, and yarn. As we have pointed out, tools used in inquiry are personal voice, intuition, imagination, emotional feelings, caring, and reason. Some of the tools used in quilting help straighten the materials, shape them to size, and hold them in place, much like reasoning helps us order and untangle our thoughts. Needles help carry the thread or yarn in and out, working it through the materials. Similarly, our intuition helps us move through our thoughts and feelings and make sense of our experiences. Quilters use their emotional feelings, imagination, intuition, caring and reasoning, communication and relational skills, and enlarged thinking skills to help them decide which materials to use and what designs to create. With the help of all of these tools and skills, they are able to construct quilts of knowledge.

The criteria used to help quilters decide what to include and omit in their quilts are usually based on the quilt's intended use, what supplies are available, and the desired aesthetic appearance. For quilts of knowledge, criteria would include such measures as clarity, coherency, cohesiveness, comprehensiveness, and beauty: Does this work? Do these ideas make sense and go together? Are they inclusive and beneficial? Are they elegant—do they appeal to us aesthetically? The ultimate warrant for quilts of knowledge is the loom itself—reality.

We think the quilting bee metaphor offers several advantages. Quilting is usually done with many people involved; it is not associated with being a solitary activity, although it is possible for someone to make a quilt all by themselves. Quilting with others is much more fun! In a democratic classroom, people can choose to work by themselves or with others, although they are always encouraged to participate and contribute to the community. And when we construct knowledge, we may spend time alone working on ideas and solutions to problems, but for those ideas to make a contribution to knowledge, they eventually must be shared with others. Our ideas do not come out of a vacuum, either; they come from our experiences and transactions with others.

Another quality of quilting bees that makes them a helpful metaphor is that they are events full of activity, both physical and mental. Quilting bees remind us that we use our whole bodies, not just our minds, to help us construct knowledge. We do not rely on just one sense to help us gather ideas. Many past epistemological theories have described reason and knowledge in relation to images of sight and vision. We can "see" this in our language, for when we say, "I see clearly now," we mean "I understand." Using sight as a metaphor for knowledge emphasizes the knower as someone who stands back, alone, disengaged, to see better. Quilting, as a metaphor, may tend to draw one's attention to sight if we just focus on its products, the quilts. But **quilting bees** point to the process of quilting and people being together enjoying each other's company. Quilting bees are social events. Even though the finished product, the quilt, is usually beautiful to look at and appeals to our sense of sight, quilts are also wonderful to feel, and the weight of a quilt around our body functions to cover us, protecting us from the elements and keeping us warm.

We also like the metaphor of a quilting bee because it does not necessarily conjure up images that imply order and unity. People have historically used nearly any source of material one can think of to make quilts, and though many of us have seen quilts that follow a strict pattern and design, we have just as easily seen quilts that seem not to have much order to them at all. Often quilts are made that do not contain any of the same colors, textures, or material patterns; they appear to be more of a hodge-podge, where the only unifying theme is "whatever was available."

A few caveats about the quilting bee metaphor: (1) Some people may associate quilting as being a gender-specific activity, one that women and girls participate in; and (2) some people may not like to sew and will not find the metaphor helpful for that reason. Some males and nonsewers may find that it is not a very helpful metaphor for them, in terms of envisioning a democratic classroom community. We urge people to allow quilting the opportunity to be a metaphor full of possibility and to check their assumptions concerning it, just as we will be attempting to do, as we use it. Certainly males do participate in quilting bees, and quilting, like weaving or sewing in general, is not gender-specific to females. Quilting is an activity that many people consider a craft and an art. People of all ethnic backgrounds from around the world have participated in quilting historically. These are some of the reasons we like it so much as a metaphor. However, other metaphors may work better for anyone who is having difficulty identifying with quilting bees, say, community picnics, barn raises, choral groups, or dances. We challenge you to find another metaphor if this one does not work for you.

Tools for Quilting

We learned in Chapter 2 that current work in philosophy, from critical theorists, feminists, postmodernists, and pragmatists, for example, describes critical thinking as an activity performed by a specific fallible person, occupying a unique body, and embedded contextually in a certain time and place. Critical thinking, in its many different forms, traditionally has been considered the kind of thinking that relies on skills such as doubting, questioning, comparing, contrasting, and judging (see Ennis, 1987, for an excellent list of critical thinking skills). Critical thinking has been viewed as a tool reasoning people can rely on to help them find the best solution to problems, to separate facts from opinions, to tell truths from deceptions, to find the most unbiased, neutral answer and the clearest, most thoroughly supported argument. Such hopes have been placed on critical thinking because it is believed people need a tool to help them be better reasoners. Without a way to reason that allows for an unbiased, neutral perspective, how can people be sure they have not tainted the information, stacked the deck, or missed a clue?

If critical theorists, postmodernists, feminists, and pragmatists are correct in their efforts to more accurately describe what happens when people quilt/construct knowledge, then there is a strong need to redescribe critical thinking theory. This chapter works on this task. We are calling our redescription of critical thinking "constructive thinking." We know that constructive thinkers acknowledge that their personal voice contributes to their knowing. But what is this subjective "personal voice"? Now that we know it is impossible to remove one's voice from one's thoughts, personal voice is a concept that deserves further discussion.

Personal Voice

We begin with the definition Belenky et al. (1986) give to personal voice. They point out 'voice' is a metaphor that the women in their study use to depict their intellectual and ethical development; developing a sense of voice is intricately intertwined with mind and self. The term **personal voice** is not used as just a metaphor for "point of view" (or "worldview"). They suggest 'voice' is an appropriate metaphor, because it stresses connection and conversation. Hearing something and being heard requires physical closeness. Following Belenky et al.'s lead, we will use *personal voice* here to mean **the self, the mind/body, the "I," one's feelings/thoughts/intuitions all rolled into one. It is the subjective, that which one cannot lose or leave out of one's thinking process**.

Important questions arise from the model of constructive thinking being developed here. For example, what is the role of personal voice, and how does it affect knowledge? Given the impossibility of being objective and impersonal in the quest for knowledge, what does thinking look like now, with personal voice included in the description? We will look at what others have said concerning such a concept, with the hope that their contributions might help shed some light. We also consider problems such a view of thinking and knowledge might present and attempt to address them.

Tacit Knowledge, Intuition, and Subjective Knowing

The first thing to note is that others have not used the term *personal voice* as we are. It is easier to find examples of people who have talked about aspects of personal voice, such as intuition. However, in discussions of these aspects, ideas about personal voice can be found, often described in terms such as "the will," "the soul," or "the subjective." Let us look at what others have said about these qualities that help make up one's personal voice.

Michael Polanyi's "Tacit Knowledge" The philosopher Michael Polanyi (1967) is our first choice for a better understanding of what the self contributes to knowledge. His concept "tacit knowledge" might refer to subjective, personal knowledge. Polanyi said, "We can know more than we can tell" (p. 4). A scientist influenced by Gestalt psychology, Polanyi has been criticized for psychologizing logic. He drew others' attention to the **shaping and integrating** that goes on in the formation/discovery of knowledge. "This shaping or integrating I hold to be the great and indispensable tacit power by which all knowledge is discovered and, once discovered, is held to be true" (p. 6). **Shaping/integrating is something done at a personal level**. It is what makes the creation of new ideas possible. Tacit knowledge, as Polanyi describes it, seems to be what one contributes to the knowing situation, although, because it is tacit, this shaping is not something one is aware of doing. It is something one does that cannot be explained or verbalized, almost as if it is unconscious.

Polanyi said tacit knowing always involves two things (two terms). The functional relation between the two terms is such that "we know the first term (proximal) only by relying on our awareness of it for attending to the second (distal)" (p. 10). One attends from something to something else. "[T]acit knowing establishes a meaningful relationship between two terms " (p. 13). This tacit knowing cannot be replaced by explicit integration of particular knowledge. Polanyi realized tacit knowledge cannot be formalized and established as "strictly detached, objective knowledge" which is the "declared aim of modern science" (p. 20).

> If tacit thought forms an indispensable part of all knowledge, then, the ideal of eliminating all personal elements of knowledge would, in effect, aim at the destruction of all knowledge. The ideal of exact science would turn out to be fundamentally misleading and possibly a source of devastating fallacies. (p. 20)

Polanyi argued that "the process of formalizing all knowledge to the exclusion of any tacit knowing is self-defeating" (p. 20). This realization points out a paradox about knowing that is as old as the Greeks. (See Plato's lesson with the slave boy in the *Meno*.) Tacit knowledge answers the paradox of how it is we can know things and not be able to tell, for it is hidden knowledge, yet to be discovered. Polanyi's description points out the fluid, developing side of knowledge, that there are things still to discover, "a still unrevealed reality" (p. 70).

What Polanyi's description of tacit knowledge also reveals is that there is a limit to how much clarity we can hope to add to this concept. If it is hidden and cannot be formalized, then we will be unable to describe "it" objectively to our readers. But we are bothered by the idea that one's personal voice is something one would not be aware of, that 'personal voice' remains unknown, like it is unconscious. If that is true, then a problem for this transactive model of constructive thinking is, What is the value of knowing that the self contributes to knowledge? If the self cannot learn about itself and become aware of its own inner workings, if there is a side of knowledge that must remain unknowable, then there is little or no hope for improvement on those contributions. (There is little hope in the assumption that one can have a partial understanding of how one thinks, no hope for the hidden aspects that remain unknowable.) For example, as a self, one may be biased toward certain experiences and unwilling to consider them valuable contributions to knowledge (e.g., dreams). According to Polanyi, when people have experiences and test out possible ideas, they make connections, integrate the different experiences, to come out with the solutions. But if they are biased against dreams and unwilling to consider them valid experiences, then they will not let them contribute to possible solutions. And people will do this without being aware of it.

The model of constructive thinking being developed here includes a personal voice that has the chance of becoming aware of its own workings. The awareness can certainly improve, and most likely takes a lifetime to do so, but the important point is that it is possible to make one's own contributions conscious to one's self. This is an important quality of personal voice, as it makes it possible to change, grow, adapt, and improve one's voice, as one becomes more aware of cultural biases. This view of personal voice, as we describe it, acknowledges that people are egocentric, in Piaget's sense of not knowing as young children that we even have a point of view that is different from others' (before developing a sense of self), and people are egocentric in the postmodern sense of being forced to view and experience the world through their own eyes (see Chapter 2). To believe selves can become aware of our ethnocentricity and our biases and prejudices due to acculturation, we need for personal voice to have the possibility of becoming conscious, and not remaining tacit and unknown.

Nel Noddings and Paul Shore's "Intuition"   Nel Noddings and Paul Shore (1984) write about intuition in *Awakening the Inner Eye: Intuition in Education*. They describe intuition as *a capacity*, or **a mode**. "The intuitive mode is characterized by engagement of the will, involvement of the senses, receptivity, a quest for understanding or meaning, and a facilitative tension between subjective certainty and objective uncertainty " (p. xiv). The intuitive mode is like what the British philosopher Sir Alfred North Whitehead called "romance," meaning "when the learner is intrigued by the material" (p. 32). It is **a direct, immediate, inward-looking receptivity** (p. 45). It is the dynamic motivator for the quest for meaning and understanding (p. 52). "[I]t is a capacity that makes contact, that participates in the creation of representations, that is capable of 'receiving' representations when the Will is disposed to this intense form of receptivity" (p. 55).

Intuition is nonrational, "a form of nonreflective consciousness" (p. 26). It is a source of knowledge but not necessarily true. "[O]ne of the distinctive qualities of intuition may be its personal, subjective, and therefore mutable quality" (p. 15). Noddings and Shore assert that it is not valuable or feasible to verify intuitions through reason or experience. Subjecting intuition to such analysis forces intuition into a rational mold, which is what Carl Jung tried to do (p. 26). "[I]ntuition itself is consciousness supreme and unanalyzable" (p. 54).

Intuition, as Noddings and Shore describe, shares the qualities that Polanyi mentions with tacit knowing, in that it is unanalyzable and not something that can be formalized and operationalized. It does not fit the scientific paradigm of thought. And yet intuition is something that we are conscious of, unlike how it is seen in Polanyi's view. "No mental mode could be more fully conscious than the intuitive mode" (p. 54).

Intuition has "two important features . . . : its object-giving function and its experience-enabling function, . . . [and] it precedes and makes possible the experience from which knowledge is constructed " (p. 49). Intuition is not something we understand "from experience but, rather, is that which makes experience comprehensible" (p. 50).

> The hallmark of the intuitive mode is seeing without glasses, hearing without filters, touching with ungloved hand. The immediate character of intuition does not imply accuracy, rightness, or moral goodness. It does imply commitment and clarity. (p. 57)

Noddings and Shore's description also sounds like Polanyi's tacit knowing, because tacit knowing always involves two terms, and the functional relation between the two terms is such that "we know the first term (proximal) only by relying on our awareness of it for attending to the second (distal)" (Polanyi, 1967, p. 10). One attends to something else, but that attention comes from something (one's tacit knowledge). This would imply that tacit knowledge gives meaning and helps us experience life; it is object giving and experience enabling, as Noddings and Shore describe intuition.

For Noddings and Shore, intuition is "exactly that part of intellect that connects body and mind" (p. 204). Something other than intuition controls and directs intuition, which is what they call "the Will." Is this the soul? Personal voice? What they have described as intuition begins to sound like a connector or transmitter, a bridge or pipeline between the soul and the world outside (including one's own physical body as part of "the world outside"). Noddings and Shore say the Will is "that central self or being that manifests itself as motive, desire, feeling, and the like" (p. 67). Will is not an object for intuition; it controls and directs intuition. Other words they use to describe the Will are "the thing-in-itself" (p. 58), "that which is more directly known than anything else" (p. 58), and "the dynamic center of self" and "the heart of being" (p. 59).

It is beginning to sound like our search for personal voice is to be found more in the Will than in intuition. Another quote by Noddings and Shore confirms this suspicion: the Will and reason "strain against each other in the productive tension between subjective certainty and objective uncertainty" (p. 89). If objective uncertainty is critical thinking, as described earlier, and subjective certainty is intuition, as presented by Noddings and Shore (or Polanyi's tacit knowledge), then reason seems to be represented by the mind, and Will is more likely the spirit or soul. Noddings and Shore close with this summation:

> We found that intuition is an object oriented capacity, one that organizes the material of inner and outer perception into representation for both reason and Will. It is driven by the Will's quest for meaning. It is, in a deep and poetic sense, the eyes, ears, and fingers of the soul. . . . The intuitive mode, as we described it, is characterized by the commitment of the Will, receptivity, involvement of the senses, the quest for understanding, and a tension between subjective certainty and objective uncertainty. (p. 202)

In our inner eye, we see personal voice as more like what Noddings and Shore describe as the Will. Our personal voice has access to all sorts of different materials and tools (experiences, feelings, thoughts, intuitions), for the quilts being constructed (the knowledge). Intuition is one of our tools that we use to help quilt knowledge. It helps the quilter decide what colors and types of material to select. Intuition helps us make connections from one idea to another, as a needle glides thread through pieces of material and ties them together. Reason, with logic, is another such tool, like straight pins to straighten and order the quilting.

Belenky et al. on Subjective Knowing   Belenky et al. (1986) present a theory of epistemology based on 5 years of research interviewing women from all classes, races, family backgrounds, and levels of education. Their theory strives to present women's ways of knowing, consciously seeking to include ways of intellectual development that do not fit the male experience. Of the five categories Belenky et al. discuss, the ones that might shed some light on personal voice are intuitive knowing and constructive knowing.

Intuitive knowing is presented as developmentally third on the list of five: from silence, to authority, to subjective knowledge (intuition), to procedural knowing (critical thinking), to constructive knowing. Thayer-Bacon (1992b, 1995c) has discussed the problem of presenting these as a hierarchy of knowledge. We are saying that constructive thinking is what happens whenever someone is inquiring, not just something the brightest, furthest developed, and most educated people do. We also have problems with how Belenky et al. present personal voice as different and separate from self (note their title: *The Development of Self, Voice, and Mind*) when in fact we think they are one and the same. But let us present what they say, and then critique it.

Subjective Knowledge. For a subjective knower, "truth and knowledge are conceived of as personal, private, and subjectively known or intuited" (Belenky et al., 1986, p. 15). At this stage of development, according to Belenky et al., a woman[3] begins to hear herself think and becomes aware that she has a unique perspective. (Again, this sounds like Piaget's concept of egocentrism. For Piaget, awareness is something one learns through interaction with other people; one must learn this awareness to develop a sense of self. See Chapter 2.) Subjective knowers discover "that first hand experience is a valuable source of knowledge" (p. 61). Truth is viewed as something that is subjective and personal ("what works best for me"; p. 70). Truth is an intuitive feeling, an experience, something felt. "These women do not see themselves as part of the process, as constructors of truth, but as conduits through which truth emerges" (p. 69). Truth takes on a relativist perspective; it is different for each person and depends on one's own point of view.

As we read what these women have to say about their sense of self, we realize they feel fragile and vulnerable. They talk about longing for escape and release; they feel lonely, alienated, isolated and distant from others. They express feelings of rebellion, that they find reasoning stifling and do not trust it. They have a general distrust of "logic, analysis, even language itself" (p. 71) but in a prejudicial way. Their antirationalist attitudes come from a perspective of not knowing reason well. It is as if they are developing an emergent sense of self and sense of agency and control, and they do not want reason to come along and steal their voice away.

This description reminds us of what can happen between students and teachers in a classroom. Students will often refuse to submit their thoughts to the scrutiny of the class, not answering the teacher's questions. They fear people will make fun of what they say, not listen well, misunderstand, or show the flaws in their young and undeveloped thoughts. So, instead of venturing into the public world, students keep their thoughts private. A subjective knower sounds like a child who has learned she or he has a perspective but has not yet realized that everyone does. Nor has the child realized that one is entitled to a perspective, and no one can take it away. The child also has not realized that everyone's perspective is partial and potentially flawed, for people are all contextual beings.

Subjective knowers are becoming conscious of the workings of their own minds. And if Noddings and Shore are right that intuition and reason struggle against each other, in the development and expression of our personal voices (our

Wills), then perhaps subjective knowers are learning about their intuitive side, at the expense of their reasoning side. (Belenky et al. label this reasoning approach "procedural knowing." Others have called it "critical thinking"; see the later section "Critical Thinking Theory.") Ironically, we learn we have a self, a voice, by interacting with others and finding out others do not see or experience the world in the same way we do. Learning that we have a voice can make us feel isolated and disconnected from people and other living beings. If we pull away from others because we fear having our voice silenced or we feel a loss of voice or confusion about our voice in the chaos and din of other voices, we will feel more isolated and separated from others. To try to strengthen our subjective personal voices, we lose connections with the outside world of others and lose our public voices.

To construct quilts of knowledge, each quilter must begin with a personal voice, a Will that motivates one to quilt at all. The development of intuition helps each of us hear our own voices more clearly. But we learn who we are with the help of other voices. As we learned in Chapter 2, knowledge does not start as something personal and private, or it would not be possible to reach out and communicate one's knowledge with others. We begin with a public language, and then internalize it to create our own. We then develop our own voice, but each of us can only grow and develop so far on our own. Our own contextuality and partiality limit our potential for growth. People need others to help see, hear, think, and feel more. Also, people need to be able to contribute their voices back into the conversation with others. Just as an individual's growth is limited and needs interactions with others to enlarge it, communities are limited in their growth and need unique voices added to their conversations to enlarge their views.

Constructive Knowledge. What distinguishes a constructive knower from a subjective knower, according to Belenky et al., is that the constructive knower attempts to integrate her personal voice and public voice. A constructive thinker knows she has a point of view and has grown comfortable with that knowledge. She no longer fears that others may take her voice away from her, nor does she worry that her voice is not perfect and seems unclear at times. She has learned to live with ambiguity and internal contradiction and with conflict, trusting that her knowledge will continue to grow and improve. She no longer fears reason but has learned to use it to help her construct knowledge, just as she has learned to use her intuition to help her. She no longer tries to rid herself of her voice, as procedural knowers (critical thinkers, in the traditional model) do, for she knows this is impossible. Instead, she gathers great strength and enthusiasm from knowing that she, like anyone else, has the opportunity to contribute to knowledge.

As we will see, other critical thinking theorists have allowed that one's subjective, personal voice contributes to the construction of knowledge, but they have only done so in a negative way, to point out how one's voice can lead one astray or cause one not to attend to necessary information (see especially Paul, 1990; Siegel, 1988). They have not acknowledged that, like it or not, we cannot get rid of our personal voices. Our personal voices do contribute to knowledge, which is true for each of us, even hard-core scientists or logicians. Rather than viewing **personal voice, or the Will, the soul, "the dynamic center of self" and "the heart of being"** (as described by Noddings and Shore, 1984, p. 59), as negative or good, we need to realize that 'personal voice' just is. It is us, what each of us is, what each of us has to give to the world.

Imagination

We have learned so far that all of us, as inquirers, or quilters contributing to quilts of knowledge, evolve a personal voice and use reasoning and intuition to help us. Our personal voice is what we use to express ourselves, but it is also what limits our expressions. How do we learn to envision the world in new ways? How do we gain insight into how others perceive the world and how others perceive us? We will find in the skills section of this chapter that communication skills and relational skills help us gain insight into ourselves and others. But being able to communicate and relate to others depends on us being able to use our tools of imagination, intuition, and emotional feelings. With this in mind, we need to turn to a further exploration of the creative, imaginative, intuitive sides of inquiry, by focusing on imagination.

What Others Have Said about Imagination Many consider creative thinking as free and imaginative thinking that relies on tools such as intuition and the use of one's emotional feelings. In contrast, critical thinking is presented as analytical, logical thinking that is used to evaluate the worth of creative ideas. However, Sharon Bailin (1988) describes critical thinking at its finest as creativity, our means for achieving extraordinary ends. Rather than connecting creativity "with arbitrary novelty, irrational processes, or rule-breaking," she connects it with "significant achievement viewed as a product of skills, rules and rational processes" (p. 109). Bailin presents the case that imagination and skills gained from knowledge, rules, and methods of inquiry are intimately connected. She agrees that imagination is "crucial for creative achievement" but describes the two as "closely interconnected, with imagination manifested in the execution of skill and skill involved in the development of an imaginative vision" (p. 109). As our skills further develop, so does our ability to express what we imagine and to interpret those expressions to others.

Critical thinking helps us define and redefine our tasks. Many have described it as the tool that limits our visions and encourages us to only see the world in fixed ways, but without some sort of tool to help us decide what to leave in and what to leave out, an ordering, straightening sort of tool, it is difficult to imagine how we would be creative. What may be a problem for us, which does begin to affect our abilities to be creative, is when we stop seeing critical thinking as a tool and think it is more than that. What can help us keep critical thinking in perspective? One idea is to highlight other tools we have available to help us think creatively, such as our emotional feelings and our intuitions, as we are doing here.

Gregory Bateson (1991) describes how "logic is a very poor model of the world of mental process" because it is linear and breaks down when confronted with paradoxes of abstraction (p. 204). Bateson sees systems as circular and self-corrective, and he begins to look at what happens when learning-to-learn is disrupted. Critical thinking may help us see the form and pattern in the living world, but we must be very careful to notice the feedback we receive that does not fit the theories we develop for explaining the living world, or critical thinking may become a limiting, harmful tool instead of a helpful tool.

The disruptions in patterns, the differences, are what inspired Bateson's "double-bind theory." Instead of focusing on the products of knowledge, he focuses on the process. He describes the symmetrical and complementary relationships of the world, the integrating dance of an "ecology of mind." Where did Bateson find his inspiration to see new forms and patterns in the world? He worked with other cultures, schizophrenics, dolphins, alcoholics, and computers (cybernetics). He found inspiration in steam engines (the governor), "scismogenesis" (evolutionary change), and Lewis Carroll's paradoxes in "Alice in Wonderland" (such as the bread-and-butter fly and the game of croquet with flamingos as mallets and hedgehogs as the balls).

Elizabeth Minnich (1990) uses what she calls "a spiraling logic," not to compel agreement but to invite it. She searches for touchstones, not conclusions, and tries to create an open space for thinking and modes of knowing. Like Bateson, Minnich points to the paradoxes and faulty generalizations we have created. She also uses stories like "Alice in Wonderland" and "The Emperor's New Clothes" to help create open spaces. She seeks serious engagement with differences and points out how "[b]oth absolutism and radical relativism make it possible, even necessary, to avoid serious engagement with differences" (p. 167). Her goal "is not necessarily to undo all universals and the very idea of universals. It is to particularize accurately, to demystify the functions of power and hierarchy . . . it is false universals, faulty and mystifying abstractions, that concern us" (pp. 180–181).

Evelyn Fox Keller (1985) describes how the Nobel Prize–winning genetic scientist, Barbara McClintock, respects difference and complexity. McClintock does not discard what does not fit into our logically patterned world; she tries to figure out why it does not fit and is challenged by the material to find "the larger multidimensional pattern into which it does fit" (p. 164). As McClintock views nature, "the complexity of nature exceeds our own imaginative possibilities" (p. 162). Like Gregory Bateson, McClintock describes how she focused on the function and organization (how genes function in relation to the cell) rather than on mechanics and structure, as other geneticists were doing. She looked for a bigger picture; she tried to understand the process.

McClintock kept in mind that critical thinking and logic are just tools. She saw how we tend to forget this by trying to impose our view on the material we are studying rather than letting the material tell us (p. 162). She saw as arrogance how philosophers and scientists try to structure and order, straighten and discard, what does not seem to fit. McClintock "listens to the material" (p. 176). She describes her studying of plants as a relationship where she strives to respect difference by attending to that othering. As Keller reports, "In the relationship she [McClintock] describes with plants, as in human relations, respect for difference constitutes a claim not only on our interest but on our capacity for empathy—in short on the highest form of love: love that allows for intimacy without the annihilation of difference" (p. 164).

Mary Catherine Bateson (1989) recommends that "[w]e need to sustain creativity with a new and richer sense of complementarity and interdependence," that we need to reject forced choices, embrace multiplicity, and accept ambiguity and asymmetry (p. 114). She points out how we tend to see difference as weakness or discrimination. We seek equality (symmetry) and sameness rather than compassion. We view someone as wise if she or he is focused and has a singular purpose, but Bateson suggests that multiple commitments and interests, having the capacity to be distracted and divided, actually offer ways to open our attention.

If we think of critical thinking as being like straight pins helping us order things and put them in place, we can also think of critical thinking pins as holding something in place while we allow ourselves to be distracted and interrupted, knowing that when we come back to our thinking, we will be able to see where we left off. Because our attention was pulled in a different direction, when we come back, we may see what we were working on in a new way. We may see something that before missed our attention.

In *Peripheral Visions,* Bateson (1994) helps us imagine a new vision of learning through participation in new and unfamiliar experiences. Seeking new experiences helps us open our minds/hearts/souls to the world, for each situation offers multiple interpretations. Some of these interpretations are obvious, but some are at the edge of our awareness, "seen through peripheral vision." Bateson suggests, just as her father Gregory did, that rather than seeing difference as a weakness or problem, we need to try to see it as a source of strength. Rather than trying to shape the world purposely, our mode of action needs to be one of response. It is not enough just to develop our abilities to reason, though important. A willingness to be distracted and interrupted, to explore our imaginations, intuitions, and emotional feelings, as well as develop our skills to communicate and relate with others and the world around us, helps us learn how to be receptive and attentive and opens us up to seeing the world in new ways.

Maxine Greene (1995) has made her career in philosophy of education centered around imagination and the arts. She uses characters from novels as examples and metaphors to help illustrate her points, defending the value of literature as a source for understanding since she began her career. Greene argues in *Releasing the Imagination* that "imagination is what, above all, makes empathy possible. . . . [I]magination is the one [cognitive capacity] that permits us to give credence to alternative realities" (p. 3). We use our imagination to open new possibilities, break through barriers, and help us be surprised by the unexpected. Our imagination helps "decenter us" and keep us wide awake and aware, intensifying our realizations and reminding us that what we know is provisional and temporary. As Greene describes her method of provisional interpretations, "All we can do, I believe, is cultivate multiple ways of seeing and multiple dialogues in a world where nothing stays the same" (p. 16).

Unlike Maxine Greene, who has looked to art and literature over her entire career, John Dewey (1934/1958) turned to art as a way of describing experience late in his career. He was greatly disturbed with how art had been removed from life and experience and placed on a pedestal. It is through experiences that art is created. He described how balance and harmony are attained through rhythm, and "form is arrived at whenever a stable, even though moving, equilibrium is reached" (p. 14). However, to have aesthetic quality, we need flux and rest, disturbance and harmony. Tools like critical thinking, intuition, and emotional feelings help us achieve harmony (symmetry) and stir us into creative action and redescription (asymmetry).

Like Barbara McClintock and Mary Catherine Bateson, Dewey believes, "The esthetic or undergoing phase of experience is receptive. It involves surrender" (p. 53). He describes imagination in terms of process:

> It is a way of seeing and feeling things as they compose an integral whole. It is the large and generous blending of interests at the point where the mind comes in contact with the world. When old and familiar things are made new in experience, there is imagination. . . . Philosophy is said to begin in wonder and end in understanding. Art departs from what has been understood and ends in wonder. (p. 270)

According to Dewey, "Art is the living and concrete proof that man [*sic*] is capable of restoring consciously, and thus on the plane of meaning, the union of sense, need, impulse and action characteristic of the live creature" (p. 25).

What have some of our most creative people taught us, in terms of imagination and its role in constructing knowledge? They do have some advice that we can sum up for teachers and future teachers:

- Skills, rules, methods, and knowledge are directly connected to imagination and creativity.
- Critical thinking may help us see the form and pattern in the living world, but we must be very careful to notice the feedback we receive that does not fit the theories we develop for explaining the living world.

What methods will help students learn to reenvision and redescribe our world? If teachers take the advice of some of our most creative people, it appears that many suggestions can be made:

- Respect difference. Be interested and empathetic, listen to the material, so that we can attempt to understand difference rather than destroy it.
- Reject forced choices, embrace multiplicity, and accept ambiguity and asymmetry.
- Focus on the process.
- Create open spaces by seeking new experiences and allowing ourselves to be divided and distracted at times.
- Look for a bigger picture; develop a new and richer sense of complementarity and interdependence.

Many philosophers and scientists say that they have their creative ideas when they are not working. They develop their skills, further their knowledge base, and become very adept at higher-order thinking. They study problems and develop questions, which they then research and test for possible solutions. But often the solution is not what they thought it would be, and their answers to their problems are found other than in the lab or library. Archimedes found the answer to his problem in the bathtub. Newton found his answer when he was lying under an apple tree. Einstein was in an elevator. Many of our most creative thinkers say they have developed their imaginations through playful activities (re-creational activities).

We would like to suggest that encouraging play is a vital method for furthering creativity, as vital as developing reasoning skills. Play offers the opportunity for the kinds of suggestions recommended to emerge. Play opens spaces and helps us be able to look for bigger pictures. It encourages us to focus on the process, the playing, rather than the product, for we find that if we do not enjoy the process, we no longer want to play. When we play games, for example, we understand the value of rules, for they allow us to play the game and have others be able to play with us. But we can also understand that although rules in a game supply us with a framework and a common language, they also are always a source of friction with players, for there is room for different interpretations of the rules and differing perspectives of what occurs as the players play. Sometimes rules need to be adapted and changed, and sometimes the framework is transcended and new games are created.

As authors, we find ourselves continually searching for metaphors to help us with our reenvisioning and redescribing efforts. The more we are willing to play, the better we can understand how to explain what we are trying to say. The more we allow ourselves to explore other areas of knowledge (e.g., anthropology, sociology, women's studies, literature, the arts) and experience the world in new ways, the more we come back to our issues of concern with a fresh perspective. The more we allow ourselves to go off in directions that may seem to be interruptions, embracing multiplicity, the more we can see interconnections and patterns and overlaps. Our imaginations challenge us and disrupt us, even getting us to attempt to "think about the unthinkable," as researchers such as Deborah Britzman (1995) are trying to do with work in Queer Theory.

This is how we hope the metaphor or a quilting bee is functioning in this chapter. Imagination plays a clear role in quilting. Quilters are often limited on what they will be able to create by such factors as time, size, and available materials. But there is still great room for creative expression. Using our imagination helps us create quilts of knowledge we will continue to enjoy and see in new ways for years to come.

How does imagination help us be empathetic of others? What role do our emotional feelings play in the quilting of knowledge? Let us turn to this tool now for a closer look at the role it plays.

Emotional Feelings

Alison Jaggar (1992), in "Love and Knowledge: Emotion in Feminist Epistemology," points out that a "gap" exists between reason and emotions. She traces this gap all the way back to Plato and the ancient Greeks. She uses her article as a way of beginning to bridge this gap "through the suggestion that emotions may be helpful and even necessary rather than inimical to the construction of knowledge" (p. 146).

What are emotions? As Jaggar uses the term, **emotions** is distinguished from **feelings**, which describes "automatic physical responses and nonintentional sensations, such as hunger pains" (p. 148). Feelings are all the sensations we experience physically, such as pain when we are bumped into, coldness when a blast of cold air blows in our faces, or wetness when we go for a swim. Most of us, in our daily conversations, use the word *feelings* to stand for physical sensations that are automatic responses and nonintentional as well as for such things as "like," "love," "hate," or "fear," what Jaggar defines as emotions. When we equate emotions to feelings, Jaggar warns that we risk denying that emotions have **intention**. Because people are so used to using the terms interchangeably, we have decided to use the term **emotional feelings** to describe **feelings that are intentional**.

One of the very interesting points Jaggar makes is that "at least some emotions are historically or culturally specific" (p. 150). What this means is that we learn about emotional feelings and the having of them through our contextual lives, the setting into which we are born and the people who surround us. Emotions are in part socially constructed, historical products. "[T]here are complex linguistic and other social preconditions for the . . . existence of human emotions" (p. 150). Even though emotional feelings are not completely within our control, they have intrinsic and instrumental value. Emotional feelings are necessary for human survival, for they prompt us to act appropriately. We use our emotional feelings as "ways in which we engage actively and even construct the world. They have both mental and physical aspects . . . in some respects they are chosen, but in others they are involuntary; they presuppose language and a social order" (pp. 152–153).

We can understand the historical and cultural influences on emotions when we notice that people from warmer climate zones, such as the Mediterranean and Caribbean areas, are viewed as being more emotional and people from colder climate zones, such as England and Scandinavia, are considered less emotional. We can see socially constructed influences on emotional feelings when we consider these from a gendered angle as well. In some cultures (e.g., Spain, Italy, Puerto Rico), boys and men are encouraged to express their emotions, and it is not unusual to see them crying or yelling when they are upset, whereas girls and women are encouraged to express themselves in a more reserved manner. In other cultures, such as the United Sates, the reverse is true, as Americans tolerate little girls, even women, crying but belittle boys and men for expressing emotional feelings.

Jaggar reminds us that children are taught by their social community appropriate ways of expressing emotions recognized by their culture. "By forming our emotional constitution in particular ways, our society helps to ensure its own perpetuation" (p. 159). Emotional feelings presuppose values, and values presuppose emotional feelings. We can see this in examples of cultural views on romantic love. "In some cultures, romantic love does not exist at all" (p. 151). When an emotional feeling does not exist in a culture or is discouraged from being expressed, this limits or "blinds us to the possibility of alternative ways of living" (p. 159). This hegemony on emotional feelings that our culture holds over us is incomplete, though. People may experience emotional feelings that our culture has not sanctioned. Jaggar calls these unsanctioned emotional feelings "outlaw emotions" (p. 160). People who express emotional feelings that their culture has outlawed find themselves facing serious repercussions, such as being labeled effeminate, queer, weird, or just plain crazy. However, outlaw emotional feelings also serve to motivate new investigations and change our perceptions.

Although our emotional feelings may help us understand others' perspectives, they may also limit our understandings because what we feel emotionally is so affected by the context of the settings in which we have grown up. "Emotions are only partially within our control as individuals" (p. 163). Jaggar relates the embeddedness of emotional feelings to how they affect our views of each other as well as observations that we think are not affected by emotions. Positivist science in the Western world has presented the scientist as a dispassionate, unemotional observer of events that are carefully recorded and reported. However, we are beginning to realize that emotional feelings and values are logically and conceptually connected; "certain emotional attitudes are involved on a deep level in all observation, in the intersubjectively verified and so supposedly dispassionate observations of science as well as in the common perceptions of daily life" (p. 154). The model of the scientist as being a dispassionate investigator is a myth. In fact, emotional feelings are necessary to the possibility of reliable knowledge, for our emotional feelings are "neither more basic than observation, reason, or action in building theory, nor are they secondary to them" (p. 165). They are inseparable from the other tools we have been describing that we use in quilting knowledge.

Does this mean all emotional feelings are good or that our emotional feelings are epistemologically indisputable? No. For example, fear and hatred close us down from furthering our understandings, for they limit our willingness to be self-reflective. Like all the tools available for our use, emotional feelings can be misleading and self-deceptive, especially because they are so contextually bound. Even as we become more aware of our emotional feelings and how they affect our knowing, because emotions are not completely in our control and are so habituated to how we respond and negotiate our ways through the world, what we have learned is not easily unlearned. Jaggar suggests that rather than trying to suppress our unwanted and unwelcome emotional feelings, we should acknowledge them and critically examine them. "We can only start from where we are" and strive to be self-reflective, recognizing "that our efforts to reinterpret and refine our emotions are necessary to our theoretical investigation[s]" (p. 164).

Do we continually rely on any particular emotional feelings to help us in our inquiring efforts as we strive to quilt knowledge? We think so. Jaggar focuses on a purified form of "love" as being necessary for knowledge. She refers us to female scientists such as Jane Goodall (chimpanzees) and Barbara McClintock (genetic work with corn) and how they describe their inquiry as requiring affection, kinship, and empathy. Because of all the negative connotations associated with "love" as being an emotional feeling that biases us and blinds us from clear understanding, we would like to point to the emotional feeling of "caring." Many might argue that *caring* as a term is no better than *love*. As we begin our description of caring as a vital emotional feeling for inquiry to take place, we want to acknowledge that our "care" is probably not very different from Jaggar's pure form of "love."

What is caring, and how does it function as an emotional feeling that helps us in our efforts to inquire? We have seen how Noddings defines caring in terms of being receptive and feeling with the other (other people, other life forms, or even inanimate objects). We also have found out that Noddings does not describe caring in terms of "empathy," for empathy can be taken to mean a projecting of oneself onto others. For her, caring is a move away from the self toward being attentive to and receptive of the other.

Joan Tronto (1989) has also written about caring, and her views will help clarify some issues with this emotional feeling (see also Tronto, 1993). Tronto takes issue with Noddings's suggestion that caring occurs with abstract ideas as well as with living beings. She points to the original English meaning of "care" as a burden; to care implies an ongoing responsibility and commitment. "If caring involves a commitment, then caring must have an object. Thus caring is necessarily relational" (p. 173). So far Noddings would agree with Tronto. However, Tronto's next move is to distinguish between "caring about" and "caring for." She makes this distinction based on the objects of care, arguing that "caring about" refers to objects that are more abstract, like ideas and jobs, whereas "caring for" refers to "a specific, particular object that is the focus of caring. . . . Caring for involves responding to the particular, concrete, physical, spiritual, intellectual, psychic, and emotional needs of others" (p. 174). Tronto presents the case that "traditional gender roles in our society imply that men care about but women care for" (p. 174).

Why make this kind of distinction between "caring about" and "caring for"? Tronto's reason is to make the case that the **activity** of "caring for" others is a moral act. As such, it is deserving of our attention and efforts to broaden our understanding "of what caring for others means, both in terms of the moral questions it raises and in terms of the need to restructure broader social and political institutions if caring for others is to be made a more central part of the everyday lives of everyone in society" (p. 184). She believes that by making this distinction, she reveals more about caring and traditional assumptions of gender difference. Noddings also distinguishes between "caring about" and "caring for"—however, not to draw our attention to social norms of gender roles but rather to get to the carer's degree of commitment. Unlike Tronto, Noddings wishes to claim that we can care for ideas. Both Noddings and Tronto write to convince us that caring is worth serious consideration. What we are trying to argue is that their commitments and efforts, their caring about "caring," is due to emotional feelings that they have.

Noddings and Tronto write about caring in the context of ethics. They do not examine caring from an epistemological angle, as Jaggar and Thayer-Bacon do. Yet, their focus on caring and valuing of "it" as a research topic have epistemological results. Emotional feelings such as caring affect us, as quilters of knowledge, because our emotional feelings help us choose what questions we want to address and try to understand. They also affect how we address those questions. Emotional feelings such as caring are what motivate and inspire us. They are what make us feel unsettled and troubled about issues and problems. They are what make us feel excited and give us the desire to carry on with our efforts to understand. Emotional feelings stir us up and bring us to the quilting frame, desiring to construct a quilt of knowledge. They are also expressed through the colors we select, the feelings we have about the topic and how we choose to approach our expression of knowledge. In the movie *How to Make an American Quilt,* the friends of a woman about to get married are making a wedding quilt as a gift for her. Love is the emotional feeling that motivates them to start quilting. And the theme of love is expressed by each woman in a different quilted square, expressing their emotional feelings about love through the colors they use, the designs they create, the stories they strive to tell.

As we pointed out in Chapter 1, by caring, we do not mean caring for another person, such as liking or loving someone. **For us 'care' simply means the ability to be receptive and open to others' ideas and willing to attend to them, to listen and consider their possibilities.** Care does **not** entail that a person like or agree with the others' ideas. Care does mean a person is open to possibly hearing the other's voice more completely and fairly. To put this definition of caring into concrete terms, when you, the reader, chose to read this book, an expression of care occurred; you deemed this topic of value and interest to you, worthy of your close inspection, and you have agreed to be present and attending to these words, generously hoping that the book will be one of value to you. In the process of choosing to occupy yourself with this book, you have also become more acquainted with us, the authors.

Our position is that without caring, one cannot hope to be a good constructive thinker. Caring is necessary to be sure that ideas have been fairly considered and understood. Critical thinking is also necessary to be a good constructive thinker. So are the skills of communication and relationality. All of these together help quilters of knowledge be constructive thinkers (as described in this chapter). These skills are intertwined and affect each other, but we will try to pull them apart so that we can examine them more carefully. Of course, the goal is to better understand them so that as teachers we can help our students develop and improve on these skills, therefore helping our students, and ourselves as teachers, be better quilters of knowledge.

Skills for Quilting

Caring and Critical Thinking

As we are beginning to understand, a problem with traditional models of critical thinking has been the focus on the logical thought process, at the exclusion of emotional feelings, intuition, and imagination. These subjective qualities have been judged to be misleading, and the critical thinker has been advised to attempt the exclusion of subjective qualities such as emotional feelings from rational arguments, although rational passions have been allowed (see, e.g., Peters, 1971). We have found it is true that some emotions can get in the way of good critical thinking. For example, anger can stop a discussion, or fear can keep someone from even expressing reasons to defend a position, or love can cause someone to overlook an important flaw in an argument. But other emotions, such as caring, are necessary to help one be a good critical thinker.

An underlying problem is the notion that people, critical thinkers, can divorce themselves from these subjective qualities such as their emotional feelings and just think. When a person chooses to think, one does not just think but thinks about something or other. One responds to a concern, ponders a question or a nagging doubt, because one is feeling something. One feels disquietude, interest, intrigue. If one is just adding up sums, balancing a checkbook, or averaging grades, the thinking is pretty mechanical and step-by-step. But this would not be considered critical thinking. Critical thinking is used when doubts, concerns, and problems arise, reasons need to be sought, and possible solutions need to be sought. As soon as a person needs to do this kind of thinking, subjective qualities such as emotional feelings come into play. This is because the person has to make judgments and decisions, choosing which facts to attend to and which ones to leave out. The person has to rely on caring.

Critical Thinking Theory

Critical thinking is what philosophers have always depended on as their main tool for reasoning and attempting to find truths. It has been presented as **thinking that relies on skills such as doubting, questioning, comparing and contrasting, judging**. Since the days of Aristotle, with his categorizing of knowledge and systemizing ways of judging arguments through logic, critical thinking has been designed as a process based in logic where facts are separated from opinion. The process of critical thinking has been viewed as one in which the critical thinker remains objective, distanced from what is being examined. The hoped result of using critical thinking has been to be able to find Truth and, since the days of Descartes, Certainty.

More recent changes in critical thinking theory have shown that being a good critical thinker does not involve just having mastered **logical skills** but also having the **disposition** to use those skills. One can better understand this change by taking a closer look at critical thinking theory as it is currently being expressed, by Robert Ennis and Richard Paul. As we do, we will examine whether caring is considered a necessary ingredient. Then we will compare these theories with the notion of constructive thinking.

Robert Ennis Robert Ennis is usually credited as rekindling the current interest in critical thinking, with an article he wrote for *The Harvard Educational Review* in 1962 titled "A Concept of Critical Thinking." He originally defined critical thinking as "the correct assessing of statements" (p. 83). The focus of this article was to identify 12 aspects and three dimensions of critical thinking and elaborate a system of criteria to be applied in this form of thinking. The goal behind identifying aspects of critical thinking is to avoid making errors and to enable us to assess statements correctly. His list of proficiencies is the most detailed, complex, and useful to be developed.

In 1987 Ennis revised his definition of critical thinking, in response to criticism, to "**reasonable reflective thinking that is focused on deciding what to believe or do**" (p. 10). This definition is not meant to exclude creative thinking, but the focus is on critical thinking as a practical activity, with reasonable belief or action as its goal. Ennis still focuses on listing 14 dispositions and 12 basic types of abilities required of a critical thinker. This newer definition includes abilities and dispositions, rather than just abilities, as his earlier article seemed to suggest, to ensure that it is not enough just to have the necessary skills to be a critical thinker; one must also have the tendency to use these skills.

Does one find reference to caring as a necessary disposition in Ennis's description of critical thinking? His list of dispositions a critical thinker must have include: seek a clear statement of the thesis or question; seek reasons; try to be well informed; use and mention credible sources; take into account the total situation; try to remain relevant to the main point; keep in mind the original and/or basic concern; look for alternatives; be open-minded (defined as using dispositional thinking, dialogical thinking, withholding judgment if the evidence and reasons are insufficient); take a position (and change a position) when the evidence and reasons are sufficient to do so; seek as much precision as the subject permits; deal in an orderly manner with the parts of a complex whole; use one's critical thinking abilities; and be sensitive to the feelings, level of knowledge, and degree of sophistication of others. This last disposition, being sensitive to feelings, sounds like it could involve caring, from Ennis's point of view, until one looks for further clarification and finds "The 14th disposition, to be sensitive to others, although not strictly speaking constitutive of critical thinking, is important for any critical thinker. Without it, critical thinking often comes to naught" (p. 16). For Ennis, being sensitive to feelings does not help one be a better critical thinker but helps one be able to use the results of one's own critical thinking successfully. Ennis offers no further explanation of these dispositions except to say that they are essential for the critical thinker (p. 16).

Ennis's list of abilities required for a critical thinker are of the logical sort: focusing on a question, analyzing arguments, asking and answering questions of clarification and/or challenge, judging the credibility of a source, observing and judging observation reports, deducing and judging deductions, inducing and judging inductions, making value judgments, defining terms and judging definitions in three dimensions, identifying assumptions, deciding on an action, interacting with others (in terms of employing and reacting to fallacy labels, logical strategies, rhetorical strategies, argumentation) (pp. 12–15).

In contrast, for constructive thinkers, as we are describing here, knowledge of themselves and their perspectives, and awareness of their own contingent situatedness and how it has affected their views, are just as important as reasoning skills. Knowing what they bring to the conversation and that they affect the knowledge that is being developed is empowering and humbling for constructive thinkers. They try to "open their hearts and minds to embrace the world" (Belenky et al., 1986, p. 141). They try to share who they are with others as well as listen attentively, with sympathy, openness, and care, to their stories. One could say that constructive thinkers attempt to commune with others they are trying to understand and gain knowledge from; that communion is a real exchange, with valued contributions being made from all involved in the epistemic experience. Constructive thinkers attempt to believe the other(s) to make sure understanding has taken place before they use their critical thinking skills (as Ennis has presented them) to doubt and critique. The judging and assessing is a vital part of constructive thinking, but so is the caring and the awareness of one's own personal voice (Belenky et al., 1986).

We can anticipate problems with Ennis's list of characteristics. His focus is on logical skills, and the abilities he mentions are ones most of us would consider to be abilities required of a logical thinker. But where is mention of the need to know oneself and what one contributes to the knowing? Where is the mention of emotional feelings and relational skills that are necessary to help open not just one's mind but also one's heart to the world, including objects and other people? Where is the mention of emotional feelings and a need to be caring? If caring, being open and receptive to others' ideas and willing to attend to what another has to say before passing judgment and doubting or critiquing others' ideas, is really a necessary ingredient for critical thinking, we should be able to find caring in Ennis's description, though maybe in a hidden or disguised form. Here is where we think it is hiding within his list of dispositions: seek reasons; try to be well informed; take into account the total situation; look for alternatives; be open-minded; be sensitive to the feelings, level of knowledge, and degree of sophistication of others.

To seek reasons, a person has to make decisions concerning what to attend to and what not, which opens the door for emotional feelings. What should I be engrossed with and be receptive to, and what can I afford to discard or leave out? In trying to be well informed, constructive thinkers must be aware of the fact they will reach a place where they feel that they have enough information, and they should be cautious and concerned when they reach that place. Do they really have enough? Have they informed themselves as much as possible, or have they neglected something because they deemed it not valuable or important, worthy of their care? Taking into account the total situation is another way of saying "Try to be well informed of the context and not leave anything out; try to be concerned and attentive to all you can." It could also mean "Be aware of your own voice and what you bring to the epistemic experience."

Looking for alternatives is a way of warning constructive thinkers that they need to stretch their concept of what they deem important or worth attending to, not to look just for the obvious. And being open-minded certainly can be redescribed as involving caring, for it means being willing to enter into dialogue and conversation with others, being careful to respect them and value their contributions to the discussion. To be open-minded one must try to be generous and inclusive, both of which are qualities of caring as defined earlier. Finally, though Ennis says being sensitive to the feelings, level of knowledge, and degree of sophistication of others is "not strictly speaking constitutive of critical thinking," this quality certainly fits the description of a constructive thinker (Ennis, 1987, p. 16). For Ennis, these qualities help ensure success for the critical thinker, but we hope you are beginning to see that being sensitive to others' feelings can also mean that the critical thinker has deemed the others important and that the others might have some valuable insight to offer and should be considered part of the process itself, not just the outcome of it.

Richard Paul   Richard Paul (1990) calls attention to the possibility of degrees or levels of critical thinking, one that is weak and one that is strong. Weak-sense critical thinking is "disciplined to serve the interests of a particular individual or group, to the exclusion of their relevant persons and groups," and strong-sense critical thinking is "disciplined to take into account the interests of diverse persons or groups" (see Paul's glossary). With Paul's distinction between weak- and strong-sense critical thinking, he makes us very aware that saying one is or is not a critical thinker, as other theorists have tended to emphasize, is incorrect, or at least insufficient. One can use critical thinking skills just to find fault with others' arguments and support for one's own, or one can use those same skills to attempt to understand others' points of view more clearly and to reflect on one's own point of view more critically.

Paul points out the need for a critical thinker to have a certain disposition, indeed, have certain character traits, such as intellectual humility and suspending judgment, intellectual courage and good faith or integrity, and intellectual perseverance and confidence in reason (p. 307). We saw that Ennis made changes in his definition to include dispositions, maybe in response to Paul's point. Central to Paul's theory is the notion that people by nature are egocentric and ethnocentric and that our tendency is to be irrational; we have to work very hard to be rational, critical thinkers—it does not come easily.[4]

A problem with Paul's distinction between weak- and strong-sense critical thinking is confusion about what he means by strong-sense critical thinking. Weak-sense critical thinking, because it is by definition not consistently being applied to one's own thinking, would not be labeled critical thinking by other theorists. With strong-sense critical thinking, at times Paul stresses a combative approach to critical thinking that follows the more traditional paradigm. At other times he stresses a nurturing, supportive approach to critical thinking that leans in the direction we favor, by taking into account feelings and what the knower brings to the knowing. Paul's more traditional version of strong-sense critical thinking leaves one always feeling like one has begged the question; hedging occurs because of uncertainty that one has ever thought strongly enough. This version of strong-sense critical thinking functions best as an ideal, which Paul recommends. (This version of strong-sense critical thinking can be compared with Belenky et al.'s separate procedural knowing, discussed later.)

Paul's more nurturing strong-sense critical thinking, in emphasizing the need to understand other people's perspectives and worldviews, leans in the direction of relationships and caring. It leans toward stressing interconnections, related-ness, and qualified relativism. (This version can be compared with Belenky et al.'s connected procedural knowing, discussed later.) One can find the possibility of a constructive thinking perspective, and the need for caring, in Paul's critical thinking theory, as he describes it himself. Though he does not use the term *caring,* he calls attention to the need for including diverse voices and believing the strongest version of another's perspective before dismissing it. His focus is on being fair-minded and open-minded, and the caring that we are describing as an essential ingredient of good critical thinkers is exactly the quality that makes it possible for one to be open-minded and fair.

Another problem with Paul's theory, and what ends up getting in the way of his recognizing thinkers as constructive knowers, is his notion of the self. Paul recognizes the thinker's subjectivity in a negative way. For Paul, our natural tendency is to be egocentric, meaning self-centered, and to use reasons to score points, defeat others, and make our own point of view look good. The fact that we have perspectives ultimately makes us selfish and just gets in our way. His distinction between weak- and strong-sense critical thinking focuses on whether the skills of critical thinking are used to support one's own position, and these remain extrinsic to one's character or, if these skills become intrinsic to one's character, are used to add insight into one's own affective and cognitive processes. Paul's stress is on removing the self from the critical thinking process, to try to understand others' points of views fairly and to apply the same critical thinking skills on ourselves that we use to judge others' positions.

It is easy to anticipate a constructive thinker's response to Paul's theory—that in trying to remove oneself and understand others' standpoints, one will end up "feeling like a chameleon," able to remove one's own voice to understand others' but losing, or at least weakening, one's own identity in the process (Belenky et al.'s terms). Also, a postmodernist would add that removing the voice is impossible. Whereas Paul is concerned with the development of strong-sense critical thinkers, our concern is for the development of constructive thinkers as members in rational, caring communities. **Constructive thinkers are doubters and believers, much like Paul's strong-sense critical thinkers. And they are feelers as well as thinkers; they think with their hearts and minds. They also know by use of their personal voice**.

As can be seen from the small survey of some current critical thinking theories presented here, including personal voice and emotional feelings in a model of critical thinking has been attempted. Learning logical, rational skills is not enough; one must recognize that critical thinkers are people, and as people they need to have the disposition to use their critical thinking skills, to be good critical thinkers. The recognition of personal voice and emotional feelings has been made in an attempt to show the problems they can create for a consistent, strong-sense critical thinker. We are presenting the case that personal voices are developed through social relationships with others and are all we really have.

The distinction between an inner, subjective, personal, feeling voice and outer, objective, expert, reasoning voice is not nearly so sharp as traditional critical thinking theories, even modern ones such as Ennis's and Paul's, would have us believe. In the end, these theories still rest on an epistemic paradigm that can be traced back to the Greek models discussed in Chapter 2. Arguments such as Rorty's and Noddings's push us to embrace a new perspective on knowledge, like the one we argued for in Chapter 2, that is relational and relies on emotional feelings as much as thoughts, subjective voice as much as objective voice.

Constructive Thinking Theory

We discussed Belenky et al.'s "subjective knowing" and "constructive knowing" in our earlier discussion on intuition. Let us turn to their *Women's Ways of Knowing* again for some insight on how emotional feelings (in particular, caring) relate to critical thinking. We already know what the five epistemological categories Belenky et al. (1986, p. 15) present are. Of these five categories, the two we wish to examine more carefully are procedural knowledge and then again constructed knowledge.

For Belenky et al., procedural knowledge, or reasoned reflection, is **the voice of reason**. It is a humbler, softer, more powerful voice. Procedural knowers seek to understand other people's ideas in the other people's terms rather than in their own terms. Procedural knowers believe intuitions may deceive; they can be irresponsible or fallible. They also believe some truths are truer than others, truth can be shared, and one can know things one has never seen or touched. Procedural knowers learn to engage in deliberate, systematic analysis. They also learn that truth is not immediately accessible. They speak cautiously, acquire and apply procedures for obtaining and communicating knowledge, look at different perspectives and worldviews, and learn to become more objective. Procedural knowledge focuses on the development of skills and techniques for finding truth, emphasizing method and form, not content. Procedural knowers are practical, pragmatic problem solvers. They are critical thinkers, relying on a traditional Enlightenment perspective of knowledge.

Within procedural knowledge, a distinction is made between separate knowing and connected knowing. Carol Gilligan's (1982) work was the guide for these two ways of knowing. In **separate knowing**, "the separate self experiences relationships in terms of 'reciprocity,' considering others as it wishes to be considered" (p. 102). The goal is to doubt, to assume that everyone, including oneself, may be wrong (p. 104). It takes on an adversarial form, a debate, in which the goal is self-extrication, to avoid projection by suppressing the self and taking an impersonal stance. The voice is specialized and speaks a public language (pp. 108–109).

Connected knowing "builds on the subjectivists' conviction that the most trustworthy knowledge comes from personal experience rather than the pronouncements of authorities" (pp. 112–113). It allows the self to participate and develops procedures for gaining access to other people's knowledge, through empathy. Instead of stressing doubting, it stresses believing. The connected knower refuses to judge but rather tries to understand the other person's situation and ways of thinking, by using personal knowledge. Personality adds to the perception; therefore, to be an adept connected knower, one must know one's own point of view. Self-analysis is required for complex connected knowing. Like Nel Noddings's "care," connected knowing entails "generous thinking" and "receptive rationality." "Authority in connected knowing rests not on power or status or certification but on commonality of experience" (p. 118). Connected knowing is leaning in the direction of constructive knowing and can be compared with Paul's strong-sense critical thinking. One can see, with the ideas of waiting to judge, being generous and receptive, and stressing self-analysis, that this form of procedural knowing is beginning to move away from a traditional perspective for critical thinking and in the direction of what we are presenting as constructive thinking.

Belenky et al. (1986) point out that using either of these forms of knowing is still procedural knowledge. The goal is to seek to understand other people's ideas in the other people's terms rather than in one's own terms. Procedural knowers are able to remove their own voices to understand others' points of view, but in the process, their own sense of identity becomes/is weak. Constructed knowledge is an effort to reclaim the self and integrate personal knowledge and expert knowledge. For constructive knowers, becoming and staying aware of the workings of their minds is vital to their sense of well-being. Theories are viewed as models for approximating experience. To be a constructed knower, one needs a high tolerance for internal contradiction and ambiguity; one needs to learn to live with conflict. The constructed knower has to abandon the either/or thinking of traditional critical thinking and search for a unique and authentic voice. She moves beyond systems but puts systems to her own service. "When truth is seen as a process of construction in which the knower participates, a passion for learning is unleashed" (p. 140).

Belenky et al. present these categories in a certain order, and in their descriptions of the different categories, the ways of knowing end up sounding developmental, as if these categories are hierarchical and one builds on the other. This is especially the case with the last three categories, as subjective knowing helps one build a sense of self, a personal voice; then procedural knowing helps one develop an expert, reasoning voice; and then constructive knowing helps one learn how to incorporate the personal voice and the critical thinking voice. We do not wish to present constructive thinking as developmental and a result of critical thinking. What we are arguing is that the traditional Enlightenment model for critical thinking (Belenky et al.'s "procedural knowing") is limited and deceptive because it does not allow for the self, yet it is impossible to get rid of one's voice and be "objective." We also are saying that the only way one can be sure of being a good constructive thinker is if one allows that emotional feelings such as receptivity and caring are vital to the process of critical thinking.

Are there ever times when it is valuable to be as objective as possible, given the limits of that possibility? Are there times when procedural type thinking, critical thinking as it has traditionally been presented, is what a thinker needs to strive for? Or when caring can get in the way of critical thinking? We want to be as clear as we possibly can here: we are ***not*** recommending that critical thinking be reduced to just emotional feelings and subjectivity and that we should do away with logic and scientific problem solving as we have known it. Certainly, at the point when decisions have to be made and criteria have to be applied to help one make the best decision possible, trying to be objective can help one make a better decision rather than being immersed in emotional feelings of fear, concern, and so forth.

At the level of assessing reasons, critical thinking as we have traditionally known it is an invaluable tool. And this kind of reasoning has been powerful at helping hold people accountable to standards of fairness and principles of equity in situations in which people were being mainly subjective and discriminatory, not objective and fair. (We are thinking specifically of the use of critical thinking to help correct situations in which sexism or racism has occurred.) It is important to always keep in mind, though, that we are human beings, and not machines, so being completely objective is never possible. We do not operate with a button to turn on or off our emotional feelings or thoughts.

As to a potential conflict between caring and critical thinking, as we said earlier, caring can be harmful to critical thinking, if by caring one means strong feelings of affection. The example of a doctor trying to perform surgery on a loved one is helpful here. Also, couples turn to outsiders for counseling advice when their marriage is in trouble because their emotional feelings are so strong they cannot step back and objectively reason through their problems to judge what they need to do to improve their relationship. They need an outsider's perspective of the situation and some professional advice. A teacher who is having serious behavior problems with a child and is feeling very upset and angry will often ask another teacher, the principal, or a counselor to observe the classroom to help the teacher see more objectively what is the best way to help the child and what might be happening to exacerbate the situation. But, as we have pointed out, the caring we are drawing attention to is not a feeling of affection, or lack thereof, but rather an attitude that says, **"I am willing to listen. I am open to try to understand what you are saying. I value your perspective and what you think. Your reasons matter to me."**

All of us have probably experienced times when people, usually authority figures, acted like they cared and were receptive to our ideas and our point of view, when really they were not at all. Parents, bosses, colleagues, retail salespeople, and even teachers and researchers are examples of people who have set about a task with an agenda already in mind, believing they knew the answer before asking for your thoughts on the matter and not listening to what you had to say, especially if it disagreed with their set agenda. People often go through the motions of acting like they care to receive more information or reasons, when really they are not open to attending to those reasons at all.

We think most of us would agree that an example of a good teacher—or a boss who is pleasant to work for, or a researcher whose work is held in high esteem—is one who is willing to listen and consider others' perspectives and alternative points of view. This is the kind of caring we are suggesting is invaluable to being a good constructive thinker. This kind of caring, the ability to attend to others—whatever they are—is not in tension with critical thinking but rather helps ensure its success, for it is as necessary as the ability to reason.

How is it possible to care for all people's ideas? Is it not the case that a person can only care for so many? Yes, certainly, because we are all finite beings, we are limited in what we can accomplish. But as long as we are attempting to be reasonable and expand our knowledge and grow, we must be willing to listen to new ideas and question the old ones. In attempting to listen and question fairly, we are relating to other people's thoughts in a way that is value giving, and in so doing, we are caring. The quality of caring, just like the quality of rationality, is an ideal to strive for; both qualities are necessary for us to be good constructive thinkers, and both qualities are ones we can always improve.

As educators, we can add to our students' abilities to think critically by attempting to develop our students' natural aptitude for caring. We can encourage them to open not just their minds but also their hearts, so that they are more receptive to finding solutions to problems, by working together in collaboration. We will come back to more suggestions on how to help students develop their abilities to think critically and to care at the end of this chapter.

Communication Skills and Relational Skills

We now are back to where we began this chapter, with the awareness that communication skills and relational skills are vital to the quilting of knowledge. This is because constructing knowledge is a social affair, just as quilting bees are social events. Human beings learn all the skills we need to construct knowledge through our social interactions with others. We develop our sense of self, as well as our language skills and thinking skills, through our relationships with other human beings. Consequently, knowing how to relate to others and being able to communicate with others will definitely affect the quality of our quilts of knowledge. As we improve on these skills of communication and relationality, so do we improve on our abilities to imagine, intuit, emotionally feel, and reason, for they are all interrelated and affect each other.

Communication skills involve the ability to communicate and explain to others what you are thinking and feeling as well as the ability to listen and understand what others are trying to communicate to you. Communication occurs orally, through people speaking out loud (as with a professor lecturing while students listen) and talking to each other (as with small- or large-group discussions, where conversations take place). Communication also happens in written form, as when a professor uses overhead transparencies or articles to communicate to students or when students keep journals or write essay exams. We use all sorts of technology to help us communicate with each other: telephones, answering machines, fax machines, computers, the Internet, and e-mail systems. These forms of technology help us speak to others and hear what others have to say. We also communicate silently, through body language or even through silence (facial expressions, how we are sitting or standing, gesturing). Sometimes ignoring someone's efforts to communicate and not responding is the most powerful form of communication available.

Let us turn to what others have said about communication to help us understand how it helps us inquire and construct knowledge. Suzanne Rice and

Nicholas Burbules are excellent sources for a discussion of the importance of communication in the development of knowledge (their focus concerns the development of reason; see Burbules, 1993; Burbules & Rice, 1991; Rice & Burbules, 1993). Aristotle is one of their sources for inspiration, as well as John Dewey. From Aristotle, they derive the idea that there are dispositional "communicative virtues" that enable communication to take place. (Remember in Chapter 3 how we came across Aristotle's idea of intellectual virtues and moral virtues? Communicative virtues are like Aristotle's moral virtues, ones we develop through the actual practice of use.) From Dewey's argument that our communicative relations affect our very ability to think, Rice and Burbules (1993) derive the stance "the quality of our conversational and dialogical relations is thought to have profound implications for our well-being as humans" (p. 36).

Rice and Burbules acknowledge the political side of communication, when acts of care are not taking place, but rather acts of exclusion and manipulation. These political acts of power lead to people being silenced and denied the ability to participate in communicative relations. These manipulative acts lead to the distortion of peoples' efforts to communicate and misrepresentation or loss of their meaning. Rice and Burbules (1993) do not think that if people have communicative virtues, these alone will allow people to overcome "numerous obstacles that block and distort communication; yet lacking the communicative virtues, one will be excluded from, and may exclude others from, numerous communicative contexts" (p. 37). In explaining what these communicative virtues are, Rice and Burbules are hoping they can serve as a regulative ideal.

The communicative virtues are "patience, tolerance for alternative points of view, respect for differences, the willingness and ability to listen thoughtfully and attentively, an openness to giving and receiving criticism, and honest and sincere self-expression" (Rice & Burbules, 1993, p. 35). Rice and Burbules do not present these communicative virtues as abstract universals but rather as "virtues . . . encountered in actual efforts to make ourselves understood, and to understand others" (p. 37). They are practical preconditions for establishing and maintaining relationships.

How do we acquire these virtues? We acquire them pragmatically, by practicing them. As Aristotle explained, we become patient by doing patient acts. The communicative virtues are not expressed the same way—universally, either—as people from different cultures express patience and tolerance in different ways, for example. These virtues do not stand on their own; they work together to "promote open, inclusive, and undistorted communication." Rice and Burbules (1993) describe the communicative virtues as being like a "cluster" or "constellation" of virtues in relation with each other (pp. 37, 38).

What is the value of describing communication in terms of dispositions and virtues rather than as skills, as we describe them? Rice and Burbules hope for communicative virtues to serve a powerful function of helping to regulate social relations so that they are not oppressive or destructive but rather democratic. They seem to hope that communicative virtues will serve many of the same functions that others have argued critical thinking ideals can serve, as criteria to help us decide what to leave in and what to leave out, what is "good and right" and what is "wrong" and in need of change. Even though Rice and Burbules say they are not presenting communicative virtues as universal truths, their presentation of the communicative virtues suggests these qualities can serve a role of power and decision making. As René Arcilla (1993) points out in a response to Rice and Burbules's position, the virtue role begins to sound like a self-righteous will to power and "risks convicting itself of hypocrisy, and prompting a more consistent discourse of virtue, one which tries to reach out to others 'like ourselves'. But what about the 'others' who want to compel us to be like *themselves*?" (p. 47).

Most of us would probably agree that if we promoted these "virtues" in our classrooms, they would make life easier for a classroom that is striving to be democratic in a diverse culture. However, there is a danger in promoting patience, honesty, and tolerance as "communicative virtues." When we strive to be virtuous, we strive to be right. This suggests we have a "God's eye view" of what is right. Such a view denies the very contextual, practical, culturally differ-ent aspects of communication that Rice and Burbules describe. Striving to be right suggests that we, as teachers aiming to establish democratic communities in our classrooms, know what is right. It also suggests that because we know what is right, eventually all of us will agree on this, once everyone has had the opportunity to learn what is right. Yet, having a democratic community does not entail that the people participating in that community will be able to, or need to be able to, reach a consensus. Communication is important in a democratic com-munity to make sure the members **understand** each other. They do not need to **agree** with each other. In fact, when we disagree with each other, we encourage further conversation about issues and experiences that we may have taken for granted or not even noticed. Communication that acknowledges differences must be humble and cautious; it cannot assume to be right.

As we have tried to highlight from the very beginning of this book, many femi-nist, multiculturalist, and postmodern scholars have asked the question, Is it our goal with a democratic community to make life easier? Is our aim to strive for consensus in our classrooms? We are uncomfortable assigning the communicative qualities Rice and Burbules describe as "virtues," for we fear such a description leads us away from acknowledging that our view of communication is limited and contextual. We found in Chapter 3 that when Socrates and Meno discussed what virtue is, they could not answer that question. Rice and Burbules present themselves as people who are able to answer the question, What is virtue? Otherwise, why call patience, openness, and so on, virtues? We wish to maintain a stance of humility, which is why we choose to describe patience, openness, and the like, in terms of "skills." It is not that we dis-agree with the qualities they highlight; we strongly agree that respect for difference and the willingness and ability to listen thoughtfully and attentively, for example, are vital communication skills. However, by describing these as "skills" rather than "virtues," we remove the moral tone the word *virtues* suggests and allow these quali-ties to remain open to continual reexamination and redescription. Whatever we sug-gest as communication skills will need to be open for discussion!

Communication skills are intertwined with relational skills. People learn how to relate to each other as they learn how to communicate with each other. For example, one of the communicative virtues Rice and Burbules (1992) note is "honest and sincere expression" (p. 35). Each of us learns what is considered honest and sincere expression within the social contexts in which we are raised. Perhaps people in your family show their love for each other by sharing their deepest fears and worries with each other. Being willing to share this information is a sign of trust and openness, and to not do so would be considered lack of honesty and lack of love. In someone else's family, talking about deepest fears and worries may be considered a lack of respect for others: people do not burden others with their concerns in this family; they keep them to themselves. Keeping silent about fears would not be considered dishonest or insincere but rather a sign of maturity. We begin to understand that what Rice and Burbules describe as communicative virtues are not individual to you or me but are rather properties of the relations themselves (Leach, 1992). How we view these properties and enact them depends greatly on the relations we have with others and what we have learned from our contextual situations.

Qualities such as honesty, respect, trust, and caring are as important for relationships as they are for communication. Another important aspect of relationships is **availability**. It is very difficult to get to know someone without both people being available for the relationship. Getting to know someone requires developing common grounds for communicating with each other by establishing shared meanings and understandings. Getting to know each other takes time. Also, because we continue to change as we participate in new experiences and learn more, maintaining a relationship means continuing to be available to each other. Relationships need availability to begin as well as to develop and be maintained.

Another quality that seems to be essential to the establishing and maintaining of relationships is **commitment**. Commitment is especially important for longer-term continuation of relationships. When people in a relationship are committed to that relationship, it means they are willing to try continually to maintain the relationship. Relating to other people is hard work! Miscommunication occurs all the time in relationships. People make mistakes and misunderstand each other; people upset and insult each other, without necessarily even being aware that they are doing harmful things that hurt their relationships. If people commit to being willing to do the hard work required to maintain relationships, it helps establish a sense of trust and valuing in the relationship and makes people feel more secure. They know they can make mistakes and recover from them. People can open up to each other, thus improving their communication with each other. They can take risks and learn from those efforts. When people feel more secure, they can be more honest and vulnerable, willing to share their personal voices with each other. Such sharing is always risky, for it exposes people to each other and to the possibilities of being vulnerable to potential pain, misunderstanding, and harm. Because we are all fallible human beings, we will make mistakes. Commitments reassure us that our relationships will continue, even after we make mistakes.

The better people are able to relate to each other, the more people will develop all of their skills for quilting knowledge. Quilters need to be able to turn to others for their input. How does this look? What do you think I need to use next? Will you help me sew for a while? I need to rest from this; I need to step back and listen and watch, before continuing. We will see in our discussion of diversity and difference from a cultural perspective, in Chapter 5, that many of the troubles we have with other people are due to our inabilities to communicate and relate effectively with each other. We often misunderstand or misinterpret others' meanings because we are embedded in our own contexts and limited in our understandings of the world because of our own experiences and interpretations of those experiences. In our quilting bee, as we interact with others we are working and playing with, we learn more about ourselves and why we favor certain patterns and colors over others. We are continually reminded that we are fallible, socially constructed beings who need to reflect continuously about how we understand the world and who we are so that we will become more aware of our own contextuality.

In summation, we have discussed the tools and skills necessary to be constructive thinkers. Some of these are ones that our better schools already spend much time helping students develop. Our better schools, as they exist, value and encourage students' abilities to reason and think critically (although certainly many scholars, such as Paul, continue to make the case that schools need to value these critical thinking skills more and help students improve on these abilities more). Yet, as our schools exist, some of the tools and skills we have discussed are not encouraged even at our best schools, and, if we look closely, we can see that schools have developed elaborate rules and structures to discourage or even punish students for trying to use these tools and skills in their work. Take relational and communication skills, for example. We punish students for trying to relate to each other and communicate with each other. We tell them to sit down and shut up. We reassign them to other seats if they are sitting near a friend and acting in a friendly manner. We discourage interaction because we say it takes time, distracts other students, and gets everyone off-track from the valuable curriculum we are trying to teach, instead of seeing that interaction as a precious **part** of our curriculum. When we punish students for relating and communicating with each other, we are teaching them, through our hidden curriculum, that these are not important skills to learning.

What about tools we use as constructive thinkers such as intuition, imagination, and emotional feelings? Do we encourage these? Teachers complain bitterly of the lack of creative and interesting ideas from their students, and yet it is a marvel what students are able to accomplish given the lack of support and opportunity to develop the skills necessary to quilt ideas! How many times have we heard teachers tell their students what colors to use in their art, that cows are not purple and skies are blue? Even in art, we teach our students to make the exact same picture. How many times have teachers given all of their students the exact same ditto sheet to fill in exactly the same way, and teachers have marked the sheets wrong or given lower grades if students vary on their thought processes or expressions of ideas? When students are being imaginative, think of all the times we tell them to stop that fantasy play: "Please grow up and act more mature!" We tell them to stop making things up and stick to reality and the facts, not realizing that "reality and facts" are not nearly as fixed as we assume and that through our abilities to imagine and "make things up" we are able to be creative and think of new ideas.

We would like to end our discussion of skills and tools used for quilting knowledge by considering the criteria we use to help us decide what to use and what not to use, what to leave in and what to leave out of our quilts.

The Criteria for Choices

What criteria are available to quilters to help them decide the colors, textures, patterns, and overall materials and designs they will create? First, we have learned that people are limited in their quilting of knowledge by their environment, which includes their experiences with the world and each other and their human capacities. As Jane Flax (1983) points out, "[T]he boundaries of knowledge are our experiences and our human abilities" (p. 249). Because people are social beings formed in relationships, those relationships will cause people to be formed certain ways and not others and will limit the possibilities of quilted knowledge. Second, we have learned that criteria for how to choose ideas are fallible, as they are human constructions, and therefore subject to change and improvement. As Sandra Harding (1993) describes this, "[T]he grounds for knowledge are fully saturated with history and social life rather than abstracted from it" (p. 57).

Plato spoke of what is real, the Forms, that people are able to discover through remembering what their souls already knew before they took on a bodily form. Aristotle spoke of correspondence as a criterion, that through one's outer experiences and inner thoughts, one could test to see how the two corresponded with each other. Coherence and certainty have also been used as criteria for judging ideas, as have extendibility and exclusivity. Modern-day scientists search for accurate representation, reliability, predictability, and probability. Pragmatists such as Dewey, James, Habermas, and Rorty have presented the criteria "what works and makes possible action or furthers communication" as the most people can hope for, given the fallibility of human beings. Quilters' views concerning criteria change as their knowledge expands.

Flax (1990) expresses a responsibility to make arguments clear so readers can respond to them and the conversation can continue:

> To pursue promising ways of understanding our experience is not necessarily to seek "truth" or power in an Enlightenment sense. Rather it entails commitment to responsibility and a hope that there are others "out there" with whom conversation is possible. . . . Such a wish can be independent of and unmotivated by any notion of "undistorted communication" or communicative competence. (p. 223)

Lorraine Code (1987) also speaks about epistemic responsibility. As we learned in Chapter 2, Code's realism is "grounded in experiences and practices, in the efficacy of dialogical negotiation and of action" (p. 39). Her criteria for making decisions are the pragmatic criteria of practice and effective action. Alison Jaggar (1983), as a social feminist:

> asserts that knowledge is useful if it contributes to a practical reconstruction of the world in which women's interests are not subordinated to those of men. Whether or not knowledge is useful in this way is verified in the process of political and scientific struggle to build such a world, a world whose maintenance does not require illusions. (p. 385)

What criteria are available to help quilters decide what to quilt? That which is most trustworthy, which can only be derived through interaction with others. The more voices that are included and considered, the more each of us can trust that we have considered all available information and can hope to make a sound judgment. That anyone can hope to arrive at a judgment that is a consensus/integration of others voices is probably not possible. It is likely not even desirable. Not all of us are going to agree on the rightness of judgments made by individuals or communities. However, discussion of the ideas is something quilters can strive for, through caring relationships and honest, sincere, respectful communication with each other. Quilting knowledge depends on an educated, equally respected, autonomous, interactive democratic community of imaginative thinkers/feelers/intuiters who are able to appreciate and use the knowledge they have had the opportunity to quilt.

Implications for Education

We turn in this section to a discussion of ways schools can begin to help solve some problems in democratic classroom communities, often through prevention by helping students develop the tools and skills they need to quilt knowledge. Here we are looking at issues concerning structure, curriculum, and methods of instruction.

Personal Voice

To help students develop their own personal voice and realize that they have something valuable to contribute to the quilting of knowledge, educators can do many things.

1.   Teachers need to encourage students to recognize and develop their own unique voice and continually improve self-awareness skills. How does a teacher encourage the development of students' personal voices? To begin, students must feel welcome in their classrooms, that they are in a safe environment. Although many may think this is accepted pedagogical wisdom, certainly it is not regularly practiced in all classrooms.[5] Students need to feel that their teacher is an approachable person. Students must feel they can talk and be heard. Through interactions with others, students learn about and develop their own voice. Stu-

dents must be able to take risks and expose their views to the scrutiny of others. To make this possible, a teacher needs to establish some ground rules of good faith in the classroom. In this place, students can trust that people will care.

2. If awareness and development of one's personal voice occurs through interaction with others, then it is important that time be allowed in school for students to have the opportunity to talk to each other. Teachers may think students already have the opportunity to do this, but research shows students spend most of their time listening, and teachers do most of the talking (Sizer, 1984). When teachers do allow time for talking, it is usually guided and directed to specific questions, often seeking certain responses, deemed the "right" answers. Students need the opportunity for "real talk," during which no one tries to dominate the conversation but, rather, people share the processes of their thinking and how they arrived at their ideas. (We will discuss "real talk" more later, under "Relational and Communication Skills.") Allowing students the opportunities for conversations (in which people try to understand/believe what is being said, as well as critique/doubt the speaker) should help them develop their personal voices, as well as furthering their communication skills, relational skills, and reasoning skills.

3. Students need to feel comfortable attending to their intuitions and emotional feelings as well as their experiences and ideas. They are all tools for the construction of knowledge. In most American classrooms, teachers focus on ideas and link them to experiences, but intuitions and emotional feelings tend to be viewed as useful for expression in art and music classes. Yet Polanyi draws attention to the shaping and integrating that is done at a personal level by all people, which affects knowledge. And Noddings and Shore point out that intuition is the dynamic motivator that drives people to seek meaning and understanding. Belenky et al. teach us that people need to understand and express their feelings and intuitions to hear their own voices clearly. Without the use of intuition and emotional feelings, the expression of one's personal voice is surely muffled.

Intuition, Imagination, and Emotional Feelings

We made suggestions for encouraging imagination in the section on imagination, taking the advice of the authors discussed. We want to suggest that the advice offered there is valuable also for developing the tools of **intuition** and **emotional feelings**. In the imagination section, we encouraged teachers to allow their students the opportunity to play and to see play as a valuable part of the curriculum rather than a "waste of time." Play means different things for different age-groups and different cultures. It seems always to involve rules and structure and the breaking/bending of those rules or the stretching/reshaping of the structures. It is this opening up and freeing of expression that is so valuable with play. Any ways that teachers can think of to help encourage students to be expressive and playful we believe will help students further develop these tools of intuition, imagination, and emotional feelings.

Children seem to be naturally playful, all around the world. Adults tell them "No, don't do that" or "No, that's wrong." Adults serve an invaluable service of acculturating their children and socializing them so they can survive in their society. But adults also limit and bind children's imagination, intuition, and emotional feelings by the very acculturation and socialization we teach them. Our best advice is to become more aware of this process, through exposure to alternatives, and allow yourself as well as your students to be playful.[6]

Relational and Communication Skills

Teachers have a tremendous possibility of helping students develop their abilities to communicate and relate to each other (thus further developing their constructive thinking skills) by allowing students time to relate to each other by talking with each other in class. Yet, we are not taking advantage of the wonderful chances we have; students are not given time for self-expression in their classrooms. By talking, we do not mean teacher-led class discussions in which teachers are asking leading questions, searching for specific answers, or trying to teach certain topics. We mean giving students time for "real talk," for conversation, in which teachers are willing to share their views and reasoning processes with students and to listen to students' points of views about topics the students find important.

We suggest that children need to practice and improve their communication skills and relational skills. This practice will not only improve their ability to communicate and relate; it will also improve their thinking abilities. They need a chance to be heard and to learn how to be good listeners. Teachers may ask, "Why do you think I am not taking advantage of this opportunity you say I have to help students develop into better critical thinkers in my classroom? It seems to me that my students spend a **lot** of time in class talking! As a matter of fact, I think I spend plenty of my time trying to get them to be quiet!"

We distinguish, however, between talking that traditionally goes on in the classroom, such as teacher-led discussions (which we label "didactic talk") or disruptive, distracting talking (which we might label "noise"), and talking that is free-flowing but stimulates reflection (which we call "real talk"). Real talk is when people share ideas and the process of their thinking. People explain their position and how they arrived at that place. Real talk is a conversation based on cooperation and reciprocity as opposed to domination. As we have already discussed, one of the skills necessary for students to engage in this activity is being able to listen sympathetically to what people have to say. Students need to learn how to listen in a caring way, in which they are being generous and receptive to others' ideas, before they judge the ideas as right or wrong.

As Richard Paul points out, what often happens with critical thinking skills is that people use these skills to show what is wrong with another point of view. We would like to encourage teachers to help students learn not just to doubt and test ideas but also to withhold judgment and wait patiently for an idea to develop. Real talk encourages people to suspend their disbelief in other people's positions to try to understand them. If students can suspend disbelief long enough to make sure they understand an idea before judging it right or wrong, they may find a kernel of truth that they can help develop to fruition. The ultimate goal of constructive thinking is to try to understand each other and find solutions to problems.

Teachers may find that in encouraging real talk in their classrooms, some people may become vehement in expressing their views and intimidate other students. This situation could be a very real concern, but it is also one of the things that teachers can have the students discuss. How do they respond when they are talking to someone who becomes very forceful and insistent about what they have to say? How do they handle that type of situation? This could help students learn ways to cope with individuals who have opinions very different from their own. Remember, our ultimate goal is to encourage understanding, not to insist on agreement.

Real talk encourages self-reflection and awareness because students have to be clear about their own points of view to be able to share them with others. The value of real talking is that it gives us the opportunity to learn from each other and grow. We can learn to reflect on and alter our own views, improving them rather than just adopting another's point of view. Because this kind of talking is sharing, the learning is real and meaningful to us.

With didactic talking, what teachers do most of the time, a person holds forth on a topic. A conversation does not take place—the teacher does all the talking, and the students do all the listening. Didactic talking certainly has its place; it is a quick, efficient way to get a lot of information across. It is also necessary to use didactic talk at times when one has to explain a new concept about which others may have no prior knowledge. A base of knowledge needs to be established before one can use real talk and a conversation can take place. We are not recommending that teachers completely do away with lecturing or the presenting of new ideas, just that teachers also need to find time in their schedules for free-flowing conversation to take place. The problem in classrooms right now is that many teachers rely almost exclusively on didactic talking, and when this happens, it is harmful in several ways: the students stop being engaged in the learning and begin to be passive receptacles for whatever information the teacher is supplying. A teacher who does all the telling while students do all the listening moves away from teaching and toward indoctrinating. Then students are not likely to learn how to be critical, reflective thinkers (Peters, 1966; Scheffler, 1973). The students learn to be passive listeners. Also, when teachers do all the talking, students are not being allowed to get to know each other better. Remember, it takes time (availability) and commitment (a willingness to persevere) for students to practice their relational and communication skills.

We do not recommend a special technique or method that is new and unique. The conversation must be real and vibrant and alive, and the topics of conversation must be ones students want to discuss. As soon as "methodologies" are introduced, the conversation tends to become "canned" and stilted. Most classroom discussions are rarely alive and vibrant conversations. The difference seems to be the amount of structure involved. Students end up feeling like the teacher knows the answer and is looking for that specific answer from the students. We recommend there be time in the classroom for teachers and students just to talk to each other. We want to encourage teachers to open up to their students and share their ideas and how they arrived at those ideas. Furthermore, we want to encourage teachers to stop talking and to listen to what their students have to say.

Ideally, students will express their thoughts and feelings about whatever topic is being discussed. One benefit of using real talk is that there is no one right answer. Therefore, students are free to share their actual understanding of the topic and how they reached that understanding. Teachers do not need to worry about evaluating their students while the class is talking. No formal evaluating is going on. Yet, for the teacher this is an opportunity to observe and note students' mastery of concepts and their thought processes and to learn about any areas of misunderstanding or confusion. During the conversation, the teacher will probably get ideas for future lessons.

Should teachers make comments and provide input while their students are talking? Certainly, this is a conversation, and you, as a teacher, are hopefully an active participant in the conversation, though not a dominating force. Should teachers worry about whether their students will still get the basic curriculum if they allow them to "really talk"? You should find that the basic curriculum is better understood, because students will be developing their ability to think constructively, and in doing so, it will positively affect all areas of understanding. Remember, this is not a new or special technique. This is talking. Any place where topics and questions will come up, conversations and discussions can develop if teachers allow this to happen. At first, you may feel hesitant to "give up the time" you would have used for didactic talking to allow real talk to take place. We challenge you to try it. We think you will find that the students learn even more than they were learning and that their enthusiasm will increase. They will remember the ideas and issues because they were interested and engaged in the conversation. They will question and ponder what is being said. You might find that your view of the students and their view of you changes as mutual respect and trust increase.

Conclusion

We would like to close with some suggestions for further discussion. The traditional Enlightenment paradigm for critical thinking has emphasized people's ability to reason and solve problems. A relational model of thinking emphasizes people working together, each contributing their own perspectives and each attempting to understand the others, to solve problems. For educators, this means many things, in terms of ways we need to change our curriculum and instructional methods.

We have argued that critical thinking involves more than learning specific knowledge (information) and skills of logic. To be a good constructive thinker, a person needs to learn as much as possible about her or his own personal voice and what it contributes to the way she or he views the world and other people, and the person needs to develop and enhance her or his ability to care for others.

Being a caring person, just as being a rational person, seems to be something we can always work on and learn more about.

Some of the ways to encourage constructive thinking are being discussed at great length right now in education journals and conferences. Methods of instruction that would encourage constructive thinking are cooperative learning, peer tutoring, and allowing in classrooms much time for Socratic dialogues, conversations, discussions, debates, and just talking to each other ("real talk"). Children need opportunities to get better at working with each other, collaborating, sharing resources, and helping each other. These methods will certainly enhance their relational skills and communication skills, as well as help build a sense of trust and respect. They need chances to hear each others' stories and learn about each others' perspectives. This will help them learn more about themselves and be able to view others as we's instead of they's. They need opportunities to read and be exposed to other cultures and diversities and to be encouraged to view diversity in a positive, affirming way rather than as problematic. Multicultural education programs that affirm diversity help enhance constructive thinking because they encourage the development of relational skills and the need for everyone to contribute to the conversation. They affirm the benefits of widening our circle of friends and acknowledge the worth of all people, which will certainly help students develop their abilities to be caring.

Students need confirmation of themselves as knowers and as members in a democratic community of constructive thinkers (confirmation and community are prerequisites rather than consequences of development). People need to develop faith in reason, intellectual humility, courage, integrity, empathy, and perseverance (all character traits Richard Paul points out in his theory). Teachers need to be more like partners and coaches, not judges. They need to get to know their students better, in smaller classroom settings, where the opportunities to express concern and nurturance toward their students, as well as the possibilities of teaching them reasoning skills, are greater. Teachers need to find the courage to think out loud with their students, providing models of thinking as a human, imperfect, and attainable activity. The need is for midwife-teachers (like Socrates) rather than banker-teachers (as Freire labels our current type of teachers) who deposit knowledge in learners' heads. The teacher needs to draw knowledge out of the learner, assist in the emergence of consciousness, preserve the student's fragile newborn thoughts, support the evolution of the student's thinking, and focus on the student's knowledge, not theirs, as teacher. (Many of these recommendations come from Belenky et al.'s work.)

These are just a few ideas; there are many more. The fact that several of these suggestions are being widely discussed is encouraging indeed. We are hearing about methods and curricula that stress the development of not only critical thinking but also caring. These methods emphasize the notions of working together as caring, reasonable democratic communities. With the giving and receiving that is required by these methods should come much growth and reward. Democratic communities certainly help develop a strong sense of relationship and connection to the people and world around us. Considering the constructing of knowledge as being like a quilting bee has hopefully helped the reader understand tools and skills that are used in constructing quilts of knowledge, as well as appreciate the beauty (and utility) of what results from constructive thinking. The quilts of knowledge we construct together are beautiful to behold!

In the Classroom

Activity 1

Think of a problem that is complex and demanding and will never be easily solved. After contemplating the essential ingredients of the problem and defining it as clearly as possible, come up with as many ideas as you, by yourself, can think of for solving it. Once you have created a list of solutions, each developed fully enough to be understood by someone else, meet with a group of four to six of your classmates to brainstorm ideas for dealing with the problems that you each have created. Each person will define his or her problem for the other members. Taking each of the problems one at a time, try to see how many possible solutions the group can create. Compare the group's list with the one that you made when working as individuals. Look not only at the quantity of solutions but the quality.

Now, as a group, think about what you have learned as a result of this exercise. What can you say about group thinking as opposed to individual thinking? If there were differences in the two lists, to what would you attribute these differences? How could your group have been made even more effective?

Activity 2

Take something you have learned this term as a student—an idea, a concept, or theory that you found to be challenging and complex. Once you are confident that you understand the idea, concept, or theory, write out a concise but complete explanation as a way of helping you further crystallize your learning. Now, try to explain whatever it is that you have now learned to at least three different individuals, all people who are not studying the topic that you have chosen but who you feel are likely to be able to understand, given your capacity to explain the topic fully. With the first person, ask that they listen to everything you are going to say without asking any questions or seeking any kind of clarification. When you have finished what you have to say, ask that they explain what you have told them and whether they understand it.

With the second person, do not allow any questions or comments as you explain; ask that he or she wait until you have said everything that you have to say. At that point, the person may ask any questions, and you should attempt to answer as best you can for as long as they have questions. You should then seek to find out how well this person has understood what you were attempting to explain.

With the third person, encourage questions as you offer your explanation; attempt to create a dialogue in which the two of you are discussing the topic and the other person feels free to seek clarification or additional information in any way they feel might be helpful to their understanding. After your discussion is complete, see how well this third person has understood what you have said.

Give everyone a letter grade indicating how well you feel they have mastered the topic that you have been trying to explain.

What have you learned as a result of giving these explanations to three different individuals? What do you think this has to say about the ways that you might be able to be most effective as a teacher in a classroom?

Activity 3

We have used the metaphor of a quilting bee to describe the construction of knowledge. We presented the construction of knowledge as having different people contributing in many different ways, all the while sharing a particular frame or structure. We have hoped that this metaphor has allowed you to see that there is a structure and that there are many ways to put together the various pieces that we think of as being knowledge.

The metaphor of a quilting bee is, of course, only one metaphor that might be used to describe the construction of knowledge. Contemplate the kinds of qualities that are necessary for communities to evolve knowledge. Try to imagine another metaphor that would encompass all of those qualities in a way that would be helpful in explaining what knowledge is and how it is constructed.

Activity 4

Saying what is really on our minds can often be very uncomfortable. We may think that other people will laugh at us or disagree or think that we simply do not know anything. In schools, these feelings are often intensified by the fact that you are in a sizeable group, with people you may not know well or feel a bit uncomfortable being around. For example, when a teacher asks a question of a student in a class, that student may be hesitant to answer, fearing that what he or she says will be seen in a negative way.

Think about a school situation in which you felt safe enough to actually say what you were thinking and/or what you believed, as opposed to saying what you thought the teacher, or some other person, wanted you to say. Try to detail, as much as possible, the situation and the dynamics of the group you were in at the time. What can you remember about the situation and why you felt that it was OK for you to be open and honest? What would you say are the key ingredients that make people comfortable enough to say what they believe and know? What can you do, as a teacher, to create a classroom environment in which your students will feel free to open up and honestly say what is on their minds?

Notes

Different threads of thought in this chapter have been published in Thayer-Bacon (1992a, 1993a, 1995b, 1995c) and Bacon and Thayer-Bacon (1993).

1. This quote is in reference to Dewey's "principle of interaction," which he later termed "transaction." See Chapter 3 of *Experience and Education*.

2. The metaphor of a quilting bee is one often found in multicultural writings, with many claiming quilts have African roots, but quilts seems to be common to people around the world. Many, such as Minnich (1990), discuss the metaphor of "weaving" through such terms as *tapestry* and *quilt,* and Minnich refers to multicultural research as well.

3. We use feminine pronouns here, as Belenky et al.'s study was conducted with women.

4. Paul discusses his notion of egocentrism in most of his writings, but a good example can be found in "Critical Thinking and the Critical Person" (pp. 114–115 of his 1990 book) or in "Dialogical Thinking: Critical Thought Essential to the Acquisition of Rational Knowledge and Passions" (1987).

5. For example, see Sizer's (1992a) discussion of the hidden curriculum in schools that teaches students to be docile. For another angle, see Kozol's (1991) report of the physical conditions of some American schools.

6. For further research on play, see Block and King (1987), King (1979), Sutton-Smith (1979, 1985), and Weininger and Daniel (1992).

CHAPTER 5

Cultural Diversity in a Democratic Classroom

Let us go back to the classroom, where we began in Chapter 1. We have focused on students and teachers in classrooms, but we realize many people who are educators do not necessarily work with students in classrooms. Counselors see students when they visit teachers' classrooms or when the students come to their offices. Reading and speech/communications specialists meet with students in regular classrooms or pulling them out of that room into the specialist's room. If you are one of those people or are planning to be, we wish to encourage you to translate what we say about classrooms to your own setting and situation. The overall ideas and issues concerning cultural diversity in this chapter should prove meaningful for educators in any situation, as all students and educators are encultured people.

We begin this final chapter by restating our philosophy of education. Like all teachers, we have a professional obligation to teach to the best of our abilities the concepts and skills of the subjects we are hired to teach. We hope that the students we have will learn these concepts and skills. We hope they master the content of the curriculum and are able to demonstrate their mastery through their discussions in class, the presentations they make, the journals and papers they write, and so forth. However, we hope for more. Even if the students in our class do **not** master the curriculum, we hope they can experience being members of a caring, democratic community while in our classroom. This is **not** to say mastering the curriculum is not important—it is; rather, it is our position that people who are treated as valued members of a democratic community have greater chances of mastering curriculum and learning how they can contribute further to knowing. This goal of nurturing democratic communities in our classrooms is what guides us as we design our classroom environment and consider what we will include in our curriculum and what methods we will employ. The hope that our classroom will be a caring, democratic community is something for which we are willing to fight and toward which we continue to strive. This hope is what shapes how we view ourselves as teachers and how we view our students. We are not willing to teach in a setting where our efforts to reach this goal will be continually thwarted; that is how much this aim of education means to us.

Why is the aim of nurturing a democratic community in our classroom so important to us? We hope those reasons are clear at this point, but let us recap them. In Chapter 1, we learned that individuals and communities are interactive, interrelational, and interdependent. Democratic communities are a form of community that recognizes these qualities of individuals, as well as others, and strives to highlight and encourage them. Democratic communities strive to include the voices of all their members, for everyone needs to contribute to a democratic community for it to thrive. We learned in Chapter 2 that making room for everyone to participate and recognizing the value of everyone's contributions ensure we will all be enriched and further our growth and understanding. In Chapter 3, we learned that democratic communities are nonrepressive and nondiscriminatory. They encourage people to care for each other and strive for justice. By doing so they ensure that their members have chances to interact freely with each other and develop shared interests. They aim to be flexible and adaptable to their members' needs so their members, and their community, are able to flourish. In Chapter 4, we learned that democratic communities offer their members innumerable ways to practice and develop their skills and abilities as knowers so they learn how to be able to participate and add their contributions to the fabric of knowledge.

We believe that if we can model and help create a democratic community in our classroom, our students (and we, as teachers) will walk out of our classroom with a better understanding of how we all affect and need each other. We believe we will all walk out of our classroom better able to reason with and care for each other. We hope that if the students learn nothing else in our classroom, they will learn and help teach all of us how to live together in a democratic society. This is our ultimate goal, and we will close this chapter by returning to a further discussion of the goal: living together in a democratic society.

Our Classroom

All teachers begin their school year with situations that frame the "reality" within which they must attempt to do their jobs. For example, they are assigned a certain room in which to teach, in a specific building. They are assigned unique individual students. They are given a specific list of skills and objectives they must attempt to ensure their students meet. They receive a defined schedule they must follow, when school starts and ends, when their students will have gym or lunch or music class. They are given whatever resources have been allocated to them: books, desks and tables, shelves and file cabinets, computers, paper and pencils, glue, staples, and paper clips. Although all teachers start with these "givens," what teachers do with these givens differs greatly from teacher to teacher. Not all teachers allow these givens to define the parameters of their jobs. Some take what they are given and work with that to their best of their ability. Others strive to change these givens so that they can change the parameters of their jobs, as well as what they do within their reshaped parameters.

Take, for example, Corla Hawkins, who teaches in the Chicago area. Jonathan Kozol (1991, pp. 47–52) tells us about Mrs. Hawkins in *Savage Inequalities*. He describes her room as looking "like a cheerful circus tent" (p. 48).

> The classroom is full of lively voices when I enter. The children are at work, surrounded by a clutter of big dictionaries, picture books and gadgets, science games and plants and colorful milk cartons, which the teacher purchased out of her own salary. An oversized Van Gogh collection, open to a print of a sunflower, is balanced on a table-ledge next to a fish tank and a turtle tank. Next to the table is a rocking chair. . . . In the center of it all, within the rocking chair, and cradling a newborn in her arms, is Mrs. Hawkins. (pp. 47–48)

The newborn in Mrs. Hawkins's arms belongs to one of her parents, who wanted to help in the classroom but had no one to care for her baby so she could volunteer her time. Mrs. Hawkins invited the parent to bring the baby with her. Mrs. Hawkins informs Kozol she has bought the materials in her room "because it never works to order things through the school system" (p. 49). She is resourceful, like many creative, industrious, caring teachers learn to be, always keeping their eyes open to "finds" at flea markets and garage sales, and continually finding ways to convince local families and businesses to make donations. She works hard to make her room an exciting, stimulating place, a place that is inviting and comfortable for her students and their families.

Whether Mrs. Hawkins or the many other great teachers we hear about regularly should have to pay for their own supplies for their classrooms on their meager salaries is an issue Kozol debates, as do many others. We bring her up as an example to remind us that what teachers start with as givens in their school year are not necessarily unalterable or fixed. We also point to teachers like Corla Hawkins (and also Herbert Kohl and Jessica Siegel; see Kohl, 1984; Freedman, 1990) because we want to make the case that nurturing a democratic community can happen in any classroom setting. The aim of education we describe does not have to occur only in wealthy suburban schools—it can happen anywhere. This does **not** mean we think our larger society should not support teachers' in their efforts to nurture democratic communities by offering them the resources to make their jobs easier. The conditions in which many of our students are forced to attend school are deplorable and shameful. We agree with Kozol (1991):

> All our children ought to be allowed a stake in the enormous richness of America. Whether they were born to poor white Appalachians or to wealthy Texans, to poor black people in the Bronx or to rich people in Manhasset or Winnetka, they are all quite wonderful and innocent when they are small. We soil them needlessly. (p. 233)

Not having the proper resources cannot act as an excuse for not striving to nurture democratic communities in our classrooms. We believe our aim is too important, for all students in our schools. We also believe that efforts to reach our aim are not wasted, even in less than ideal situations. Therefore, we will describe how to take our theoretical aim, our philosophy of education, and apply it in a classroom setting that is less than ideal. We will choose a setting where our givens are meager and limiting, and our goal will be difficult to reach. Please note, though, that our aim for education commits us to more than just striving to reach it within our classroom. Although we work under less than ideal conditions, our aim to help students learn how to live in peace and harmony with each other by experiencing membership in a democratic community also commits us to strive to persuade society at large to make conditions more ideal and support us in our efforts.

Here is the description of our assigned classroom and the school building that contains this classroom from *Savage Inequalities*. Kozol (1991) describes school conditions in East St. Louis; the Chicago area; the New York City area; the Camden, New Jersey, area; Washington, DC; and San Antonio, Texas, to name a few. We will use a school in the North Bronx, Public School 261 in District 10 (pp. 85–88).

The school is in a former roller-skating rink, with a capacity enrollment size of 900, but 1,300 are enrolled there. There are low ceilings and no windows in all of the rooms Kozol describes except on the top floor. For those rooms with no windows, there is no ventilation system. No playground for recess is available. Children are able to use a small gym once or twice a week. About 700 books are in the library, and 26 computers are available for the 1,300 students to use. There are no reference books. In this school, the cultural diversity numbers are "90% black and Hispanic; the other 10% are Asian, white or Middle Eastern" (p. 87).

On the top floor of the school (Kozol does not specify, but this appears to be the third floor) in the one room that has windows and high ceilings is our 6th-grade classroom. Thirty students are in the class, but the physical space is shared with 29 bilingual second graders, two teachers, and two teaching assistants. The room is a size that would hold 20 students in a wealthier suburban school. File cabinets and movable blackboards are available to divide the room.

Many teachers do not find out what room they will have until the school year begins. However, let us assume in this case teachers know their room assignments by August, so they do have some time to prepare the environment. The first task will be to meet with the bilingual 2nd-grade teacher, Maria Garcia, to discuss how this space will be shared.[1] Several options exist. The room could simply be subdivided, using the file cabinets and movable blackboards to create a wall within the room. Or, the room could be partially subdivided with some areas left open to both age-groups. Or, the room could be kept completely open. Jed Jones, the 6th-grade teacher, and Maria are aware that in this space they will have 59 children with different styles of learning. Some will need a highly structured environment that is quiet and has minimal distractions, so they can concentrate and learn. Others will learn more by discussing and working with their fellow students in small groups. Many find that the opportunity to work with concrete manipulatives and learning centers will work better for them, but some will find they lose sight of abstract concepts in tactile experiences and are better off learning about the ideas in a more isolated way. Jed and Maria can assume that the 29 Spanish-speaking second graders will need to practice reading and speaking in English, and some of their teaching must focus on auditory skills and oral practice of languages.

Jed suggests that he and Maria create places that are closed off, for privacy and quiet, and that they also devise places where the room is more open. Maria's husband and brother have a carpentry business together and offer to build shelf units that are able to be assembled in a variety of ways. Some of them will have solid backs, for privacy, and some will be open. Jed offers to paint the walls a cheery, soft yellow. He and Maria get permission from the administration to bring their own materials and furniture into the room and to paint and decorate the room.

Jed and Maria decide to pick a theme for Room 302 and decorate and design the room around that theme. Because the 2nd grade is bilingual, their native language being Spanish, and sixth graders study cultures around the world, they select the theme "The World as a Community." Jed offers to visit travel agencies to collect posters of famous sites from around the world. At a shared open end of the room, a huge world map is mounted on the wall to which both classes will be able to refer. Jed and Maria would like to think of all 59 students as being members of the same community, those who are in Room 302.

Jed offers his sixth graders as potential tutors for the second graders, suggesting that Maria assign a buddy for each of her students. He also suggests the second graders should teach the sixth graders Spanish, assuming they are able to get the OK to do this from the school administration and parents involved. This suggestion is called **two-way bilingual education**. It lends itself very well to cooperative learning and peer tutoring and supports the goal of striving to nurture a democratic classroom community, given the conditions in which Jed and Maria are asked to work. Two-way bilingual education is being used in the United States, and the research on these programs has shown many benefits. Children remain fluent and continue to further their abilities in their native language, while they also develop fluency in the second language. They learn the curriculum content in their stronger language, so they do not lose ground in subject areas. They learn to be more sensitive to cultural differences and appreciate the difficulty of being fluent in two languages. They also learn to view being bilingual as an asset rather than a deficit that must be overcome (Collier, 1989;[2] Nieto, 1992). Of course, having Jed and his sixth graders learn Spanish from the second graders and their teacher is a controversial proposal. Not long ago, it was against many school districts' policies to use any language but standard English.

Maria is a talented gardener and cook. She offers to bring in a variety of plants, and her husband recommends suspending the plants from the ceiling in hanging baskets because floor space is at a premium. Maria and Jed jointly invest in a step stool and watering can so students will be able to care for and study the plants. Maria also offers to organize monthly international lunch meals that the students will plan and cook with the help of parent volunteers. The second and sixth graders will share these meals together, and families will also be invited. Jed offers to organize a guest speaker schedule that will be coordinated with the meals, so that if Puerto Rican food is being prepared, he will invite someone to come talk to the students about Puerto Rico. Of course, his first source for guest speakers will be the students and their extended families.

Jed is great with animals! He volunteers to bring in his fish tanks from home, and he and Maria make plans to have the classes each adopt one to help maintain. They both intend to have each class adopt a pet as well, but they decide to wait on this so that they can discuss the idea with their perspective classes to find out whether they would like a pet and, if so, allow each class the opportunity to choose the kind of pet they want. Maria's husband designs the open shelves so that fish tanks can sit on them safely, and the future pets will also be housed there. This adds to the room's sense of shared space and privacy, aesthetic beauty, and resources to study and learn about. Plants and animals offer students other life forms to learn to share in the responsibilities of caring for, study and learn about, and enjoy.

Jed and Maria each try to create quiet places in their room(s) that are beckoning to students. Maria finds an old bathtub that she cleans, paints, and decorates with throw pillows as a place where her students can be by themselves for quiet time. Jed finds an old desk that he repairs and decides will be a writer's desk, each drawer filled with different types of paper and ideas/activities for writing. He installs one of the building's 26 computers on this desk. How is it he talks the administration into giving him one of the computers? He makes the case that the sixth graders, as the oldest students in the building, need to learn how to use the computer the most. Also, he offers to be the adviser for a school newspaper that all the sixth graders in the school will help produce. They will use the computer before and after school hours for that purpose.

Jed also brings in a beanbag chair and places it and the desk in a tucked-away corner of the room, for writing and reading. He hopes that some of his students and family members will be able to help him create a loft area, to enlarge the room and add another quiet area. Under the loft will be the 6th grade's own mini–resource library, and above will be a place for individuals or small groups to work on research projects. Jed and Maria use their file cabinets and shelf units to help create areas within their rooms where materials will be stored and learning centers can be developed. They plan to get the students involved in creating the materials for their learning centers.

Both teachers bring in area rugs they find on sale, to help make the room feel more comfortable and to subdivide it. Maria donates a rocking chair, which she keeps on her side of the room. Jed brings in a portable playpen, found at a flea market, which he stores behind one of the shelf units. This "baby equipment" is supplied so the school year begins by sending parents and their children a strong message that they are welcome in Room 302 and the teachers will make an effort to accommodate their needs. Maria has tables for her students where they may sit and work, Jed has desks. They both talk about ideas for arranging these but know that where students sit depends a great deal on the students. It is time to begin to meet the students.

Jed Jones's Students

In Chapter 4 of Myra and David Sadker's (1991) book *Teachers, Schools, and Society,* they discuss demographic trends and how this translates to classrooms in the United States. They describe patterns of fertility, immigration, changing families, age, poverty, and educational loss. They then set up an interesting scenario.

Imagine this: You have graduated from your teacher preparation program, signed the contract for your first teaching job, and now you stand before your very first class. As you survey your 6th-grade students, you see that 15 boys and 14 girls are present. Seven of your students are Hispanic, six are black, four are Vietnamese or Chinese, and 12 are Anglo. You know from reading background records that six are learning disabled, and muscular dystrophy has confined another to a wheelchair. One of the children has been identified as exceptionally gifted. About half of your students are from single-parent homes. While a third of the children come from middle-class back-grounds, the remaining two-thirds are from working-class or poor families. (p. 117)

Now we begin to have an idea of who will be in this 6th-grade classroom. Let us assume Jed and Maria are assigned these students before the school year starts, so they are able to read their files and familiarize themselves with their backgrounds, as Sadker and Sadker suggest. Of course, as many teachers know, even this is an ideal, for often teachers do not find out who they will be teaching (or where or what they will be teaching) until after the school year starts. There are pros and cons to reading what others have written about future students. Some think that doing so changes how the teacher views the student, that the teacher becomes prejudiced by others' assessments of the students. These people prefer **not** to read about their students' pasts and choose to start the year with a fresh perspective. For teachers or parents who have had to invest a great deal of time and energy into getting a school to diagnose a child and find out why she or he is having trouble learning in school, from their perspective not reading a student's folder can be a very limiting and ineffective approach. It sets up the situation in which each school year the teacher is potentially rediagnosing a problem rather than acting on previous knowledge to begin the year with a plan to help continue and further that child's development.

Even if a student has been misdiagnosed or comes from a 5th-grade class viewed as a behavior problem or an unmotivated learner by the previous teacher, this is still valuable information for a new teacher to have. If Jed knows this, he will also know that the student walks into his class with problems from last year that need to be solved or with which the student and he must find ways of coping. All sorts of reasons could cause a student to have previously had a bad classroom experience. Maybe the student did not get along with the teacher, the teacher was using a style of teaching that did not address the student's needs, the student had problems at home that year, or the student was suffering with health problems. Jed will likely not know this from reading the student's file. However, he will know that the student had problems, and the student will be bringing her or his past experiences into Jed's classroom. If he reads student files and knows the student with whom he is having problems did **not** have problems in her or his previous class, this information becomes a warning: "What am **I** doing wrong as a teacher, or is there something going on this year for this student of which I am not aware?"

If Jed can find out who the students' past teachers were, he can research their teaching styles and the curricula they taught. Test scores and grades may help identify students' strengths and weaknesses, academically. If Jed can find out more about the students' cultural, religious, and family backgrounds, for example, he can begin to research and learn more about cultures and religions he may not be familiar with, as well as begin to think about how he will incorporate these cultural differences into his curriculum. The theme chosen for his classroom, "The World Community," makes this easier to do. Knowing the context of his students' lives will help Jed anticipate potential issues he will have to address and potential resources available to help him. Of course, what Jed learns about his students can be faulty, misleading, limited information, and he has to remind himself to assess this information critically and place it in perspective. The best sources of information for who these students are are the students themselves.

Jessica Siegel (Freedman, 1990) began the school year by asking her high school students to write autobiographies. She learned a lot about her students through this assignment. Some teachers, especially preschool and special education teachers, try to make home visits or invite their students into the classroom for an open house before school starts. Many teachers send out a letter to all of their students before school begins, introducing themselves to their students and explaining what they can expect on the first day of school. As a teacher who is trying to nurture a democratic community in his classroom, Jed will try to learn about his students in as many ways as he can. He will also begin his school year with activities that help the students come to know each other and him better.

To get to know some of the students in this classroom, we will meet some of the students Sonia Nieto (1992) interviewed in *Affirming Diversity* and Jessica Siegel taught in Samuel Freedman's (1990) *Small Victories,* as well as some of our own former students. Our own students' identities have been disguised to protect their privacy. For many of the other teachers' students, we will fill in details with the help of our own students.

Before introducing the students, it is important to say something about labels, as descriptors, as this is a controversial issue that all teachers should be aware of, especially teachers who are striving to create a democratic classroom community where their students will feel safe, welcomed, and affirmed for who they are. Labels are constructed by people, and their meanings change, in the context of different historical settings. For example, Maria Montessori used the label "idiot" in her turn-of-the-century writings. At the time she was writing, *idiot* was a scientific term for children we would currently label as being mentally challenged; in the 1960s these children were labeled mentally retarded. To call a child an "idiot" is a very insulting label today, but it was considered a technical term in Montessori's times. Her first job as a physician was to be responsible for the health of the idiots in her city's insane asylum, many of whom would today be living in group homes or independently.

Ethnic and racial labels change with time too. People whose ancestors were forcefully brought to America from Africa as slaves have been called by many terms over time, often as terms of respect: Negro, Colored, Black, African American. Some people of African descent identify with and are comfortable with one of these terms; some identify with none of these and prefer to be called "Americans." Some people whose ancestors are African prefer to be known by their religious affiliation, as Jewish, Muslims, Buddhists, or Christians, for example. Many

Caucasian people in America do not identify with being called European American or White but also prefer to be called "Americans." Currently we label people whose ancestors are native to the continent of North America Native Americans. We used to call them Indians or Red Skins. However, if you ask these people what they prefer to be called, many will say Indigenous people or their tribal name. They do not identify with being "American" or "Canadian" but rather think of themselves as Navaho, Hopi, Shoshone, or Cherokee, for example.

The same is true of people from Latin American countries. We may call them Latinos, Hispanics, or Latin Americans. Often you will find, if you ask them, that they prefer to be identified by the name of the country from which they came: Mexicans, Puerto Ricans, Spanish, Portuguese, Brazilians, Cubans. Our best advice, so as not to insult the people with whom you work, is to ask them what they prefer to be called. Give people the opportunity to name themselves, and respect their preference.

Similarly, some people prefer to be called Ms. Smith, not Miss Smith or Mrs. Smith. Others consider calling a married woman Mrs. Smith a sign of respect. However, if a woman has hyphenated her name when she marries to keep her maiden name as well, it is safe to assume she wants to be called by that hyphenated name, not some shortened version of it. When in doubt, ask people to tell you what they prefer being called.

For our student descriptions, we will use the labels the authors offer, if given. If not, we will use the labels of the country of origin, if known. If unknown, we will use the most respectful label we know, given our level of knowledge and the historical context of our times, acknowledging that labels change. We mean no offense, only respect.

Jessica Siegel's Students

Aracelis Collado (pp. 60–61, 307–311) Aracelis's family is from the Dominican Republic. Her mother came to the United States alone and sent money home to her children until she was able to return to her homeland and bring her children to America (Aracelis was age 5). She is the oldest girl in her family of five children. She started sweeping and cleaning at age 8, to help her family out. Her mother works in a garment factory. When her mother gave birth to her last child, many years after her previous childbirth, the pregnancy was a risk to her health because of her age and other factors, and she almost died. Aracelis was 9 or 10 at the time. Her mother did finally recover and come back home. Aracelis's father died when she was 12, and when her mother went back to the Dominican Republic for the funeral, Aracelis began to take on laundry and cooking chores to help her mother. Aracelis is a pretty girl, and she was first proposed to at age 12, by a man from the Dominican Republic who was 23 years old. She is drawn to older, more mature men. As a teenager in Jessica's class, Aracelis has a boyfriend who wants to get engaged. She loves him but says no, as she has begun to want to go to college and have a career, not get married at age 18. Aracelis's file says she is so self-assured, so controlled, perfectly kind, but almost aloof (p. 61).

See Wai Mui (Chapter 8) See Wai's family came to the United States from China when he was 10 or 11 years old. In China the family of six lived in a rural village and were too poor to afford to send See Wai to school until he was 9 years old. When See Wai starts school in the United States as an 11-year-old, he has had less than 2 years of formal schooling. "The school compromised by placing him in a fifth-grade class for English as a Second Language, and there he learned the alphabet and the family members and the different types of transportation" (p. 199). His family is still just as poor as they were in China. See Wai works after school until 10 P.M. in the garment factory to help his family out. The family works hard and pays back their debts, and when See Wai is entering 6th grade his family gets a sidewalk vegetable stand, and See Wai is free to study in the afternoon and evenings. He is talented in art and language arts; he is much more interested in literature than in math and science, which is a problem for him because of his limited knowledge of the English language. His parents send him to school with the advice to "dress drably and say little . . . he would do best to listen and obey" as "one without experience" (p. 199).

Carlos Pimentel (Chapter 12) In Jessica's class, Carlos is the star of Seward Park's basketball team and doing very well, but his life has not always been like this. He is from a rural hamlet in the Dominican Republic, raised as a young boy by his mother, Bernandita. He did not know his father as a young child because his father was in the United States trying to make a way for his family to come join him. Carlos is biracial, his mother being Spanish (White) and his father being Black. He did not realize the impact of this until he met his father when he and his mother flew to New York. Carlos feels like he loses his mother to his father, for he has never had to share her before. He hates his father, whom he sees as a harsh man. Ramon (father) keeps trying to discipline Carlos, using physical punishment, as he fears his son is slipping away. Carlos also hates the United States and wants to go back to the Dominican Republic. Education-wise, Carlos attended a Catholic boarding school in the Dominican Republic, and when he enrolls in an American school, he is in 2nd grade. He is teased for being a poor ignorant hillbilly. In 5th grade, Carlos first smoked marijuana. He lost interest in school and failed the 5th grade. "By the time he reached 6th grade, he was getting high three or four times a day, beginning after breakfast, and carrying a carpet knife for protection and cachet" (pp. 285–286). What turns Carlos's life around is the Ascension Church to which Ramon turns for help, after having surgery for throat cancer. The man who leads the Los Buenos Amigos youth group there, Cipriano Lintigua, helps Ramon and Carlos explore their problems and begin to communicate with each other. He also helps Carlos understand his father cares about him and that he should feel proud for being a Dominican Republican. This happens when Carlos is in junior high school.

Sonia Nieto's Interviewed Students

Rich Miller (pp. 50-59) Rich is being raised by a single mother, with his brother and sister. His Black family is strong and very close. His mother is a kindergarten teacher who got her college education as a nontraditional adult student. She believes very strongly in the value of an education and both of Rich's older siblings are in college. She knows how to help her children get the education they need, which can be seen by how she fights to keep Rich in advanced classes, even when he acts up and tries to get kicked out. Rich says his mom is "really bossy to her children . . . because she desires those things for us to go on . . . she's very persistent . . . it's out of love and persistence, so I'm trying to bear with it" (p. 55). Rich is very involved in his church and has a talent for music. He likes gospel and classical music and plays the organ, piano, and violin. Rich is an independent person who has a great sense of personal responsibility. He is willing to work hard and likes challenging teachers. He is "comfortable setting [his] own standards" (p. 56). He does not have a lot of friends, but those he does have are close, encouraging and supporting him. "Rich has also learned that Blacks have to work harder to get anywhere and that White teachers have lower expectations of Black students" (p. 56). He blames his "race" for being lazy and unproductive.[3] As Nieto points out, he has absorbed the cultural beliefs around him and "has learned to 'blame the victim,' although he himself becomes one of them" (p. 57). Yet he does also have tremendous pride in his culture.

Marisol Martinez (pp. 124–132) Marisol is Puerto Rican by ancestry, as both of her parents were born in Puerto Rico. Marisol was born in the United States. She was fluent in both Spanish and English before she entered school. As a result, she was never in a bilingual education program. She lives in a housing project with both of her parents and a brother and three sisters. Marisol has older siblings who are adults and live on their own, making Marisol's parents older than most of her peers' parents. Neither of her parents work because of health problems. Her parents and older siblings have all graduated from high school. Education is important to them. Her family is very close-knit, and her parents are actively involved in their children's lives. Marisol feels that she has a good relationship with them and that she can talk to them about anything. She is a confident, ambitious student who "wants to be somebody" (p. 125). She is also independent and self-reliant, feeling she needs to make her way on her own. She is proud of her heritage but, at the same time, is embarrassed about being Puerto Rican, "I know that Puerto Ricans are way, way badder than the whites. . . . You know, the way they act and they fight" (p. 127). She "has never learned anything in her classes about being Puerto Rican," and her tastes in food, music, holidays, and so forth, all reflect assimilated "mainstream" America (p. 130). She is trying to be successful and a "good student" while at the same time trying to maintain her culture. "[S]he has accepted the limited role of women within society," dreaming to be a model or a nurse (p. 129).

Hoang Vinh (pp. 141–151) Vinh is from Vietnam. He is living in the United States with his uncle and four younger siblings, two brothers and two sisters. His parents still live in Vietnam. They are not allowed to leave their country because the father worked for the U.S. government during the Vietnam War and is seen as an

American sympathizer. The parents sent their children to the United States, hoping they will have a chance for a better life. The children are lonely and sad, coping with all that is so new and hard. Their uncle supports all of the children and "constantly motivates them to do better," taking "his role as 'surrogate father' very seriously" (p. 141). They are poor and hardworking; the children go to school and go home to study. Vinh works in the summers to help support his family. The family is Catholic and actively participates in their religion. Vinh sees the United States as being materially rich but spiritually poor (p. 147). The children also strive to maintain their Vietnamese culture by speaking only Vietnamese at home, cooking and eating Vietnamese food, and writing weekly letters in Vietnamese to their parents. The parents and uncle "constantly stress the importance of an education and place great demands on Vinh and his brothers and sisters" (p. 142). Vinh loves school and strives to be a good student but has very high standards for himself. Although in Vietnam he considered himself smart, once he entered American schools he began to feel that he was "stupid" because of his struggles with English. As Nieto describes Vinh, he is 18 and has been in the United States for 3 years, which means he would not have been in this country when he was in 6th grade. We are taking literary license to include him in Jed Jones's class.

Yolanda Piedra (pp. 181–187) Yolanda was born in Mexico, her parents both being natives to Mexico, and she did not learn English until she was 7, when her parents moved to the United States. Her parents are separated, her father having gone back to Mexico. She lives with her mother, who works in a candy factory, and her two siblings, a brother 1 year younger and a sister who is 3. Yolanda has many family responsibilities helping her mother because she is the oldest child and a daughter. Her mother is very strict, limiting the children's social interactions and worrying about their safety. Yolanda says her brother is "wild." "Her [mother's] constant message to all of them [the three children] concerns the importance of getting an education" (p. 181). Yolanda is proud of her culture, and her family strives to maintain it in their home. "She is a fortunate young woman in the sense that . . . her elementary school . . . has been quite affirming of her culture and her language" (p. 187). Yolanda was in a bilingual class in 2nd grade, much like the one that shares the room with Jed and her 6th-grade class. Her file says she is a successful student and "is enthusiastic about school and becomes noticeably enlivened when talking about learning and wanting to 'make my mind work,' as she says" (p. 181).

Students from Thayer-Bacon's Classrooms

Herbert I. McDonaugh Herbert (who says, "You can call me H.I. for short") is a very bright boy who also has an extreme learning disability. His IQ test score is around 140, and his performance level is around 90 (a 50-point discrepancy between what he is capable of understanding and what he is able to show he knows on a piece of paper). He is funny, entertaining, and very well liked by the other children, although they often miss his jokes because of a lack of under-standing. H.I. is someone teachers might label "the class clown." H.I.'s ancestry can be traced back to Great Britain and Northern Europe. His father is an insur-ance agent, and his mother works as a secretary in his father's office. He has one older sister in high school who is also very bright but does not have any learning disabilities. H.I. is not very athletically inclined (he has trouble with eye-hand coordination), but he is willing to try for all he is worth, and he loves to play games, even if he is incompetent, often trying instead to be silly. H.I. cannot write in a manner that anyone but his mother or teacher can read. He has a great deal of difficulty copying anything off the board, as he loses his place and misses let-ters and words easily. He also has trouble spelling, often reversing letters and not being able to remember how letters sound long enough to spell them correctly by the time he writes them down. In math he has difficulty keeping his numbers lined up so he can compute the problem and get the correct answer. He has learned how to read, though, and is an avid reader. He is a very hard-working guy who is incredibly patient with himself and usually able to maintain a sense of humor about his "handicaps." H.I. says all he needs is a secretary to go with him through life or a portable computer. He will also tell you all the famous people in the world who have had learning disabilities. He loves to learn and is confident he will be able to have a successful life. His family is very supportive of his efforts and considers him a very intelligent child. One of the main ways he has learned to compensate for his learning disability is by enhancing his ability to learn by auditory means. H.I. remembers whatever he hears; he is a great listener.

Anthony Anthony can trace his ancestry to the Mediterranean area of Europe. He is large and muscular, strong and athletically inclined. Tony is a serious child, quiet and sullen, and also has a learning disability. He struggles with controlling his temper; he gets angry and frustrated easily and considers himself "stupid" because he struggles and has so much difficulty in school. At times he shows signs of depression. He is usually the oldest in his class, as he was delayed in entering school because of a lack of readiness, and he has been delayed from advancing; he spent 2 years in 3rd grade, because he was reading at a 1st- to 2nd-grade level. He enters 6th grade not feeling very good about himself, and he knows learning is harder for him than it is for others. He has developed ways of avoiding doing work and will quietly try to "disappear" in a classroom. He has many problems similar to those experienced by H.I.—trouble spelling, writing, and copying work from a blackboard. He struggles with reading, because the let-ters reverse on him, and he has problems with his short-term memory, so that he has to continually relearn how to read. This is probably his greatest handicap. His greatest asset is his family. They are not as highly educated as H.I.'s and struggle with parenting skills. Tony's father, a carpenter, was raised in a family with an alcoholic father, and Tony's mother, a secretary, was raised by a parent diagnosed as schizophrenic. Both of his parents have trouble expressing their emotions and showing their feelings of care. They are willing to seek help, though, and have sought family counseling. They have also had Tony tested and are working with an eye specialist and are paying for him to be tutored. His younger sister shows signs of having the same kind of problems he has. Both children are suspected of being "mildly mentally challenged." Tony is very skilled with his hands and has learned how to do carpentry work from his dad. He is also fascinated with machinery and is teaching himself how to repair cars and other equipment. Tony knows how to fix whatever breaks down in school and is often asked to help keep things running.

Lakisha Lakisha is a special education child who can be mainstreamed into a regular classroom. (In Sadker & Sadker's [1991] description, the classroom has a child in a wheelchair with muscular dystrophy. We suspect the Bronx school Kozol describes has no elevator to help a student in a wheelchair reach a third-floor classroom, so we have changed the special needs child to one who has epilepsy). Lakisha, whose ancestry can be traced back to Africa, has a type of epilepsy that causes petit mal seizures. These are hidden, not noticeable by most people, even Lakisha. Epilepsy is a neurological disorder in which seizures result from "an uncontrolled burst of neural transmissions" (Kirk & Gallagher, 1989, p. 503). She loses momentary consciousness when she has a seizure, but because this happens so quickly, it appears as if she has just lost her attention or is daydreaming. Fortunately for Lakisha, her family noticed her tendency to "drift off" and learned that Lakisha would not remember she had done so. They also noticed how she appeared to be "spacey" and not able to concentrate for long periods of time. She was also tired and worn out after a particularly "spacey" day. They took her to the doctors, and she was diagnosed as being epileptic. She is on medication, which helps control and minimize her seizures, but it does not make them go completely away. Her doctors are continually readjusting her medicine as she will get used to what she is taking and the medicine will begin to be less effective. The medicines produce side effects, which mostly adds to her feeling of tiredness. Like most people with epilepsy, Lakisha has a normal intelligence range. However, like many children with special needs, her needs do affect her life and schoolwork in that she tends to lag behind others and needs to have instructions and directions reexplained if she has "missed them." This is tricky, as Lakisha often does not know she has missed something, and so everyone has to be on the lookout for these occurrences. Lakisha has a very sweet, uncomplaining temperament and a supportive family environment. She is childlike in manner, acting younger than her age.

Ira Greenberg Ira lives with his mother, father, and one brother. His family is Jewish, and they practice their religion, which means Ira goes to temple, speaks Hebrew, and attends Jewish day camp in the summers. He has been taught a profound care, respect, and love for his culture, religion, and family. Because of his pride in his Jewish faith, Ira remains unassimilated and often feels isolated from his peers at school. He feels a sense of responsibility for his family and community. He is willing to speak up against discrimination when he is witness to it. He has positive support from his family and peers and through school activities. Ira is not very athletically inclined, but he is a gifted artist and writer, which has earned him his peers' respect. He has created his own cartoon character and has learned how to make drawings and turn those into comic "flip books" and comic filmstrips. He publishes and sells his own monthly newsletter, which includes comics starring his own character, around school and the community. Ira is highly capable on the computer and what many children might call a "computer geek" or "nerd."

Emilie Emilie traces her ancestry to Europe. Although she is not classified as a special education child, she does have an unusual physical condition that affects her life. She has Turner's syndrome, which in Emilie's case means she has mosaic sex-typed chromosomes. She has XX chromosomes and XY chromosomes. This condition has affected her physical size and will affect her ability to have her own biological children naturally. She is small, and at her full adult size she will be under 5 feet tall. She takes hormones to help increase her size and enhance her female sexual development, but the hormones do not enlarge her size, just help her reach her fullest height at a younger age. Emilie's mother worries about her daughter's safety because of her small size. Emilie is big in the personality department, however, and has learned how to speak up for herself and make sure she does not go unnoticed. She is a bright, inquisitive student who is successful in school. She has good study habits and is a thorough, careful scholar. She has many interests, especially theater, dance, and music, all being areas in which she is talented. She does not test well on IQ or proficiency exams; she always scores in the average range. She also struggles with mathematics. Her test scores do not reveal her talents in the arts, and her high grades are due to her hardworking nature. Emilie has one sister who is 2 years younger but catching up to her in size. Her father is a musician, and her mother is a librarian. Education is something that is highly valued in her family but not necessarily "schooling," which her father sees as mostly detrimental and likely to kill any creativity Emilie might have. Her parents support Emilie's interests by signing her up for outside activities such as dance and piano lessons; she is also involved in local theater productions for children. Emilie is a good-natured, kind, mature-acting student who will go out of her way to help others and is easily hurt by what others might say or do to her (especially regarding her size).

Morrison Torry Morrison is another girl in Jed's class who does not test out as gifted and talented, but it is obvious to some of her teachers that she is. Her test scores are higher than Emilie's: she scores in the 80th percentile, whereas Emilie tends to score in the 70th percentile, but those scores would still not classify her as gifted. Her teachers have recommended her anyway as her giftedness shows up through her work. She is highly imaginative and creative, which can be seen especially in her artwork and her incredible abilities to concentrate and explore topics in which she is interested. Morrison does not have the same kind of study habits as Emilie does. She will work hours on something she is interested in but avoid or do minimal effort on schoolwork she finds boring. Unfortunately, depending on who she has as teachers, she may show great flashes of creativity and brilliance, or she may appear to be a bored, lazy, apathetic student. Like Rich Miller, Morrison is being raised by a single mother, who has two younger boys to raise as well. Morrison is Black and poor and, at home, has many family responsibilities helping her mother, as do her younger brothers. Her mother is an elementary teacher, who also attained her teaching certificate as a nontraditional adult student. Morrison's mother marches to school regularly to fight for her daughter's right to a quality education. She does not let her "get away" with being lazy and tries to push her daughter to want to succeed. Often the mother and daughter fight and disagree. It seems to Morrison that her mother is always taking classes, and she knows education is highly valued in her family. Even her father, whom she sees on weekends, has worked his way through college on the GI bill. He works for a trucking company. Morrison does not have access to the kinds of outside classes Emilie has. However, she insists she does not want art lessons and refuses to take them when she is offered free lessons, saying they will "kill" her interest in art. Morrison is stubborn, independent, and very self-reliant. She prefers to explore on her own, which she does daily as she works to develop her own style. She has a great deal of style, taking old clothes and recycling them into something new. Her file is very inconsistent, in that Morrison has high grades and low grades, and she has teachers who have only praise for her and teachers who found her "uncooperative and difficult."

Sadker and Sadker (1991) describe a classroom with only one student labeled as "gifted and talented." This is contrary to our experience and appears to be contrary to Siegel's and Nieto's experiences also. We have already described many students who are talented in a variety of ways, although their test scores may not show this, including H.I. McDonaugh, who has an IQ of 140 but whose learning disability affects his test scores dramatically. One student enrolled in Jed's class is labeled clearly "exceptional" owing to teacher recommendations, grades, and test scores. This is Claire Bridger.

Claire Bridger Claire's ancestry is European. She is physically big for her age, in height as well as weight. As a sixth grader, she is the size of many adult women. Her mother is 5 feet, 8 inches tall, her father is 6 feet, 2 inches tall, and she appears to be on her way to being tall herself. As a 6th-grade girl about to enter her teenage years, her size is uncomfortable and embarrassing for her, but if her mother is any indication, she will grow up to be a very attractive adult woman. Her mother is a housewife, who sings in their church and occasionally with a band. Her father teaches in a local community college. Claire has a younger sister who already shows signs of being a talented dancer. Claire has a very sharp mind; she has always gotten straight A's in school in all subjects and scores in the 99th percentile on all performance-based tests. She has excellent study habits and is a hard worker. She carefully and conscientiously does her assignments quickly and with ease. She thrives on competition and is a natural leader with her peers in her classes. Claire's one weakness is in learning how to be a kind and caring leader; at times she can be bossy and not very tactful with children she does not like or judges as inferior. Because she is highly respected and esteemed by her peers, Claire's opinions and actions have great weight and can cause another child to feel excluded and left out. As a student, she is someone teachers are thrilled to have, and she is remembered years later. She is likely to be valedictorian in her high school class, unless she decides she does not want to be the "good student" anymore. Not only is Claire talented in all academic subject areas; she is talented in language acquisition and the performing arts, too. She is also very healthy, rarely missing a day of school.

We have not described 30 students, but we trust we have described enough that you can begin to anticipate the kinds of issues Jed will have to address in his classroom. We have described seven boys and seven girls: two students are Asian, five are White, four are Black, and four are Hispanic, counting Carlos as being both Black and Hispanic. Two students have been identified as having learning disabilities, and one has epilepsy. Many are gifted and talented in a variety of ways, but only one has officially been classified as such. They are an exciting, complex, challenging group of people to work with. Jed Jones has his work cut out for him.

Issues to Address in Room 302

We left Jed considering how he should arrange the desks in his room. After reading his students' files, he decides to begin the year by offering students the opportunity to choose their own desks, and he will observe how their choices work and make adjustments as needed. He takes the 30 desks and arranges them so that 10 are single and spaced throughout the room; he creates three groups of four desks together as square shapes, two sets of three desks together in "T" shapes, and two sets of paired desks in rectangular shapes. This setting will offer many opportunities for groupings and can always be adjusted as needed. If there are not 10 students who prefer to work alone or who need to be alone to get any work done, he will pair some of them up or combine them with other desks that are already grouped together.

In terms of the methods of instruction Jed will use, he has a tremendous variety of students at very different ability levels. Tony is oldest in the class but still learning how to read. See Wai just started to learn English last year and has only 3 years of formal education, 1 in the United States. Carlos and Vinh are also struggling with English. Three students are fluent in Spanish and English and will be great assets to Maria: Aracelis, Marisol, and Yolanda. Then Jed has students who are reading around grade level and others who are reading at high school or college levels. He decides that he will use a mastery approach to math, teaching each student on an individualized basis, creating a sequential filing system (similar to SRAs[4] in reading) so that all students can proceed at their own pace. He will group students for lessons on new concepts with others closest to their own abilities. He plans to give students weekly assignments they must complete by Friday, so they will continue to progress and practice their skills. This lets him address the wide variety of ability levels and, at the same time, allows his students some freedom in choosing when during the week they will work on their math assignments.

For language arts, Jed plans to read to his class, maybe after lunch, as a "settling back in" activity. He will read stories from around the world, going along with his classroom theme for the year of "The World as a Community." He knows he needs to include stories from China, Vietnam, Puerto Rico, Mexico, the Dominican Republic, Israel, Africa, and Europe, to reflect his class. Jed will also ask students to write in a daily journal. He will not grade students' journals; instead, he gives credit for completing them daily. He plans to read the journals as a way of getting to know his students better and to help him diagnose the kinds of language skills his students have, and he makes comments about where they need work. The students will be encouraged to work on their journals whenever they want, but at the end of the day those students who have not made journal entries will be required to do so.

The whole class, including Jed, will read silently together for about 30 minutes each day, whatever they like. Jed knows 15 minutes of reading each day is not enough time. For students who find reading difficult, like Tony, it is easy to stall and avoid reading for 15 minutes, but not so easy (and much more boring!) to avoid reading for 30 minutes. The possibility of avoiding reading is further diminished by the fact that students can choose to read whatever they want. Jed intends to ask students to write a one-page essay every night, with him alternately choosing topics or having it be a "free-choice" night. He plans to use "writing partners," with students reviewing one another's writings by reading, discussing, and making comments and suggestions to each other, to further develop their writing skills.

Language arts and mathematics lessons will be taught in the mornings, when students are least tired, but students will be able to choose when they work on their assignments, based around their own work and study patterns. Friday will be "catch-up" day for any who have not managed their time well and still need to complete their assignments. Those students who have completed their weekly assignments will be able to choose their own work. Jed intends to build a class library and have art shelves stocked with different supplies, as well as having learning center activities, educational games, and props for dramatic performances available for those students who are interested. He hopes to enlist parents to help him find old clothes, hats, and so forth, for props.

Jed plans to use the afternoons for the subjects students tend to find the most interesting, the cultural subjects of history and geography, and science. He will teach these as large-group activities, with small groups within the large group at times for research projects, labs, and study groups. These subjects lend themselves to monthly, bimonthly, even year-long projects (maybe they will study recycling and continue that as a project all year long, or maybe they will learn about the weather and study the weather patterns year-round). These subjects are also easy to adapt and adjust to different student needs, interests, and skill levels, while still keeping the students together as a large group. He intends to allow students a variety of methods for demonstrating what they have learned, so they can show their mastery of concepts in ways that favor their styles of learning. The students will be creating portfolios of their work throughout the year; Jed will be evaluating each student's work, as well as using peers' evaluations, and having students do self-assessments. What subjects the students are studying, what projects they are studying, and how they are doing will be communicated to their families in a variety of ways: newsletters, phone calls, conferences, conversations before, after, and during school, whenever the family members come by Room 302.

When people walk by Room 302, they will notice a "hum" in the room. Students will be working by themselves as well as with each other. The teacher and classroom aide may be walking around checking individual students' work and offering assistance, or Jed may be having a small-group lesson in math and the students will have to turn to each other or the aide for assistance. Sometimes the room may be silent, as when they are reading or when students or teachers have requested silence so they can concentrate. At times all students will be sitting at their desks having a large-group lesson; other times some students will be moving around the room, seeking what they need to complete an activity, while classmates will be working at their desks.

We would like to turn now to more questions and issues that are likely to arise in Jed's classroom, because of the variety of cultures and personalities in it. Thirty students arrive in Room 302, bringing with them an incredible variety of experiences and personalities that make them unique. As a teacher striving to nurture a democratic community, Jed has no intention of denying students their differences. He plans to accept these differences, try to understand and respect them, and make provisions for them, so his students' differences are viewed as strengths on which they can draw rather than deficits for which they must compensate.

As we begin to talk about Jed's students' cultural differences, it is important to note that as much as possible we will keep our discussion to these specific students, to help us avoid making broad, sweeping generalizations about cultures that are easily shown to be false. All of us are affected by our own cultures in unique, individual ways. We also want to avoid creating false stereotypes. Cultures are not static; they continue to change. And they are not deterministic; individuals affect their cultures, just as individuals shape and change communities. Sonia Nieto (1992) offers a framework for looking at cultural issues in *Affirming Diversity* that we believe will be helpful for us as we try to understand what occurs in Room 302. She defines **culture** this way: "Culture can be understood as the ever-changing values, traditions, social and political relationships, and world-view shared by a group of people bound together by a combination of factors that can include a common history, geographic location, language, social class, and/or religion" (p. 111).

Nieto says that "cultural differences may be especially apparent in three areas: **learning styles**, **interactional or communication styles**, and **language differences**" (p. 111). We have already discussed learning styles (the way in which students receive and process information) and alluded to language differences (the students' native languages and how they are intertwined with their cultures), and we will continue to do so as we develop potential issues and concerns. But what about communication styles? "This area focuses on the way in which individuals interact with one another and the messages they may send, intentionally or not, in their communications" (p. 114). Communication styles involve verbal and nonverbal communication, oral and body language. They involve how people listen and hear what others have to say, whether people speak softly or loudly, who tend to be the communicators in the culture (i.e., the elders, the women), and whether people are expressive and loquacious or communicate sparingly. Communication styles even include the kinds of humor people use, as this varies in different regional areas and cultural groups too.

Some families are expressive and yell a lot, using body language and gesturing. African cultures emphasize "stage setting" as an important part of communication. Other families are very controlled and subtle in their expressions, very rarely raising their voices. Some families express feelings—for example, openly hugging and kissing each other every time they come together or leave. When they are in pain or grieving, they will wail. Others keep their feelings hidden, and a glance or shrug means a lot for them. With Alaska's Native cultures, raising one's eyebrows communicates yes, and wrinkling one's nose means no.

Researchers have identified cultural discontinuities and areas of potential conflict. They study other cultures using ethnographic methods and have been able to make recommendations for cultural-specific accommodations in classrooms. What tends to happen in the classroom is actions and messages are misinterpreted and misunderstood because of cultural differences, and these then become sources for potential conflict. Nieto (1992, p. 115) refers to four areas of potential cultural conflict:[5] **learning style, interactional or relational style, communication style**, and **differing perceptions of involvement**.

Here are historical examples of the kinds of potential cultural conflicts of which Jed should be aware. In terms of learning styles: American schools, as they have historically been designed, have favored students who are good at analytical, logical reasoning skills. They have favored students who are independent learners and who learn better through field-independent means, meaning they do not need contextual information to understand the ideas being taught and often find contextual information distracting to their learning. People who are from European and Asian cultural backgrounds tend to be field-independent learners, although this seems to vary by gender, as girls and women in general seem to be more field-dependent (or field-sensitive) learners (pp. 111–112). Other groups of people who are more field-dependent include Indigenous people who live more rural, agrarian lives, where they learn to see themselves connected to each other and the earth rather than separated from their environments.

Why do we learn differently? Some of the answers may lie in child-rearing practices, occupations, living conditions (including social class), or ethnicity. We do not know the answer to this very complex question. According to research, though, ethnicity is a more powerful influence than is social class (Nieto, 1992, p. 112). Given that people have different learning styles and we do not know why, the facts remain: some children are right-handed and others are left (yet Americans have a history of forcing left-handed children to write right-handed). Some children learn better through written words; others learn more orally (and in the United States we have a history of labeling those who struggle with the written word learning disabled). Some children are better at small-muscle, fine-motor skills such as handwriting, and others are better at large-muscle skills (we have a history of disciplining and labeling as behavior problems little boys who cannot sit still and rewarding little girls because they are better able to do these fine-motor tasks). Some children learn better through discussion, being given the opportunity to talk, whereas others need silence to concentrate. Some children learn better in cooperative groups, and others seem to need competition to motivate them and spur them on. Some children move, speak, think, or develop slower than others (yet we have a history of equating slowness with lower intelligence).

We can consider potential cultural misunderstandings and conflicts concerning relational styles and perceptions of involvement more easily if we turn to the students in Jed's class and let them help us understand.

Student and Teacher Interactions

Jed has at least two students from Asia, who likely have been taught to revere their teachers and anticipate that their teacher will have a formal relationship with them as students, as is the custom in Asian countries such as China, Japan, and Vietnam. Jed's philosophy of education is to nurture a democratic community where students feel safe and welcome to contribute to the class and where the teacher and students are able to develop egalitarian, caring relationships with each other. Vinh and See Wai may feel uncomfortable with what will seem to them an informal relationship, perhaps not worthy of respect. They will wonder why Jed does not take a more distant authority role. Why does he ask for their input and opinions? Asian relationships between parent and child, teacher and student, are more hierarchical by age—elders held in high regard—and sex—males having higher status then females.

We can try to understand an Asian perspective of the teaching relationship by looking at what Vinh has to say about teachers. He says that in Vietnam if he did not understand something, his teacher would spend all the time that was necessary to make sure she taught him and that he did understand. To him, that is a sign of a good teacher and a nice teacher. In the United States, Vinh has teachers who try to encourage him and tell him he is doing a good job rather than teach him what he is doing wrong so he can improve and learn what he needs to learn. Whereas American teachers may think they are being helpful and supportive, Vinh believes they are being dishonest and lowering their expectations of what he is capable of by giving him "false praise." They are not being nice in that they are limiting his education. He knows his English is not good, and he wants the teacher to give him the feedback he needs so he can continue to improve his skills (Nieto, 1992, pp. 142–143).

Vinh says he had teachers in Vietnam who just punished him, but he says he has had teachers in the United States who just do not care about the students and are not doing their job as teachers. By *care* he means to make sure they get to know him and help him learn. He does appreciate how his American teachers place more emphasis on the importance of him understanding the meaning of words and ideas, as opposed to simply learning how to write them. In Vietnam, his teachers asked him to memorize all the words, partly because of a lack of textbooks, but his teachers in the United States do not care so much about him remembering everything as that he understand the ideas.

Because Jed Jones is trying to establish relationships with his students, he will know them better, and they should feel like he cares more about them as people. However, Vinh helps him remember that his job as a teacher includes making sure the students learn the concepts and develop the skills they need to further their education, not just being a "nice guy." Getting to know his students should help him know their strengths and weaknesses and give them more focused feedback on where they need to improve. The Asian cultural value for respectful relationships is one Jed can discuss and encourage in his class, to help students learn how to have respectful relationships, not just with him but with all the members of Room 302. He will want to discuss with the group the difference between hierarchical relationships and the egalitarian ones he is trying to establish. Jed's philosophy of education **insists** all people should be treated with respect, and for people to have healthy relationships with each other, they need to feel they can trust that the relationships are honest and sincere.

Jed has at least four Hispanic students who have very likely been taught to respect their elders and that questioning them or looking them in the eye are signs of disrespect. This is true for Marisol, who is from Puerto Rico; Carlos and Aracelis, who are from the Dominican Republic; and Yolanda, who is from Mexico. Hispanic children are taught in general that being judged as a good person is based on how they act. As Nieto (1992) explains (Nieto is Puerto Rican):

> To be *educado* in the Latino sense of the word means not only to be educated academically but also to be respectful, polite, and obedient. This multiple definition of *educado* has a profound effect on many Latino children, who learn that to be a good student also means to be quiet and reserved, a departure from what are considered to be important characteristics of intellectually curious children in other cultures. (p. 128)

Marisol says she goes to school to learn and tries to be a good student, meaning she does her work, pays attention, behaves, and respects her teachers (p. 126). She is motivated **not** to be like many of her friends who have quit school for different reasons (crime, pregnancy, drugs, welfare). She has had teachers who ask her not to speak Spanish in class, and she views this request as an insult to her cultural heritage. Spanish is her native language, and she continues to use it in her classes. Marisol advises teachers not to be afraid of Puerto Ricans; rather, they should get to know them by talking to them. The students can teach the teachers about their culture, clear up confusions, and therefore improve communications (p. 127). Jed realizes this is sound advice for him to follow with all of his students. He intends to let his students be his resources for understanding them and considers this approach consistent with his philosophy of education.

Jed will be able to highlight the Hispanic valuing of good manners and politeness and demonstrate how these qualities help communities function in positive ways. Manners are what help us function in social groups and not get on each others' nerves or cause us to feel irritated with each other. Certainly teaching students to be polite is consistent with a democratic classroom community model. What may cause some problems for Jed and his Hispanic students are the values of obeying and being quiet and reserved. He will have to describe his democratic model as being one that encourages the students to participate in the running of it, so that they feel responsible for their classroom, they share in the care of the room and each other, and they learn how to live together as a diverse community. He will need to point out the importance of having students speak up and ask questions, while at the same time acknowledging some students may feel uncomfortable doing so, feeling like they are being disrespectful to him, as a teacher, if they do speak up. Maybe the class can have an anonymous suggestions box or an in-class mail system so students can write down comments and suggestions they feel uncomfortable saying aloud. Rotating leadership roles/jobs in the class may help all students practice their leadership skills in a way that does not have to draw attention to themselves but becomes part of being a good student, doing what the teacher has requested they all do. Getting students in small groups often may also encourage Jed's Hispanic students to speak up more.

What are the potential conflicts and misunderstandings that might occur between Jed and his Black students? Lisa Delpit (1995) can help us understand in her essays concerning this topic in *Other People's Children*. We have described four of the Black students whom Jed has: Carlos, Rich, Lakisha, and Morrison. We know from the prior descriptions that Lakisha is a shy, quiet girl. Delpit points out that research "has been conducted in classroom settings which shows that African-American girls are rewarded for nurturing behavior while white girls are rewarded for academic behavior" (p. 171). (Other research shows that White girls are also encouraged and expected to be nurturers in the classroom.[6]) Feminist scholars and Womynist scholars such as bell hooks and Audre Lorde[7] have made strong cases for the limiting of girls' education that occurs due to teachers' lowering of expectations. This is important to watch out for with **all** girls.

We have pointed out that Jed will be worrying about finding ways to make sure Lakisha is included in Room 302's community and not marginalized or silenced. He will be looking for her strengths and finding ways to let her "shine," so she will feel like she is contributing to the classroom community and gain self-confidence as well as her peers' respect. To begin with, Lakisha may choose to sit at a paired desk setting with someone like Yolanda. If she chooses to sit by herself, Jed may suggest she tries being with someone else who is also quiet.

Jed also has a tremendous asset in having Maria's second graders so close by. Often students who are shy will open up to younger children and become more expressive. He will suggest Lakisha be actively involved in developing the buddy system that Maria and he plan to set up (as well as Aracelis, Marisol, and Yolanda, who are bilingual students). Maybe working with those three other girls will help friendships develop with Lakisha, too. Jed will have to be careful to make sure the girls are not the only ones involved in the buddy system, for it can easily be mistaken as another nurturing activity for girls. Rather, he will want to emphasize their roles as leaders in organizing and coordinating the buddy system. He will want the class to understand that it is important for **all** of his students to learn the value of helping others and that through helping others they will not only be making friends but also practicing their academic skills. As all teachers know, when you can teach a concept or skill to someone else, you are sure you have learned it yourself.

Rich and Morrison are likely to demonstrate more of the stereotypical Black styles of communicating and relating in terms of being extroverted and adept at oral skills (not so much Carlos, because he was raised in the Dominican Republic and is likely to have more Hispanic cultural values than Black cultural values). Many of their former teachers may have viewed these students' oral skills as disruptive and threatening to teacher authority. Jed will, instead, value their stylish flair and find ways for them to use their oral skills in positive ways in the classroom setting (Nieto, 1992, p. 116). Jed may notice some of his Black students performing stage-setting activities before they begin a task, such as sharpening pencils and preparing papers. White teachers often mistake these activities for avoiding the task or "wasting time." When students ask teachers to repeat instructions (another stage-setting activity), this may be misinterpreted as meaning the student was not paying attention (Nieto, 1992, p. 116).

African-American culture is hierarchical in terms of parenting and siblings, and Black children are taught to expect authority figures to act with authority. As Delpit (1995) explains, "[M]any people of color expect authority to be earned by personal efforts and exhibited by personal characteristics. . . . [B]ecause authority is earned, the teacher must consistently prove characteristics that give her authority" (p. 35). If teachers act like they are students' friends, they are judged as having no authority. If teachers attempt to establish a democratic community in the classroom, as Jed intends to do, they may be perceived as "weak, ineffectual, and incapable of taking on the role of being the teacher; therefore, there is no need to follow [their] directive" (p. 36). How does a teacher act with authority?

> The authoritative teacher can control the class through exhibition of personal power; establishes meaningful interpersonal relationships that garner student respect; exhibits a strong belief that all students can learn; establishes a standard of achievement and "pushes" the students to achieve that standard; and holds the attention of the students by incorporating interactional features of black communicative style in his or her teaching. (pp. 35–36)

Sometimes Black children disobey their teachers because they misunderstand what the teacher says. Delpit (1995) points out that White teachers often tell students to do something by phrasing their request in a question format. They may say, "Would you like to get out your books for silent reading?" What they mean is "Get out your books for silent reading now." The authority figures in Black children's lives tend to phrase calls to action as statements or commands, telling them what action they should do (pp. 34–35). Although the message is very clear, to a White person, it may sound like the Black person is being too authoritarian. Black teachers are often viewed as being too teacher directed (p. 33).

Jed can be careful that his directions are given clearly and directly and, if there is no choice in what he is directing, that the message of no choice should also be clear. When he meets with the large class, he can use an interactive style of communicating, which is usually more interesting for most students, and offer all of his students the opportunity to practice their oral skills (remember, some of them know little English), while also giving his Black students a chance to shine with their oral proficiency. The need to make sure that he maintains high standards and believes in all of his students' abilities to achieve holds for all of his students, not just his Black students. Establishing meaningful interpersonal relationships based on mutual respect with all of his students is one of Jed's main goals with his philosophy of education.

What may cause some problems for Jed and his Black students are the cultural values that suggest a good teacher pushes his or her students to do their work as a sign of the teacher's authority and that a teacher shows authority by controlling the classroom through the exhibition of personal power. Jed is trying to establish a democratic classroom community in which the students have a lot of power in the class and he has a more egalitarian relationship with them. He will need to make sure all of his students understand he is not giving up power or authority as a teacher, he is still a resource and guide for them, and he is still responsible for making sure they learn the curriculum he is responsible for teaching. Rather than "giving up" his own power, he is "adding to" their power by offering them ways to contribute and make choices in their education. He is also trying to teach his students that along with freedom and choices come responsibilities and that they have just as much ownership for the success of the class as he does. Jed will need to explain that he intends to hold all students to his high standards and "push" them all but that his ultimate goal is for them to learn to push themselves.

As for the five White students described in Jed's class, he should find these students are comfortable with his democratic, egalitarian style of teaching, in that they share the same cultural background. Yet they are each unique individuals (as are the rest of the students described), and they all bring their different family values with them into Jed's class, so he will need to try to get to know them as well and look out for misunderstandings and potential conflicts. For example, Anthony comes from a family that is not very emotionally expressive, so learning to read Tony's body language will become important. His lack of expression can be misunderstood as lack of interest, boredom, or apathy. Jed will also learn much about Tony through what he writes in his journal. He learns to tell signs of Tony's depression and times when Tony feels "stupid" and frustrated. Jed will worry about how to open up space in this classroom for Tony to participate, so that Tony can make friends and feel more confident in his own abilities. One fairly obvious idea is to put Tony in charge of Room 302's "loft project" because he is a good carpenter. Jed may also want to focus on machines for part of his science curriculum and get Tony to help him create a mechanical activities center.

On the other hand, Ira, H.I., Emilie, and Claire are all very expressive White students in Jed's class who will begin the year standing out for their leadership qualities and their mastery and comfort with the English language as well as the American culture. Even though they are not the majority in their classroom, they are from the majority culture in the United States, the one with the highest status and power. Jed will have to make sure these students do not dominate the classroom but share in its responsibilities and leadership with all of their classmates. He will want to ensure they become friends with other students in the classroom "not like them" and that they treat them with equal respect, not favor or ignore them.

Jed will design activities that help students interact with each other and get to know each other better. He will suggest different pairings for subject areas such as writing or get different students working together on projects. Maybe different students will take turns being editors for the school newspaper, with See Wai and Claire in charge of assigning those various tasks. Because Morrison and Ira are talented artists, maybe they will work together to design illustrations for the newsletter and contribute cartoons. We have arrived at a discussion of student-to-student interactions, so let us turn to that topic now.

Student-to-Student Interactions

Let us assume that Jed establishes himself as a teacher who is to be respected and has authority, as well as being someone who is attentive and actively seeking to know his students in a relational manner so he can help them learn. Jed has found ways to value the cultural influences of students' views of teachers and still feel that he is being true to his goals as a teacher of a democratic community. What are some of the problems that he can anticipate and maybe prevent among the students of Room 302? Our experience is that, aside from misunderstandings that occur routinely in any relationship, many student-to-student problems happen because students feel a lack of self-confidence and well-being. They will often lash out to hurt others because they are hurting themselves. They will isolate themselves and avoid making friends, acting as though they do not like anyone, because they do not feel very likable themselves. Herbert Kohl (1984) expresses the belief in *Growing Minds: On Becoming a Teacher* that it is very important for teachers to find ways to help students make friends and feel included in the classroom community. As he puts it:

> It is essential to assume that children want to be part of the group, and that isolation is painful. Time spent trying to help someone who doesn't fit into a group is also time spent understanding the group itself. The more I teach, the more convinced I am that one of the essential roles of the teacher is to make it possible for even the most difficult and unhappy individuals to feel supported and welcome within a group of their peers. (p. 86)

Some may question why is it necessary to make every student participate and join the community. What if someone wants to be an outsider? But these questions assume the student who does not participate has a choice. Certainly, in a democratic classroom community students can and will choose **not** to participate at times. However, it is vital that they feel space has been created for them in this classroom and their presence and participation are desired. An invitation and welcome need always to be present, and then the student has a real choice about whether to participate. Being excluded from a classroom community is a painful experience. Exclusion is not by choice.

Most classrooms have a few students who attempt to lead the class by intimidating and bullying their fellow classmates. Based on the file descriptions, Jed can anticipate such action might occur with Anthony, Claire, and maybe Carlos (who joins a gang in junior high). Most classrooms also have students who tend to feel like misfits, who isolate themselves or find themselves isolated by their peers. Jed is already worrying about Vinh, Carlos, and Lakisha. H.I. and Ira also have the possibility of feeling like misfits. Many of Jed's students enter his class feeling embarrassed and ashamed because of their situations in life.

Carlos, See Wai, and Vinh feel incompetent with the English language. Vinh has the advantage of having come to the United States with a strong background in education and experiences that are more highly valued in this country, but he has family issues that affect his well-being. Vinh must live with being separated from both of his parents.

Carlos and See Wai have poor families who came to the United States from small little villages and hamlets in their native countries. They are innocent and unaware of the larger world, and as they are learning about it they are finding it a dangerous, unfriendly place. Their neighbors use and sell drugs; they commit crimes and are the victims of crimes; they are school dropouts and unemployed, many of them living on welfare. Certainly many people around them are doing well and working hard to raise themselves and their families out of poverty. But they also suffer setbacks. Carlos's father, Ramon, finds out he has throat cancer. See Wai's family loses their sidewalk vegetable stall after buying a small home, and his father must go back to working in a noodle factory while See Wai helps the family by working a cook for 20 hours each week (all while he is commuting more than 2 hours each day to Seward High School). Many of the students are victims of crime themselves or have best friends who have been beaten or shot to death.

Carlos, See Wai, and Vinh have all found out that in American schools they can expect to be teased because they sound or look different. Rich and Marisol have found that the way they can feel successful in school is to separate themselves from their culture and remove themselves from friendships with people who are not assimilating successfully into the American (White) culture. H.I. and Tony have learned that because they are learning disabled, people think they are incompetent even though they both have many skills and talents. Claire knows people resent her smartness and tease her for her abilities and size. Emilie also gets teased for her size and because she is emotional and gets her feelings hurt easily. Because she is so small, people think Emilie is younger than she is and underestimate her abilities or worry about her getting hurt and become overprotective. People behave similarly with Lakisha because of her special needs.

Morrison has learned that if you do not fit in, teachers will view you as a "troublemaker." See Wai has learned that teachers will embarrass you by getting you in trouble, even when you were asking your neighbor to repeat the instructions you did not quite understand the first time the teacher said them. Vinh has learned that teachers often assume that if you are Asian you will not need help; they think all Asian students are smart and well behaved (making the false assumption of labeling all Asians successful and a "model minority"; Nieto, 1992, pp. 148–149). Ira finds that teachers also label him a model student because he is Jewish, and they therefore assume he does not need any instructional help. As a gifted student, Claire has also experienced this treatment. She often receives the least amount of instruction in her class because teachers assume that since she is smart, she does not need to be taught, or at least not as much as the other students.

Most students seem to feel like misfits in their classes. Many do not describe going to school as a happy, positive experience. What is Jed going to be able to do about the angry, frustrating, bitter, painful feelings many of his students have about school? It is safe to assume that if he can create a classroom environment in which the students in Room 302 feel comfortable expressing themselves, what is shared in that room with each other will not always be pretty. Caring democratic classroom communities create a place where sorrow and pain will be expressed as well as joy. This is because the students learn that they can trust their teachers and peers to be open and honest and that their teachers and peers will try to be accepting and caring of them. In such an environment, students will express themselves, and the main task of the teachers and students will be to listen receptively and attentively. When they are able to open up communication and accept different styles and ways of relating, healing can begin to take place, and growth can continue.

The students in Room 302 are in 6th grade, they already have a history of experiences, and they have established behavior patterns for coping with their problems. Morrison is an expert at causing problems and hurting teachers' abilities to teach by undermining their authority. See Wai and Lakisha already know how to hide in classrooms so that they will not draw unwanted attention. Carlos is already getting high on marijuana regularly by the time he walks into Jed's 6th-grade class. He is discouraged with his failures in school and is turning to the street to find ways to feel good about himself. We all need to feel like we can be successful and that people believe in us and will help us be successful. When we feel that we can learn and master skills, we are rewarded by feeling successful, and our self-esteem improves. When we fail or get in trouble, we feel stupid and bad about ourselves and angry at whatever, or whomever, is making us feel that way.

Jed will have to work to help his students establish good work habits and positive feelings about learning. It is through the schoolwork itself that he has the best chance of changing bullies and isolated students into active, participating, helpful, contributing members of the classroom community. However, before he can tackle schoolwork, he will have to establish rules of conduct for the classroom, with the class, beginning on the very first day of school. To be consistent with his philosophy of education, Jed and Room 302 will have to decide together what the consequences will be for breaking the rules they agree on, and then the entire classroom community will have to make sure the rules are consistently followed and the consequences enacted, if rules are broken. The class may decide to have a regular weekly meeting in which broken rules are discussed and punishments are decided, as Summerhill does with its town meetings.

Neill (1960, 1992) found that the students learned to trust that their peers' judgments will be fair and equitable. Sometimes people worry that if they vote on a decision by majority rule, that approach might create a situation in which minorities will always lose or, in a classroom context, unpopular students will never get their way. We have found all sorts of ways to subvert majority votes— by giving everyone a turn, passing around a talking stone, or counting people off by numbers for grouping activities, for example. But these are still teacher-directed ideas, and one of the goals of a democratic classroom community is to get the students actively involved and feeling that they have ownership in how things go in that classroom. What Neill (1960, 1992) suggested as a structure to protect fairness was that if a student disagreed with the group ruling, he or she always had the right to request a reconsideration. He found that if students requested a reconsideration, the other students would assume they must have made a mistake and would try to reconsider their decision as fairly as they could. When students feel responsible for helping manage a classroom, they put a great deal of care into their behavior and how they treat each other. They stop viewing the teacher and fellow students as "they" and begin to see that everyone comprises a "we" in the classroom community together.

With classroom management established and considered to be the responsibility of the entire class, Jed can move on to the very rewarding task of trying to get to know his students better so he can teach them. He needs to find out their interests, strengths, and weaknesses. Even with this knowledge, Jed knows that students continue to change, and he will need to continually develop his relationships with his students so that he is aware of these changes. Still, as he begins to know them, he can begin to design his curriculum so that it taps into their interests and meets their needs. He can begin to use methods of instruction that favor his students' styles of learning. Jed will do everything he possibly can to help his students have successful learning and relational experiences while they are in his classroom.

This brings us to the other most important group of people that can help Jed be a successful 6th-grade teacher: his students' families. If Jed is attempting to nurture a democratic classroom community, he will need to consider how he will establish positive relationships with his students' families. Establishing positive, respectful relationships with the families will help Jed get to know his students better. If he can explain his philosophy of education to the families and also get them involved in Room 302, he will find that as they understand what he is doing and get to know him well enough to know that he cares about their children, they will be supportive and help him reach his goals. Let us turn to a discussion of the families of Room 302 students.

Teacher and Family Interactions

It is not unusual to go into a teacher lounge and hear teachers complaining about parents: "Why don't parents care enough about their children to get them to bed at a decent time and feed them a healthy breakfast, so they'll come to school ready to learn?" "Why don't parents teach their children manners and rules? Why do we have to spend so much time disciplining their children instead of teaching them?" "Why don't parents come in to school for parent conferences or open houses? Why aren't they more actively involved in their children's education?" Many teachers conclude that parents do not care about their children, and this conclusion is supported by what they take to be a significant amount of sound evidence.

Yet, "evidence" is culturally bound and depends on a great deal of contextual information that teachers often do not have. Is it possible that they have reached the wrong conclusion? Here is an example of teachers doing just that, misunderstanding parents' actions and judging the parents to be at fault because of different cultural views on parenting. Delpit (1995, p. 176) tells a story of Latino parents fighting with teachers in Boston. The teachers wanted the parents to bring their children to school, drop them off at the playground, and leave. A teacher's aide would supervise the children on the playground until school started. The teachers did not want any children in their classroom before classes starting so that they could prepare for the day. The parents kept ignoring the teachers' requests and bringing their children into the classroom or staying with their children in the playground area until school started. This misunderstanding escalated to shouting and teachers locking school doors, until the parents approached the school board. The children involved in this cultural conflict were 6 years old.

> What the teachers in this instance did not understand was that the parents viewed their 6-year-olds as still being babies and in need of their mother's or their surrogate mother's [the teacher's] attention. To the parents, leaving children outside without one of their "mothers" present was tantamount to child abuse and exhibited a most callous disregard for the children's welfare. (p. 176)

Kozol (1991) shares interviews he has had with many students and their family members. These are mostly poor, minority families whose children go to public schools in urban settings. One of the common complaints for parents is that they cannot get to their children's schools. Many children in the United States attend schools to which they are bused (as a way of desegregating schools). It is not unusual for children in the New York City school system, for example, to ride a bus for 2 hours each day. With the consolidation of schools and the advent of magnet schools, neighborhood schools are just a memory for most families. When children went to neighborhood schools, their parents **could** visit the schools to show concern for their children's education. Now, participating in schools involves finding transportation and time to go there, as well as usually arranging child care for other younger children.

Many teachers assume that parents just do not want to take the time to be involved in their children's education. Without knowing the context of parents' lives and understanding their other commitments, teachers have no way to make a fair judgment on this matter. Many parents, for example, are single parents trying to juggle work, child care, and sometimes their own education so they can improve their working conditions. Some have work commitments that might prevent them from attending open houses, conferences, or awards ceremonies. Most children today have stepparents or other relatives and friends who play active roles in their lives, and teachers must be respectful of these relationships. In short, teachers need to be mindful of families' unique makeup, offering alternative opportunities for parent/guardian participation. Some parental concerns and questions can be taken care of through phone calls or notes, and conferences and classroom visits can be scheduled at times convenient for working parents. Not taking the time and care to get to know families and be flexible in interacting with them can hurt and insult these vital people in students' lives.

Often teachers' assumptions of lack of care are based on a lack of cultural understanding of how parents view their responsibilities versus teachers' responsibilities. We saw that with the Latino parents in Boston described earlier. Delpit (1995) can help us understand this issue for Black families as well. African-American parents have a long history of placing their hopes for a better life in America's education system, only to find their hopes dashed again and again (Perkinson, 1991). They send their children to schools knowing that when they, themselves, were children they were likely discriminated against and many did not receive an equal education. Jed can assume his Black parents are mistrustful of American White teachers, with due cause. He also can assume his Black parents are concerned that their children have an equal opportunity for success and that they consider it his job to teach their children the skills they will need for success in American culture. "They want to ensure that the school provides their children with the discourse patterns, interactional styles, and spoken and written language codes that will allow them success in the larger society" (Delpit, 1995, p. 29).

Black parents consider it the school's job to teach their children these skills, just as it is the school's job to teach Latino children English. It is not the case that the parents are uncaring or want to abdicate their responsibilities to help educate their children. They cannot teach their children the skills that they do not know themselves, such as communication and literacy skills that are based on Standard English, anymore than Carlos's or Yolanda's mothers can teach their children what they need to learn about English.

> What the school personnel fail to understand is that if the parents were members of the culture of power and lived by its rules and codes, then they would transmit those codes to their children. In fact, they transmit another culture that children must learn at home in order to survive in their communities. (Delpit, 1995, p. 30)

Delpit (1995) suggests the way preservice teachers are taught to teach skills such as reading and writing makes sense for White students who are learning the White culture codes at home but does not necessarily work for minority students. Not only are minority children not learning the "culture of power" at home, in our schools we tend to treat what they are learning at home as detrimental. For example, a Black child who is trying to learn how to read will typically be corrected by her teacher when she uses her Black dialect to say what she is reading, as if she is misreading the words. In fact, what she is doing is a translation act as she reads, which demonstrates she is reading the words correctly and comprehends what they mean. However, correcting her results in her learning to resist reading and resent the teacher. It harms her fluency in reading as well as her enjoyment in reading (Delpit, 1995, pp. 58–59).

We teach teachers to focus on the process of writing and to encourage fluency, and Black parents feel concerned that their children do not need to develop fluency. What they need are writing skills, which they need teachers to explicitly teach their children. When teachers do not explicitly teach their students the skills they need to be successful, Black parents and students feel cheated, as if the teachers are holding them back and keeping something from their children considered of high value in the "culture of power." Jed will need to reassure his Black families that he is doing his job, that he will make sure their children learn the skills they need to know to be successful. He will need to earn these families' respect and trust, and he can begin to do so by not passing judgment on what kind of parents they are and taking a more humble stance. They can teach him much about their children, but he has to be willing to listen and **hear** what they have to say (Delpit, 1995, p. 47).

Hispanic families typically are very close-knit, and, like Asian families, the family is viewed in an extended way, not just as a nuclear family, as White people tend to view families in the United States. As a cultural group, Hispanics clearly are family centered and enjoy children. What they consider basic acts of caring for their children, others might judge to be overindulgence or overprotection. Americans tend to stereotype Hispanics as lazy and irresponsible. The media describe Hispanic families as having problems with rising crime, drug abuse, teenage pregnancies, large families, and unemployment. It is well documented that American schools have discriminated against Latino children, placing them in lower academic tracks, falsely labeling them as having special education needs, and insisting they not use their native language in the schools. These children whom we have wrongly treated are now the parents of the Hispanic children assigned to Jed's class. He cannot assume these parents will trust him or believe that he is looking out for their children. He will have to earn their trust and respect, as with all of his parents. He will have to demonstrate that he is trying to understand their cultural perspectives, in a positive, receptive, nonjudgmental way. Then they will feel safe to open up to him, and they will advise their children to give him a try and participate in class and not be afraid of Señor Jones. Hispanic parents are also unlikely to come in and complain to teachers about problems their children are having in school, out of respect for teachers as authorities, not because they do not care about their children. Instead, they will teach their children at home ways to cope with their teachers' misunderstandings.

Similarly, Asian parents are sometimes labeled as "not caring" because they do not come to parent conferences or communicate with the school about their children, either. Again, as a cultural group they feel it is their duty to treat their children's teachers with respect. From an Asian parent's perspective, questioning these teachers would be considered a sign of disrespect and possibly an insult. They may also fear that if they insult their children's teachers by questioning them, their children will suffer as a result. Of course, Asian parents, like all parents nowadays, have many commitments that may account for why they are not seen often at schools. Vinh's uncle, for instance, works full-time and takes care of his brothers' four children. See Wai's parents both work extremely long days just to keep from drowning in debt. These children all know something their teachers may not—that their families care a great deal about them and are willing to make tremendous sacrifices for their children's sakes.

So many times parents must explain to their children why a teacher did this or that and help ease their frustrations and sorrow, so that their children are able to go back and face another day of school with that same teacher. Why do we expect children to be more mature and understanding than we are as teachers? How can we make such a painful, insulting mistake as to assume these families do not care?

Jed assumes his families care about their children and know their children better than anyone else. He considers them his greatest resources for helping him understand his students and reaching their needs. He looks forward to having these parents, siblings, and other relatives as friends, as Herbert Kohl (1984) does in *Growing Minds*. Kohl talks about being invited to parents' houses for dinner and being asked to sneak Puerto Rican food into the hospital for an ailing parent. He says he often turns to the parents for advice when what he tries to do seems to hurt their children rather than help them.

Because Jed approaches parents in a respectful, humble way and lets them know that he values their insights about their children, he very rarely meets a family he cannot get along with or parents who seem to be truly abusive of their children. What is most common is that Jed's students' families are happy and relieved to know their children have a teacher who cares about their children's well-being and views their children in a positive, holistic manner. They feel reassured to know that their children will find their cultural backgrounds considered assets in Jed's class and that he will let their children rely on their experiences to help them learn, further developing their strengths as they work on their weaknesses. The students' families are pleased that he considers them valuable resources and that he plans to enlist their help, so they can find ways to support their children's education and come visit their classroom. They will want to be reassured that Jed has control of the classroom and the children will be safe. And they will want to know that he has high expectations and their children will learn what they need to know so they can be successful in America's culture. Jed finds that parents contribute what they can to help the classroom function as well as possible and to support his goal of nurturing a democratic community in the classroom.

Further Issues to Address with Our Philosophy of Education

Jed cannot, by himself, change the social conditions that cause many of the problems and hardships his students and their families must face. However, he can serve as a resource and support system for his students and their extended families, and he can help them learn the skills and tools they need to assist each other and themselves. He can also help them understand the social conditions in which they live, critique these conditions, and then develop plans of action to help make changes. These are the kinds of roles Paulo Freire has been able to play as an educator for his adult students. (We discussed Freire in Chapter 1.)

Critical theorists argue it is not enough to be a resource and guide to your students. It is not enough to show them you care, by being attentive, receptive, and empathetic to their situations. People need to work actively to improve situations, to put their theory into action (what Freire calls **praxis**). The great difficulty for democratic teachers is they cannot assume to know what kind of action their students need to take; they must let their students figure this out for themselves. Again, they must fall back to playing the resource role, or else they will be vulnerable to accusations that they are undermining exactly what they are trying to teach. For Jed, he cannot tell his students how to be a democratic community, and he cannot be a democratic community for them. If the community he creates is a truly democratic one, Jed will not be able to predict exactly how events will unfold, nor will he have control over all that happens. The students and teacher(s) will choose to be a democratic community together or not. Jed can explain the value of his goals and outline the plans he has made to help enact them, but ultimately he is dependent on his students and their families to effectively reach his goals.

Just as social conditions affect Jed's students' lives, so too do they affect his life as a teacher. These social conditions reflect American social values (meaning the dominant, majority cultural norms). Looking at these conditions will give us final pause to consider the philosophy of education presented here. It also offers us an opportunity to make some final recommendations for U.S. school systems, if we mean to support establishing democratic classroom communities within our schools like the one we have described in this chapter. These social conditions are ones Jed (and Maria) face that make their task more difficult. Let us go back to where we started this chapter, with the working conditions in which Jed and Maria must work.

Working Conditions

We situated our classroom in a real, existing school building that Kozol (1991) has described in *Savage Inequalities*. We did not choose one of the more extreme buildings he depicts, such as the school in East St. Louis that has raw sewage coming up in the bathrooms (Chapter 1) or the high school in New York City that has ceiling tiles falling on students' heads and water that cascades down the stairs of the building whenever it rains (Chapter 3). All of the urban buildings Kozol describes have very grim, miserable qualities. These are buildings teachers choose to work in and lower-class students are forced to attend (after all, school attendance is required by law in the United States). People who can have moved their children away from these schools to ones that are safer, more aesthetically pleasing, and offer a higher quality of education. We chose the setting we did to demonstrate that our philosophy of education is possible and applicable for all children in any school setting.

A democratic classroom is possible anywhere. All you really need are teachers and students who are willing to try to be a democratic community together and parents and administrators who are willing to let you try. Certainly, though, there are ways to make the process of nurturing easier, and there are ways to better support such a goal. One recommendation is to repair and improve our school buildings so that these may become places in which students and teachers can look forward to spending time, rather than places with which they "put up." Jed Jones and Maria Garcia work very hard to make their rooms pleasant, comfortable places in which to learn, and they should do so, as good teachers who care. But this does not mean they should have to teach 59 children in a space that would hold 20 students if they were in the suburbs. The cramped conditions of their space will make their jobs more difficult. Investing in safe, comfortable school buildings will improve conditions for learning and living together.

Maria should not have to teach 29 second graders in a bilingual class. Twenty-nine second graders who know English is too many, let alone 29 children who are trying to learn a second language while they are still learning their first language. Investing in manageable classroom population sizes by hiring more teachers will make it more possible for teachers to nurture democratic communities in their classrooms. Smaller classes mean teachers and students have more chances to get to know each other and learn how to get along with each other. Students also have greater opportunities to have their strengths and weaknesses assessed, and teachers can develop more individualized curricula using students' experiences and interests to help assure that they improve their knowledge. Smaller classes offer students more time and ways to practice and improve the tools and skills they need to be constructive thinkers.

Some states have already taken seriously the recommendation to hire more teachers so that classroom sizes are smaller. Indiana, for example, has a program called "Prime Time" in which elementary classrooms are not allowed to be larger than 18 to 20 students, to help students get as much assistance as they need. These education policies have measured, successful results that are the end result of a willingness to invest in education.

Of course, Jed should not have to create his own resource library for his 6th-grade students. He also should not have to share one computer with the entire 6th-grade student body. The teaching supplies and resources available to him handicap him in his efforts to nurture a democratic community. We learned that some of the best methods to help students feel good about themselves and become more actively involved in the classroom are to get them excited about what they are learning and let them work together and help each other. Jed can teach students without any books, but the better his resources are, the easier his job is going to be and the more students he will be able to help become engaged learners.

What does it say about our values, as an American society, that we are willing to spend so much to build prisons and pay for the care of prisoners, but we are not willing to invest in our children's education, especially our poor children's, to ensure they have a good start in schools? We know how to make their experiences in schools educational and how to help them feel cared for. We know how to improve their understanding and further their growth. This book is not full of startling revelations. Rather, we hope it has made a strong case for the value of working with each other and helping each other and considering the need for everyone to contribute to the quilting of knowledge. We wonder, Do we live in a society that values all of its citizens? If it does, why is it not willing to invest in their education?

Administration

People might say the administration for which Jed and Maria work is very supportive. By some standards that opinion would be right. "Support" is a relative term, though. True, they received permission to paint their room and bring in supplies. However, none of the work they did on Room 302 cost the school anything. The administration cannot afford to be supportive in terms of supplies and resources. It is also true that the administration supports their efforts to nurture a democratic community in Room 302 by defending them if a parent has questions or complaints. The administration says it is willing to allow Jed and Maria to be flexible and creative with their curriculum, but only because it is in a no-lose position with these teachers' innovative efforts. These are lower-class, minority students, for the most part, who tend not to do well in school (meaning earn good grades and high achievement test scores). The principal is pleased that the teachers care so much about their curriculum and are willing to work so hard to help their students be successful learners. Surely what they are trying to accomplish is worth the risk, for the results could be improved test scores and happy parents, both of which make the school and the administrators look good. If the students do not improve academically and the parents are unhappy, the administration can just blame the teachers. Even if the teachers fail, the administrators of Jed and Maria's school face little risk.

What if Jed and Maria were teaching in a wealthier, suburban school? In a wealthier school system, the administration would probably have to be more cautious. Major changes in curriculum and styles of instruction would need to be extensively researched and the pros and cons carefully weighed. The risks would be much higher, because these schools enroll students who are already being successful. These schools have good reputations as fine institutions for learning where people are pleased with the quality of education. Administrators in successful schools have to worry that the quality of their schools is upheld. People buy homes and decide to locate businesses in communities where "the schools are good." If a school harms the quality of the education offered by trying something new and different, it has the potential to initiate a damaging, rippling effect on the entire community, even including people who do not have children in school.

Because Jed and Maria have a clearly articulated philosophy of education and have taken the time to plan their classrooms so that what they will be doing in Room 302 supports that philosophy, if they should apply for jobs at a wealthier school system they would likely find school administrators willing to listen to what they have to offer. They have extensive research to support their philosophy of education, and they can show that they have carefully considered the pros and cons. Most likely, though, Jed and Maria might be surprised to find that some teachers are already nurturing democratic classroom communities in wealthier schools. They would probably be amazed to find that parents want their children in this type of classroom and are already convinced it will benefit their children's education. Jed and Maria might even find that administrators in wealthier school systems would hire them **because** of their philosophy of education. The goal of striving to nurture a democratic community in the classroom meets the needs of wealthier students just as readily as it meets the needs of poorer students. Teaching students to be responsible and caring and helping them learn how to be constructive thinkers are all goals toward which wealthier schools tend to strive.

The biggest concerns Jed and Maria are likely to have are whether their students will continue to learn and thrive academically (doing at least as well as they did before entering their classes) and whether they will be able to ensure their safety. Because we know from this chapter that both of those concerns can be alleviated, they should find teaching in a wealthier school system an enjoyable experience (although maybe not as rewarding or as appreciated). They would have more resources available to them and would work in conditions that are more supportive of their efforts. They would find the environment is framed in such a way that it would be easier for them to "fit in" and get on with their work. Many of the battles they have to fight in P.S. 261 would not exist in wealthier suburban schools. Their classrooms would be larger, their class sizes smaller, and they would have the supplies they need. Their students would come to school better prepared to learn, because they did not have to work as a cook the night before (See Wai), and they did not have to go with their father to the doctor to translate the type of surgery he needs (Carlos). They would probably have to address a narrower range of skills and ability levels and would have less cultural diversity in their classrooms. This means their curricula would be easier to develop and their methods of instruction would not have to be so diverse. These differences do not mean nurturing a democratic community in a wealthier school system is less valuable but rather that it may be easier to accomplish because our society already values and embraces many of the qualities of democratic communities for its wealthier citizens.

Keeping Good Teachers

Great teachers are appreciated and celebrated in poor schools in the United States, by the school's administrators, children, and parents. We can find in some of our poorest schools some of our best teachers, and if you look at them closely you will see they know how to nurture caring democratic communities in their classrooms. Teachers such as Herbert Kohl, Jessica Siegel, Corla Hawkins, and Jaime Escalante have books written and movies made about them. They help us all feel better, providing hope that we can help all children reach their full potential and contribute to our greater society. But then the book is over, the movie ends, and these teachers go back to their classrooms where they are expected to continue to make miracles happen, with little to no support from our larger society. Herbert Kohl says he has been able to teach the way he does because he takes a year off from teaching every couple of years. Jaime Escalante found that even after he was so successful teaching Hispanic students calculus that they were able to pass the advanced placement calculus test, he still had to fight the same battles over and over again. He no longer teaches at Garfield High School in East Los Angeles. Jessica Siegel no longer teaches at all.

The battles good teachers fight in poor schools wear them down. The problems they face and with which they try to help their students and parents cope are tremendous. Lisa Delpit found in her interviews of minority teachers and would-be teachers that many of them quit teaching before they even begin or leave very early in their careers. When she asked why, they said it was because they found the problems bigger then they alone could tackle. They also felt that to stay was somehow to give credence to the prejudice, lack of care, and injustice they were witnessing. As one would-be teacher said:

> After that one semester of student teaching, I felt I just couldn't work in the public school system. The system was corrupt, and I'd be fighting and fussing the whole time. No, the system was murderous. It didn't exist to educate children. I realized it was bigger than me, and I had to leave. (Delpit, 1995, p. 112)

Does our society value the need to offer quality education for all of its citizens? As Kohl (1984) points out in Corla Hawkins's case, the school where she works has many problems, and the Chicago school system in general faces serious concerns such as a shortage of teachers. The problems are not due to a lack of information about how to be a good teacher; "[t]he problems are systemic" (p. 51). People do not want jobs as teachers in conditions like those in which Jed Jones and Maria Garcia teach. The worst part seems to be that as long as we do have good teachers, even if only a few, who are willing to teach under harmful, disgraceful conditions, our greater society can avoid working to solve the problems that exist. The greater society can avoid taking responsibility for reflecting on its values and assumptions, critiquing its perspectives and plans, and amending its theories so that new plans for action can be drawn.

Several good teachers face a great many problems daily because they teach poor, minority children in a society that does not seem to care or feel the need to improve learning conditions for its poorer citizens. Given the social conditions that currently exist and the values seemingly embraced by the majority society in the United States, very often the best moral course of action good teachers can choose is to quit teaching and refuse to be a part of such corruption. Teachers who feel unable to change a corrupt system may elect not to contribute to that corruption by opting out of teaching—unless these teachers look around their classrooms one more time at the children they have come to know so well. In the end, teachers such as Herbert Kohl and Corla Hawkins come back to teach again another year because of the students. They care, and they hope that in some small way what they do helps the children they are teaching.

What Happens When the Students Leave Jed's Classroom?

The most frequent questions we are asked when we explain our philosophy of education are "How do the students adjust when they leave your classroom? How do they cope with other classrooms that are not like the democratic community they experienced with you? Aren't you setting them up for failure and disappointment when they have to move on to another classroom?" We find these questions very troubling because of what they say about assumptions people have concerning education. These questions do not say, "We disagree with what you are suggesting." The concern is not with the value or worth of teaching students in the manner we are suggesting. People do not seem even to doubt that the students will learn a lot, including learning how to get along with each other. What these concerns express to us is a sense of hopelessness, that what we are suggesting is idealistic and "pie-in-the-sky" and will never happen in our public education system. Given that nurturing democratic communities in our classrooms will never be valued in the United States, how do we intend to help our students cope when they leave our classroom and have to face "the real world"?

First, we do not feel the hopelessness that these concerns express. If nothing else, we hope that the reasons and examples we have given and the sources we have used to help support the case for why our philosophy of education is valuable will at least warrant people thinking about what they are suggesting. Even if students should only experience a caring, democratic community in one classroom, it gives them a place where they can grow and develop, where they can learn more about themselves and others, where they can feel that they are valued and have significant contributions to make to our greater society. If they do not encounter such a place again in their academic careers, will they suffer because of this one experience? We do not think so. Students will leave our democratic classroom with tools and skills that will help them for the rest of their lives (see Chapter 4). And having experienced such a community in one place offers them the knowledge that it is possible and supplies them with a model for how to help nurture democratic communities elsewhere. Besides, we do not believe our classroom will be the only place that students will ever encounter such a place. We are writing this book in a country that embraces democracy as a form of government. For all of its flaws, the United States is a country that draws people from around the world, for it is considered a land of opportunity. It is supposed to be a place where people are welcomed and diversity is embraced. It is supposed to be a "land of liberty, justice, and freedom for all," and though it is not perfect, most Americans still think that it is a place they want to live and that these tenets are worthwhile goals.

These expressed concerns are like saying to a parent, "Why be so kind and loving with your children? Aren't you setting them up for painful failure when they move out of your house and encounter the evil, ugly world that exists out there?" Parents might think you were crazy if you asked them such a question! "What are you saying—you want us to abuse our children now so they'll know how to deal with abuse when they grow up? Shouldn't we love them and treat them with kindness so they grow up healthy and strong, better able to cope with problems they might encounter?" Who is to say the world is so evil and ugly now or will be when our children do grow up? Maybe our actions will help the world be a place that will not harm our innocent, loving children. If we treat our children in a kind and loving manner, will they not grow up knowing how to be loving and kind to other people?

Helping create caring, safe, reasonable, intuitive, imaginative, emotional environments is a positive thing to do. Even people who may be concerned that this philosophy of education means we all have to agree and be alike will find that a democratic community model leaves plenty of room for people to be as diverse, unique, dissonant, disagreeable, and rebellious as they want to be. We are not saying we all have to agree or even get along with each other. We are saying that it is vital that we make room for each other and commit ourselves to attempting to listen and try to understand what each other has to say (to **hear**, as Delpit describes this). We are recommending that all of us need to practice how to be **enlarged thinkers** (Benhabib's term), and part of that practice includes enlarging our hearts and stretching our imaginations, as we attempt to understand others' worlds that are unknown to us. We are recommending that as an American society we need to reexamine our values and beliefs continually to make sure that our social institutions, such as our public schools, are indeed accomplishing the goals we want them to accomplish. If they are not, rather than preparing students for failure and disappointment, teaching them coping skills for the problems we know they will encounter in other classrooms and society at large, we recommend that we, as citizens, act to change our schools so they do meet the goals we value. Let us work to rid our schools of the problems students encounter and prepare our students for success in their lives rather than failure.

Conclusion

We have described the nurturing of a democratic classroom community because ultimately we hope that if children are taught in such a manner and in such an environment by people who care about their well-being, these children will grow up to be contributing citizens of a democratic society. As Maxine Greene (1995) points out, democracy is an ideal, always in the making. It is something toward which we strive and try to make work. We have found in this chapter and throughout the book that democratic societies are something we must continually reenvision, with the help of diverse perspectives. Democratic societies offer the opportunity for perpetual flux and change.

Like Greene (1995), we still believe "that the ground of a critical community can be opened in our teaching and in our schools" (pp. 197–198). We know that the kind of opening up that is needed relies on Noddings's concept of care; Freire's concept of trust; Benhabib's concept of respect; Belenky et al.'s concepts of appreciation and affection; and Gadamer's, Rorty's, and Freire's ideas of hope (to name a few of those who have worked on these important ideas).

We know that for others to open up and discuss their ideas, our society has be committed to creating safe spaces and making room for the promise of others' contributions. We have to find ways to guarantee that others' voices will be listened to and heard. As Noddings (1989) points out, in the Euro-Western world "educators perpetuate a system that creates strangers, rivals, and enemies" (p. 187). When people view knowing as an activity that develops out of their (our) relationships with each other, then the conditions of those relationships become very important. Now, taking care of each other and thinking about how people affect each other becomes worthy of our attention. In a philosophy of education that aims to help each individual student discover Truth, how everyone else is doing does not really matter. In an individualistic perspective, how **I** am doing is what is important, and my main worry is how others might deceive me, or steal from me, or distract me from my task of discovering Truth.

However, in a philosophy of education that recognizes the need for each others' input and that none of us alone can ever hope to find "the goods" (Truth), "the goods" become the **people** to whom we relate. As social beings who learn our languages from each other, enhance our abilities to think through interactions with each other, and develop our voices by learning what is different about our perspectives from others', those other beings in our social communities become our greatest treasures. The more we are able to work together and help each other, attend to each others' needs, and care for each other, the more we will increase our chances of living in a thriving democratic society. The goal of living in a democratic society is a beautiful and beneficial goal, for it focuses our attentions on what makes constructive knowledge a possibility for us, our most prized treasures: each other and the world in which we live. Anytime we move to embrace a democratic society, people are rewarded because knowing is further developed, and our hopes and promises of tomorrow move closer to becoming realities. As Maxine Greene (1995) says in *Releasing the Imagination:*

> All we can do is to speak with others as passionately and eloquently as we can; all we can do is to look into each others' eye and urge each other on to new beginnings. Our classrooms ought to be nurturing and thoughtful and just all at once; they ought to pulsate with multiple conceptions of what it is to be human and alive. They ought to resound with the voices of articulate young people in dialogues always incomplete because there is always more to be discovered and more to be said. We must want our students to achieve friendship as each one stirs to wide-awakeness, to imaginative action, and to renewed consciousness of possibility. (p. 43)

In the Classroom

Activity 1

We have described 14 of the students in Jed Jones's class, giving you enough background to have an idea who they are as students and the kinds of issues they are likely to face as learners. We would like you to describe one of the 16 students not represented in the chapter, giving enough details and background that you and your classmates will be able to make some reasonable assumptions about the student and the kinds of problems that she or he might be expected to have in a class like the one we have described. Make sure your student fits within the demographic classroom description Sadker and Sadker (1988) give.

If you can base the student description on a real student you know, your descriptions will be more vivid and will help you in better understanding his or her potential problems. Consider how the student you describe might relate to the teacher, Jed, or how she or he might get along with some of the other students. Try to think of specific things that Jed and the class might do to encourage your student to thrive and grow in their democratic classroom. This activity can be dramatized.

Activity 2

Looking back at the scenarios we developed in Chapter 3, choose students from Room 302 to be involved in one of those situations and then predict how the problem will play out for them in Jed's classroom. Consider how Jed and his class will try to deal with the problem and reach some manner of resolution, all the while maintaining the spirit of nurturing a democratic community in their classroom. This activity can be dramatized.

Activity 3

We have described a classroom of students and some of the issues and concerns that are likely to be present in Jed's 6th-grade class. We did not do this for Maria's 2nd-grade class, which shares Room 302 with Jed's class. Try to describe an individual student who might be in her class, using someone you have known, as a basis for your description. Think about his or her unique family situation, the kinds of problems that he or she is likely to experience as a learner, and the cultural/social concerns that will affect this student's capacity to function in an American classroom that is attempting to be democratic. Ideally, you should seek time in class to describe your student to your classmates and learn what your classmates have written about other individuals who might conceivably be members of Maria's class. As a class, you might then think about Maria's 2nd-grade classroom and flesh out what are likely to be some of the issues that may emerge based on the students whom you and your classmates have described as her potential students. This activity can be dramatized.

Activity 4

We have used the example of a classroom that has students who are of mixed ages, second graders and sixth graders, together. In Chapter 1, we described Montessori classrooms that have three consecutive ages together (i.e., 6- to 9-year-olds or 9- to 12-year-olds). Look at mixed-age groups as an innovation that might be adopted for use in our schools. If teachers strive to develop a democratic community in their classrooms, what things might happen as a result of having mixed age groups? Try to brainstorm a list of as many possible ramifications, both good and bad, as you can. Consider how mixed-age groups might affect the process of creating and sustaining a democratic classroom community as well as prepare students for life outside the school.

Notes

1. For ease of writing, the bilingual teacher we name Maria Garcia, and we, as the 6th-grade teacher, are named Jed Jones. In America's elementary schools this is the common pattern: males tend to teach the older students, and females tend to teach younger children.

2. Sonia Nieto (1992) references this paper in her discussion on bilingual education programs.

3. We label "blacks" and "whites" a race, but from a scientific standpoint there is only one race: the human race. "Race" is a socially constructed category. The problem, as Nieto (1992) points out, with using *culture* as a term to describe blacks,

instead of *race,* is that we then risk hiding "the very real issue of racism in society" (p. 17).

4. Science Research Associates is the company that publishes color-coded sequential reading materials known as SRAs.

5. Nieto refers to Gilbert and Gay (1985).

6. See Arnot (1994), Frankenburg (1995), Lather (1994), and Nicholson (1980, 1994).

7. See Angelou (1969), Davis (1981), Dill (1994), hooks (1981, 1984, 1989), Lorde (1981, 1984), McKellar (1989), Olsen (1978), and Walker (1983).

Bibliography

Adler, M. (1982). *The paideia proposal: an educational manifesto*. New York: Collier.

Angelou, M. (1969). *I know why the caged bird sings*. New York: Random House.

Apple, M. (1986). *Teachers and texts*. New York: Routledge.

Apple, M. (1996). *Cultural politics and education*. New York: Teachers College Press.

Arcilla, R. V. (1993). Against polemics, for disarming communication: Response to Rice and Burbules. In H. A. Alexander (Ed.), *Philosophy of education 1992* (pp. 45–48). Normal, IL: Philosophy of Education Society.

Aristotle. (1970a). Nichomachaen ethics. In S. Cahn (Ed.), *The philosophical foundations of education* (pp. 107–120). New York: Harper & Row.

Aristotle. (1970b). *The politics*. In S. Cahn (Ed.), *The philosophical foundations of education* (pp. 121–132). New York: Harper & Row.

Arnot, M. (1994). Male hegemony, social class, and women's education. In L. Stone, with G. M. Boldt (Eds.), *The education feminist reader* (pp. 84–104). New York: Routledge.

Bacon, C. (1988). *Teacher goal structures and student responsibility for learning: A student perspective*. Unpublished doctoral dissertation, University of California, Santa Barbara.

Bacon, C., & Thayer-Bacon, B. (1993). "Real talk": Enhancing critical thinking skills through conversation in the classroom. *Clearing House, 66*(3), 181–184.

Bailin, S. (1988). *Achieving extraordinary ends: an essay on creativity*. Dordrecht: Kluwer Academic.

Bar On, B. (1993). Marginality and epistemic privilege. In L. Alcoff & E. Potter (Eds.), *Feminist epistemologies* (pp. 83–100). New York: Routledge.

Barber, B. R. (1984). *Strong democracy: participatory politics for a new age*. Los Angeles: University of California Press.

Bateson, G. (1972). *Steps to an ecology of mind*. New York: Ballantine.

Bateson, G. (1991). *A sacred unity: Further steps to an ecology of mind*. New York: HarperCollins.

Bateson, M. C. (1989). *Composing a life*. New York: Penguin.

Bateson, M. C. (1994). *Peripheral visions: Learning along the way*. New York: HarperCollins.

Belenky, M., Clinchy, B., Goldberger, N., & Tarule, J. (1986). *Women's ways of knowing*. New York: Basic Books.

Benhabib, S. (1992). *Situating the self: Gender, community and postmodernism.* New York: Routledge.

Bennett deMarrais, K., & LeCompte, M. D. (1995). *The way schools work* (2nd ed.). New York: Longman.

Berger, P. L., & Luckmann, T. (1966). *The social construction of reality: A treatise in the sociology of knowledge.* Garden City, NY: Anchor Books, Doubleday.

Bernstein, R. J. (1983). *Beyond objectivism and relativism: Science, hermeneutics, and praxis.* Philadelphia: University of Pennsylvania Press.

Berry, W. (1977). *The unsettling of America: Culture and agriculture.* San Francisco: Sierra Club Books.

Berry, W. (1981). *Recollected essays, 1965–1980.* San Francisco: North Point.

Betham, J. (1977). *A fragment on government.* Cambridge: Cambridge University Press.

Block, J. H., & King, N. R. (1987). *School play: A source book.* New York: Garland.

Bloom, A. (1987). *The closing of the American mind.* New York: Simon & Schuster.

Bowles, S., & Gintis, H. (1976). *Schooling in capitalist America.* New York: Basic Books.

Britzman, D. P. (1995, Spring). Is there a queer pedagogy? Or, stop reading straight. *Educational Theory, 45*(2), 151–165.

Brosio, R. A. (1994). *A radical democratic critique of capitalist education.* New York: Lang.

Burbules, N. C. (1991, Spring). Rationality and reasonableness: A discussion of Harvey Siegel's relativism refuted and educating reason. *Educational Theory, 41*(2), 235–252.

Burbules, N. C. (1992). Two perspectives on reason as an educational aim: The virtues of reasonableness. In M. Buchmann & R. E. Floden (Eds.), *Philosophy of education 1991* (pp. 215–224). Normal, IL: Philosophy of Education Society.

Burbules, N. C. (1993). *Dialogue in teaching: Theory and practice.* New York: Teachers College Press.

Burbules, N. C., & Rice, S. (1991). Dialogue across differences: Continuing the conversation. *Harvard Educational Review, 6*(4), 393–416.

Cahn, S. (Ed.). (1970). *The philosophical foundations of education.* New York: Harper & Row.

Code, L. (1987). *Epistemic responsibility.* Hanover, NH: University Press of New England, for Brown University Press.

Code, L. (1991). *What can she know? Feminist theory and the construction of knowledge.* Ithaca, NY: Cornell University Press.

Code, L. (1993). Taking subjectivity into account. In L. Alcoff & E. Potter (Eds.), *Feminist epistemologies* (pp. 15–48). New York: Routledge.

Collier, V. P. (1989, March). *Academic achievement, attitudes, and occupations among graduates of two-way bilingual classes.* Paper presented at the annual meeting of the American Educational Research Association, San Francisco.

Davis, A. (1981). *Women, race, and class.* New York: Random House.

de Beauvoir, S. (1989). *The second sex.* (H. M. Parshley, Trans. and Ed.). New York: Vantage Books. (Original work published 1952)

Deci, E. L. (1975). *Intrinsic motivation.* New York: Plenum.

Deci, E. L. (1980). *The psychology of self-determination.* Lexington, MA: Lexington Books.

Deci, E. L., & Ryan, R. (1985). *Intrinsic motivation and self-determination in human behavior.* New York: Plenum.

de Lauretis, T. (1986). Feminist studies/critical studies: Issues, terms, and context. In T. de Lauretis (Ed.), *Feminist studies/critical studies.* Bloomington: Indiana University Press.

Delpit, L. (1995). *Other people's children: Cultural conflict in the classroom.* New York: New Press.

Derrida, J. (1978). *Writing and difference* (A. Bass, Trans.). Chicago: University of Chicago Press.

Descartes, R. (1960). *Meditations on first philosophy* (L. J. Lafleur, Trans.). Indianapolis: Bobbs-Merrill. (Original work published 1641)

Dewey, J. (1935). *Liberalism and social action.* New York: Putnam's.

Dewey, J. (1956). The school and society. In *The child and the curriculum and the school and society.* Chicago: University of Chicago. (Original work published 1900)

Dewey, J. (1958). *Art as experience* (2nd ed.). New York: Capricorn Books. (Original work published 1934)

Dewey, J. (1965). *Experience and education* (2nd ed.). New York: Macmillan. (Original work published 1938)

Dewey, J. (1966). *Democracy and education* (2nd ed.). New York: Free Press. (Original work published 1916)

Dewey, J. (1981). Experience and philosophic method. In J. Boydston (Ed.), *John Dewey: The later works, 1925–1953* (Vol. 1). Carbondale: Southern Illinois University Press.

Dill, B. T. (1994). Race, class, and gender: Prospects for an all-inclusive sisterhood. In L. Stone, with G. M. Boldt (Eds.), *The education feminist reader* (pp. 42–56). New York: Routledge.

Elbow, P. (1986). *Embracing contraries: Explorations in learning and teaching*. New York: Oxford University Press.

Ennis, R. (1962). A concept of critical thinking. *Harvard Educational Review, 32*(1), 81–111.

Ennis, R. (1987). A taxonomy of critical thinking dispositions and abilities. In J. Baron & R. Sternberg (Eds.), *Teaching thinking skills: Theory and practice* (pp. 9–26). New York: Freeman.

Fiskin, J. S. (1991). *Democracy and deliberation: New directions for democratic reform*. New Haven, CT: Yale University Press.

Flanagan, O., & Jackson, K. (1987). Justice, care, and gender: The Kohlberg-Gilligan debate revisited. *Ethics, 97*(3), 622–637.

Flax, J. (1983). Political philosophy and the patriarchal unconscious: A psychoanalytic perspective on epistemology and metaphysics. In S. Harding & M. B. Hintikka (Eds.), *Discovering reality* (pp. 245–281). Dordrecht: Reidel.

Flax, J. (1990). *Thinking fragments: Psychoanalysis, feminism, and postmodernism in contemporary West*. Berkeley: University of California Press.

Foucault, M. (1980). *Power/knowledge*. New York: Pantheon.

Fox-Genovese, E. (1991). *Feminism without illusions*. Chapel Hill: University of North Carolina Press.

Frankenberg, R. (1995). *The social construction of white women: Whiteness race matters*. Minneapolis: University of Minnesota Press.

Freedman, S. G. (1990). *Small victories*. New York: HarperCollins.

Freire, P. (1970). *Pedagogy of the oppressed*. New York: Seabury.

Freire, P. (1985). *The politics of education: Culture, power, and liberation*. South Hadley, MA: Bergin & Garvey.

Fuller, S. (1988). *Social epistemology*. Bloomington: Indiana University Press.

Gardner, H. (1983). *Frames of mind*. New York: Basic Books.

Gilbert, S. E., & Gay, G. (1985, October). Improving the success in school of poor black children. *Phi Delta Kappan*, pp. 133–137.

Gilligan, C. (1982). *In a different voice*. Cambridge, MA: Harvard University Press.

Giroux, H. A. (1981). *Ideology, culture and the process of school*. Barcombe, England: Falmer.

Giroux, H A. (1983). *Theory and resistance in education: A pedagogy for the opposition*. South Hadley, MA: Bergin & Garvey.

Giroux, H. A. (1988). *Schooling and the struggle for public life*. Minneapolis: University of Minnesota Press.

Goldman, A. (1994). Argumentation and social epistemology. *Journal of Philosophy*, 910(1), 27–49.

Goleman, D. (1995). *Emotional intelligence*. New York: Bantam Books.

Goodlad, J. (1984). *A place called school*. New York: McGraw-Hill.

Goodlad, J. (1991). *Teachers for our nation's schools*. San Francisco: Jossey-Bass.

Greene, M. (1995). *Releasing the imagination*. San Francisco: Jossey-Bass.

Grimshaw, J. (1986). *Philosophy and feminist thinking*. Minneapolis: University of Minnesota Press.

Gutmann, A. (1987). *Democratic education*. Princeton, NJ: Princeton University Press.

Habermas, J. (1982). A reply to my critics. In J. Thompson & D. Held (Eds.), *Habermas: Critical debates* (pp. 219–283). Cambridge, MA: MIT Press.

Hallahan, D. P., & Kauffman, J. M. (1988). *Exceptional children: Introduction to special education* (4th ed.). Upper Saddle River, NJ: Prentice Hall.

Hamlyn, D. W. (1978). *Experience and the growth of understanding*. London: Routledge & Kegan Paul.

Hanson, K. (1986). *The self imagined: Philosophical reflections on the social character of the psyche.* London: Routledge & Kegan Paul.

Harding, S. (1984). Is gender a variable in conceptions of rationality? In C. C. Gould (Ed.), *Beyond domination: New perspectives on women and philosophy* (pp. 43–63). Totowa, NJ: Rowman & Allanheid.

Harding, S. (1993). Rethinking standpoint epistemology: What is "strong objectivity"? In L. Alcoff & E. Potter (Eds.), *Feminist epistemologies.* New York: Routledge (pp. 49–82).

Hardwig, J. (1991). The role of trust in knowledge. *Journal of Philosophy,* 88(12), 693–708.

Harstock, N. (1983). The feminist standpoint: Developing the grounds for a specifically feminist historical materialism. In S. Harding & M. B. Hintikka (Eds.), *Discovering reality (pp. 283–310).* Dordrecht: Reidel.

Hegel, G. W. F. (1975). *Natural laws* (T. M. Know, Trans.). Philadelphia: University of Pennsylvania Press. (Original work published 1802, 1803)

Heldke, L. (1987, Fall). John Dewey and Evelyn Fox Keller: A shared epistemological tradition. *Hypatia,* 2(3), 129–140.

Hirsch, E. D., Jr. (1987). *Cultural literacy.* Boston: Houghton Mifflin.

hooks, b. (1981). *Ain't I a woman: Black women and feminism.* Boston: South End Press.

hooks, b. (1984). *Feminist theory from margin to center.* Boston: South End Press.

hooks, b. (1989). *Talking back.* Boston: South End Press.

Illich, I. (1973). *Deschooling society.* New York: Harper & Row.

Jaggar, A. M. (1983). *Feminist politics and human nature.* Sussex: Harvester.

Jaggar, A. M. (1992). Love and knowledge: Emotion in feminist epistemology. In A. Garry & M. Pearsall (Eds.), *Women, knowledge, and reality: Explorations in feminist philosophy.* New York: Routledge.

Johnson, D. W., Johnson, R. T., & Holubec, E. J. (1992, May). Cooperative learning: A tool for integrating students with special needs into the regular classroom. In National Education Association, *A report from education policy and professional practice,* "The Integration of Students with Special Needs into Regular Classrooms: Policies and Practices That Work." Washington, DC: National Education Association.

Kant, I. (1949). *Fundamental principles of the metaphysics of ethics* (T. K. A. Abbott, Trans.). Indianapolis: Bobbs-Merrill. (Original work published 1785)

Kant, I. (1950). *Prolegomena to any future metaphysics.* New York: Liberal Arts Press. (Original work published 1783)

Kant, I. (1951). *Critique of judgment* (J. Bernard, Trans.). (Original work published 1790)

Kant, I. (1956). *Critique of practical reason* (L. W. Beck, Trans.). New York: Liberal Arts Press. (Original work published 1788)

Kant, I. (1960). *Education* (A. Churton, Trans.). Ann Arbor: University of Michigan Press. (Original work published 1899)

Kant, I. (1966). *Critique of Pure Reason* (F. M. Muller, Trans.). Garden City, NY: Doubleday. (Original work published 1781)

Kaufman-Osborn, T. V. (1993, Spring). Teasing feminist sense from experience. *Hypatia,* 8(2), 124–144.

Keller, C. (1986). *From a broken web: Separation, sexism, and self.* Boston: Beacon.

Keller, E. F. (1985). *Reflections on gender and science.* New Haven, CT: Yale University Press.

King, N. (1979). Play: The kindergartner's perspective. *Elementary School Journal,* 80, 81–87.

Kipling, R. (1992). *The jungle book: Favorite Mowgli stories.* New York: Simon & Schuster.

Kirk, S. A., & Gallagher, J. J. (1989). *Educating exceptional children* (6th ed.). Boston: Houghton Mifflin.

Kohl, H. (1984). *Growing minds: On becoming a teacher.* New York: Harper & Row.

Kozol, J. (1991). *Savage inequalities.* New York: Crown.

Kuhn, T. (1970). *The structure of scientific revolutions* (2nd ed.). Chicago: University of Chicago Press.

Laclau, E., & Mouffe, C. (1985). *Hegemony and socialist strategy: Towards a radical democratic politics* (W. Moore & P. Cammack, Trans.). London: Verso.

Larson, R. (Ed. and Trans.). (1979). *Republic,* by Plato. Arlington Heights, IL: Harlan Davidson.

Lather, P. (1994). The absence of presence: Patriarchy, capitalism, and the nature of teacher work. In L. Stone, with G. M. Boldt (Eds.), *The education feminist reader* (pp. 242–251). New York: Routledge.

Leach, M. (1992). Can we talk? Response to Burbules and Rice. *Harvard Educational Review,* 62(2), 257–263.

Locke, J. (1894). *An essay concerning human understanding.* Oxford: Clarendon. (Original work published 1690)

Locke, J. (1960). *The second treatise on government.* Cambridge: Cambridge University Press. (Edition used originally published 1823)

Locke, J. (1970). Some thoughts concerning education. In S. Cahn (Ed.), *The philosophical foundations of education.* New York: Harper & Row.

Lorde, A. (1981, Fall). The uses of anger. *Women's Studies Quarterly,* 9, 7–10.

Lorde, A. (1984). *Sister outsider.* New York: Crossing.

Lyotard, J.-F. (1984). *The postmodern condition: A report on knowledge.* Minneapolis: University of Minnesota Press.

Maccia, G. S. (1954, July). The educational aims of Charles Peirce. *Educational Theory,* 4(3), 206–212.

Macpherson, C. B. (1973). *Democratic theory: Essays in retrieval.* Oxford: Oxford University Press.

Macpherson, C. B. (1977). *The life and times of liberal democracy.* Oxford: Oxford University Press.

Martin, J. R. (1984). Bringing women into educational thought, *Educational Theory,* 34(4), 341–354.

Martin, J. R. (1985). *Reclaiming a conversation.* New Haven, CT: Yale University Press.

Martin, J. R. (1992). *The schoolhome: Rethinking schools for changing families.* Cambridge, MA: Harvard University Press.

Marx, K., & Engels, F. (1964). *Communist manifesto.* New York: Pocket Books. (Original work published 1848)

Maslow, A. (1962). *Toward a psychology of being.* Princeton, NJ: Van Nostrand.

Mayhew, K. C., & Edwards, A. C. (1966). *The Dewey school.* New York: Atherton.

McKellar, B. (1989). Only the fittest of the fittest will survive: Black women and education. In L. Stone, with G. M. Boldt (Eds.), *The education feminist reader* (pp. 229–241). New York: Routledge.

McLaren, P. (1993). *Schools as ritual performance.* New York: Routledge & Kegan Paul.

McLaren, P. (1994). *Life in schools* (2nd ed.). New York: Longman.

McLaren, P., & Lankshear, C. (Eds.). (1994). *Politics of liberation: Paths from Freire.* New York: Routledge.

Mead, G. H. (1934). *Mind, self, and society: From the standpoint of a social behaviorist* (C. W. Morris, Ed.). Chicago: University of Chicago Press.

Mead, M. (1970). *Culture and commitment.* Garden City, NY: American Museum of Natural History Natural History Press/Doubleday.

Mill, J. S. (1947). *On liberty* (A. Castell, Ed.). New York: Appleton-Century-Crofts. (Original work published 1859)

Mill, J. S. (1950). *Utilitarianism, liberty and representative government.* New York: Dutton. (Original work published 1863)

Minnich, E. (1990). *Transforming knowledge.* Philadelphia: Temple University Press.

Montessori, M. (1972). *The discovery of the child* (2nd ed., M. Josephy Costelloe, Trans.). New York: Ballantine.

Montessori, M. (1977). *The secret of childhood* (2nd ed., M. Josephy Costelloe, Trans.). New York: Ballantine.

Morris, W. (Ed.). (1970). *The American heritage dictionary of the English language.* Boston: Heritage and Houghton Mifflin.

Narayan, U. (1989). The project of feminist epistemology: Perspectives from a nonwestern feminist. In A. Jaggar & S. Bordo (Eds.), *Gender/body/knowledge* (pp. 256–269). New Brunswick, NJ: Rutgers University Press.

National Education Association (NEA). (1992, May). *A report from education policy and professional practice,* "The Integration of Students with Special Needs into Regular Classrooms: Policies and Practices That Work." Washington, DC: National Education Association.

Neill, A. S. (1960). *Summerhill: A radical approach to child rearing*. New York City: Hart.

Neill, A. S. (1992). *Summerhill School: A new view of childhood* (A. Lamb, Ed.). New York: St. Martin's.

Nicholson, L. J. (1980, 1994). Women and schooling. In L. Stone (Ed.) with G. M. Boldt, *The education feminist reader*. New York, London: Routledge.

Nieto, S. (1992). *Affirming diversity: The sociopolitical context of multicultural education*. White Plains, NY: Longman.

Noddings, N. (1984). *Caring: A feminine approach to ethics and moral education*. Berkeley: University of California Press.

Noddings, N. (1989). *Women and evil*. Berkeley: University of California Press.

Noddings, N. (1992). *The challenge to care in schools: An alternative approach to education*. New York: Teachers College Press.

Noddings, N., & Shore, P. (1984). *Awakening the inner eye: Intuition in education*. New York: Teachers College Press.

Nussbaum, M. C. (1990). *Love's knowledge: Essays on philosophy and literature*. New York: Oxford University Press.

Offen, K. (1988). Defining feminism: A comparative historical approach. *Signs, 14*(1), 119–157.

Olsen, T. (1978). *Silences* (3rd ed.). New York: Delacorte/Seymour Lawrence.

Owen, R. (1948). *A new view of society*. Glencoe, IL: Free Press. (Original work published 1813)

Paley, V. (1992). *You can't say you can't play*. Cambridge, MA: Harvard University Press.

Paul, R. (1987). Dialogical thinking: Critical thought essential to the acquisition of rational knowledge and passions. In J. B. Baron & R. Sternberg (Eds.), *Teaching thinking skills: Theory and practice* (pp. 127–148). New York: Freeman.

Paul, R. (1990). *Critical thinking: What every person needs in a rapidly changing world*. Sonoma, CA: Sonoma State University.

Peirce, C. S. (1958). *Values in a universe of chance: Selected writings of Charles Sanders Peirce (1839–1914)* (P. Wiener, Ed.). Garden City, NJ: Doubleday.

Perkinson, H. J. (1991). *The imperfect panacea: American faith in education 1865–1990* (3rd ed.). New York: McGraw-Hill.

Peters, R. S. (1966). Reason and habit: The paradox of moral education. In I. Scheffler (Ed.), *Philosophy and education* (2nd ed.) (pp. 245–262). Boston: Allyn & Bacon.

Peters, R. S. (1971). Reason and passion. In G. Vessey (Ed.), *The proper study* (pp. 132–153). Royal Institute of Philosophy Lectures, Vol. 4. London: McMillan.

Piaget, J. (1966). *Judgement and reasoning in the child*. Totowa, NJ: Littlefield, Adams.

Plato. (1970a). The meno. In S. M. Cahn (Ed.), *The philosophical foundations of education*. New York: Harper & Row.

Plato. (1970b). *Protagoras*. In S. Cahn (Ed.), *The philosophical foundations of education*. New York: Harper & Row.

Plato. (1970c). Selections from *Republic*. In S. M. Cahn (Ed.), *The philosophical foundations of education*. New York: Harper & Row.

Plato. (1979). *Republic* (R. Larson, Ed. & Trans.). Arlington Heights, IL: Harlan Davidson.

Polanyi, M. (1967). *The tacit dimension*. Garden City, NY: Doubleday.

Prakash, M. S. (1990, May). War and peace: Education for survival, sustainability, and flourishing. *American Journal of Education, 98*(3), 278–298.

Prakash, M. S. (1994, Spring). What are people for? Wendell Barry on education, ecology, and culture. *Educational Theory, 44*(2), 135–157.

Quigley, L. (1959). *The blind men and the elephant*. New York: Scribner's.

Rawls, J. (1971). *A theory of justice*. Cambridge, MA: Harvard University Press.

Rice, S., & Burbules, N. C. (1993). Communicative virtue and educational relations. In H. A. Alexander (Ed.), *Philosophy of education 1992* (pp. 34–44). Urbana: University of Illinois, Philosophy of Education Society.

Rorty, R. (1979). *Philosophy and the mirror of nature*. Princeton, NJ: Princeton University Press.

Rorty, R. (1982). *Consequences of pragmatism*. Minneapolis: University of Minnesota Press.

Rorty, R. (1989). *Contingency, irony, and solidarity*. Cambridge: Cambridge University Press.

Rorty, R. (1991). Feminism and pragmatism. *Michigan Quarterly Review, 30*(2), 231–258.

Rousseau, J. J. (1968). *The social contract* (M. Cranston, Trans.). Harmondsworth: Penguin Books. (Original work published 1762)

Rousseau, J. J. (1970). Selections from *Emile*. In S. M. Cahn (Ed.), *The philosophical foundations of education*. New York: Harper & Row. (Original work published 1762)

Ruddick, S. (1989). *Maternal thinking: Toward a politics of peace.* Boston: Beacon.

Sadker, M. P., & Sadker, D. M. (1991). *Teachers, schools, and society* (2nd ed.). New York: McGraw-Hill.

Scheffler, I. (1973). *Reason and teaching.* New York: Bobbs-Merrill.

Seigfried, C. H. (1991, Summer). Where are all the pragmatist feminists? *Hypatia,* 6(2), 1–20.

Shapiro, H. S. (1990). *Between capitalism and democracy: Educational policy and the crisis of the welfare state.* New York: Bergin & Garvey.

Siegel, H. (1987). *Relativism refuted: A critique of contemporary epistemological relativism.* Dordrecht: Reidel.

Siegel, H. (1988). *Educating reason.* New York: Routledge.

Siegel, H. (1992). Two perspectives on reason as an educational aim: The rationality of reasonableness. In M. Buchmann & R. E. Floden (Eds.), *Philosophy of education 1991* (pp. 225–233). Normal, IL: Philosophy of Education Society.

Sizer, T. (1984). *Horace's compromise: The dilemma of the American high school.* Boston: Houghton Mifflin.

Sizer, T. (1992). *Horace's school: Redesigning the American High School.* Boston: Houghton Mifflin.

Slavin, R. E. (1991, February). Synthesis of research on cooperative learning. *Educational Leadership,* pp. 71–82.

Sleeter, C. E., & Grant, C. A. (1994). *Making choices for multicultural education* (2nd ed.). New York: Macmillan.

Snauwaert, D. T. (1992). Reclaiming the lost treasure: Deliberation and strong democratic education. *Educational Theory,* 42(3), 351–367.

Spring, J. (1994). *American education* (6th ed.). New York: McGraw-Hill.

Steiner, E. (1989). Society, government, and education: A philosophical treatise. Bloomington: Indiana University.

Stone, L. (1992). Disavowing community. In H. A. Alexander (Ed.), *Philosophy of education 1991* (pp. 93–101). Urbana, IL: Philosophy of Education Society.

Stout, M. (1992). Response to "Disavowing Community." In H. A. Alexander (Ed.), *Philosophy of education 1991* (pp. 102–104). Urbana, IL: Philosophy of Education Society.

Sutton-Smith, B. (Ed.). (1979). *Play and learning.* New York: Gardner.

Sutton-Smith, B. (1985, October). The child at play: Play is becoming steadily less physical, more computerized and, most of all, more isolated. *Psychology Today,* p. 64.

Taylor, C. (1989). *Sources of the self.* Cambridge, MA: Harvard University Press.

Taylor, C. (1992). *The ethics of authenticity.* Cambridge, MA: Harvard University Press.

Thayer-Bacon, B. (1987). *Parental views of Montessori schools.* Unpublished master's thesis, San Diego State University, San Diego, CA.

Thayer-Bacon, B. (1989). How the child reasons. *Philosophical Studies in Education,* pp. 107–116.

Thayer-Bacon, B. (1991, May). Egocentrism in critical thinking theory. *Inquiry: Critical Thinking across the Disciplines,* 7(4), 30–33.

Thayer-Bacon, B. (1992a). Is modern critical thinking theory sexist? *Inquiry: Critical Thinking across the Disciplines,* 10(1), 3–7.

Thayer-Bacon, B. (1992b, April). *Richard Paul's strong-sense critical thinking and procedural knowing: A comparison.* Paper presented at a conference of the American Educational Research Association. (ERIC Document Reproduction Service No. ED 353 280)

Thayer-Bacon, B. (1993a, Summer). Caring and its relationship to critical thinking. *Educational Theory,* 43(3), 323–340.

Thayer-Bacon, B. (1993b, April). Selves in relation: Reconstructing community. Paper presented at a conference of the American Educational Research Association (ERIC Document Reproduction Service No. ED 363 551)

Thayer-Bacon, B. (1995a). Caring democratic communities. *Philosophical Studies in Education,* pp. 139–151.

Thayer-Bacon, B. (1995b, Spring). Constructive thinking: Personal voice. *Journal of Thought,* 30(1), 55–70.

Thayer-Bacon, B. (1995c, Winter). Doubting and believing: Both are important for critical thinking. *Inquiry: Critical Thinking across the Disciplines,* 15(2), 59–66.

Thayer-Bacon, B. (1996a). Democratic classroom communities. *Studies in Philosophical Education,* 15, 333–351.

Thayer-Bacon, B. (1996b). Navigating epistemological territories. In A. Neiman (Ed.), *Philosophy of education 1995* (pp. 460–468). Urbana, IL: Philosophy of Education Society.

Thayer-Bacon, B. (1996c, July). Relational qualities between selves and communities: Implications for schools. *Journal for a just and caring education,* 2(3), 283–303.

Thayer-Bacon, B. (1997a, April). An examination and redescription of epistemology. Paper presented at an "enGendering Rationalities" conference (ERIC Document Reproduction Service No. ED401 279).

Thayer-Bacon, B. (1997b). The nurturing of a relational epistemolgy. *Educational Theory,* 47(2) (in press).

Thayer-Bacon, B., & Bacon, C. (1996a, Spring). Caring in the college/university classroom. *Educational Foundations,* 10(2), 53–72.

Thayer-Bacon, B., & Bacon, C. (1996b, October). Caring professors: A model. *Journal of General Education,* 45(4), 255–269.

Tozer, S. E., Violas, P. C., & Senese, G. B. (1993). *School and society: Educational practice as social expression.* New York: McGraw-Hill.

Tronto, J. (1987). Beyond gender difference to a theory of care. *Signs,* 12(4), 644–663.

Tronto, J. C. (1989). Women and caring: What can feminists learn about morality from caring? In A. Jaggar & S. R. Bordo (Eds.), *Gender/body/knowledge* (pp. 172–187). New Brunswick, NJ: Rutgers University Press.

Tronto, J. C. (1993). *Moral boundaries: A political argument for an ethic of care.* New York: Routledge.

Tyack, D., & Hansot, E. (1990). *Learning together: A history of coeducation in American public schools.* New Haven, CT: Yale University Press.

Walker, A. (1983). *In search of our mothers' gardens: Womanist prose.* San Diego, CA: Harcourt Brace Jovanovich.

Weininger, O., & Daniel, S. (1992). *Playing to learn: The young child, the teacher and the classroom.* Springfield, IL: Thomas.

Wiener, P. P. (Ed.). (1958). *Values in a universe of chance: Selected writings of Charles Sanders Peirce (1839–1914).* Garden City, NJ: Doubleday.

Witherell, C., & Noddings, N. (Eds.). (1991). *Stories lives tell: Narrative and dialogue in education.* New York: Teachers College Press.

Young, I. M. (1990). The ideal of community and the politics of difference. In L. Nicholson (Ed.), *Feminism/postmodernism* (pp. 300–323). New York: Routledge.

Index